~Linda + Todd~

Merry Christmas

Love,

Aggie

12-25-96

LET NOT YOUR HEART BE TROUBLED

LET NOT YOUR YOUR HEART BE TROUBLED

BOYD K. PACKER

Illustrations by Ted Gorka

BOOKCRAFT
Salt Lake City, Utah

Library of Congress Catalog Card Number: 91-70100

ISBN 0-88494-787-4

6th Printing, 1995

Printed in the United States of America

Peace I leave with you, my peace I give unto you:
not as the world giveth, give I unto you.
Let not your heart be troubled,
neither let it be afraid.

John 14:27

Contents

Hope for Troubled Hearts 1

I. Direction

1   Scriptures 5
2   In the Spirit of Testimony 12
3   The Essence of Education 22
4   "Feed My Sheep" 31
5   The Redemption of the Dead 37

II. Inspiration

6   To Young Women and Men 47
7   The Country with a Conscience 54
8   The Secret of Service 69
9   Atonement, Agency, Accountability 75
10 The Only True Church 82

III. Caution

11 Steady As She Goes 93
12 The Mantle Is Far, Far Greater Than the Intellect 101
13 A Call to the Christian Clergy 123
14 "From Such Turn Away" 129
15 Youth's Obligation to Parents 137

IV. Admonition

16 Keeper of the Faith 145
17 Moral and Spiritual Values in Character Education 158
18 Where Much Is Given, Much Is Required 175
19 The Saints Securely Dwell 182
20 The Relief Society 190

V. Understanding

21 Your Articles of Faith 199
22 Revelation in a Changing World 210
23 Can I Really Know? 217
24 The Mystery of Life 222
25 Live by the Spirit 229

VI. Assurance

26 "Let Not Your Heart Be Troubled" 243
27 Keeping Covenants 254
28 Bruce R. McConkie, Apostle 259
29 The Book of Mormon 268
30 The Pattern of Our Parentage 286

Index 295

Hope for Troubled Hearts

The fourteenth chapter of the Gospel of John in the New Testament begins, "Let not your heart be troubled." Near the close of that chapter (verse 27) the same message is repeated: "Peace I leave with you, my peace I give unto you: not as the world giveth, give I unto you. Let not your heart be troubled, neither let it be afraid."

It is characteristic of the gospel that as we ponder any theme and study it in the scriptures it broadens into all other themes until it embraces all that is true. One cannot therefore entirely separate one theme from another. A study of repentance leads one to the subject of forgiveness; a study of spiritual darkness to spiritual light; and so on.

Whatever our challenge in life, be it grief or fear, temptation or confusion, worry, health, the agony of failure, or vanity contracted from success, there is comfort and caution in the gospel. For example, once we accept the truth of the doctrine that we are the children of God, that realization changes us. Thereafter we cannot willingly injure another or transgress against him. That simple, profound doctrine has a very practical value. It brings a feeling of self-worth, of dignity, of self-respect. Then self-pity and depression fade away. We then can yield to self-discipline and to the discipline of a loving Father and accept even the very hard lessons in life.

The gospel is good medicine. Study it and there emerges just the right combination of direction, inspiration, caution, admonition, understanding, and assurance to steady and strengthen and heal. That is a testimony that the gospel is full and whole and true.

Consider these other verses from that one chapter in the Gospel of John.

> If ye shall ask anything in my name, I will do it.
>
> If ye love me, keep my commandments.
>
> And I will pray the Father, and he shall give you another Comforter, that he may abide with you for ever;
>
> Even the Spirit of truth; whom the world cannot receive, because it seeth him not, neither knoweth him: but ye know him; for he dwelleth with you, and shall be in you.
>
> I will not leave you comfortless: I will come to you. . . .
>
> These things have I spoken unto you, being yet present with you.
>
> But the Comforter, which is the Holy Ghost, whom the Father will send in my name, he shall teach you all things, and bring all things to your remembrance, whatsoever I have said unto you. (Verses 14–18, 25–26.)

The sermons in this book, on many gospel themes, were delivered over a period of many years, to differing audiences, in many places. They are published with the hope that when you read them you will share in some of the feelings of comfort and inspiration which were present when they were prepared and delivered, and will be drawn to study the gospel in the scriptures upon which all of them are based.

I

Direction

1

Scriptures

I must tell you of a work that has moved quietly forward in the Church virtually unnoticed. It had its beginning in Old Testament times and is the fulfillment of a prophecy by Ezekiel, who wrote: "The word of the Lord came . . . unto me, saying, Moreover, thou son of man, take thee one stick, and write upon it, For Judah, and for the children of Israel his companions: then take another stick, and write upon it, For Joseph, the stick of Ephraim, and for all the house of Israel his companions: and join them one to another into one stick; and they shall become one in thine hand" (Ezekiel 37:15–17).

The sticks, of course, are records or books. In ancient Israel records were written on tablets of wood or on scrolls rolled upon sticks. The record of Judah and the record of Ephraim, according to the prophecy, were to become one in our hands.

Address given at general conference October 1982.

First Printing of Book of Mormon

Two events connected with the fulfillment of the prophecy were centered in print shops. The first of these events began on the second floor of a building on Main Street in the village of Palmyra, New York. In June of 1829 Joseph Smith and Martin Harris called upon Mr. Egbert B. Grandin, the proprietor, to discuss the publication of a new book of scripture. Mr. Grandin, then twenty-three, was three months younger than Joseph Smith. Only three months earlier he had advertised his intention to print books, a very ambitious undertaking for so small a shop with only a hand-operated, cast-iron press.

Others had refused to print the book, and young Mr. Grandin, a religious man, was very skeptical himself. But as the contract was secured by a mortgage on the farm of Martin Harris, he signed it, and printing commenced in August of 1829.

No sooner had the project begun than one Abner Cole, who used the pseudonym Obediah Dogberry, began to steal pages of the work and print them with accompanying ridicule in his weekly paper, *Palmyra Reflector.*

In March of 1830 the Book of Mormon came from the press and was advertised for sale. It met such a bitter and destructive response that it did not sell, and Martin Harris lost his farm.

An epoch of scriptural history had begun. The Prophet Joseph Smith and his successors to this day would proclaim the Book of Mormon to be another testament of Jesus Christ. "Obediah Dogberry" and his successors, moved by another spirit, would, with the same methods, to this day revile it.

Latter-day Saint Edition of Scriptures

One hundred forty-eight years later, in June 1977, again in a print shop, another step occurred in the coming together of the two sticks. James Mortimer, long experienced in publishing scriptures, and Ellis T. Rasmussen, recently dean of Religious Instruction at Brigham Young University, called at the Cambridge University Press in Cambridge, England. Bibles had been printed at this prestigious press for 293 years before Egbert Grandin opened his print shop in Palmyra.

They met with Mr. Roger Coleman, director of religious publishing, to discuss the publication of a most unusual edition of the King James Version of the Bible. The printers were quite as skeptical about this proposal as Egbert Grandin had been about that of Joseph Smith and Martin Harris nearly 150 years before.

The Cambridge Press had been publishing the King James Bible since the first edition in 1611, but they had never been asked to do anything like this. The text was to remain exactly as it was—no changes, not one. But all footnoting, cross-references, chapter introductions, indexes, and so on, were to be replaced. Only the chapter and verse numbering for the sixty-six books would be retained.

And that was just the beginning. This edition of the Bible would be cross-referenced with three other books of scripture: the Book of Mormon, the Doctrine and Covenants, and the Pearl of Great Price. The printers had barely heard of them.

But there was more. A new, innovative system of footnoting was to be used. Instead of progressing from *A* to *Z* in each chapter, the letters would start over in every verse, for innumerable verses would have many footnotes.

The technical problems seemed insurmountable. Computers could help, but there was always the human factor. How could you cross-reference the Bible with any other book? To cross-reference it with the three volumes was to require tens of thousands of footnotes. Thereafter there would be hundreds of thousands of possible combinations of information. It was too big even to think about. The technical challenge alone was staggering, to say nothing of maintaining accuracy, harmony, and consistency with the biblical text itself. It could not be done!

But in that meeting also was Mr. Derek Bowen, editor, a most remarkable man. A World War II injury had left him unable to hear. Thereafter he devoted his remarkable compensating abilities to the editing, typesetting, and printing of Bibles. He was, perhaps, the one man in the world who could direct such a printing project.

All of the problems mentioned so far related only to the printing part of the project. The actual compiling and organizing of the tens of thousands of footnotes would require many hundreds of workers. This work had already been under way for several years. Without the computer it would be manifestly impossible!

That also was but a beginning. There would be a combined concordance and topical guide, listing hundreds of subjects; a Bible dictionary; maps; and a new format. New chapter headings would be written. All this would be in harmony with the sacred message of the Old and the New Testaments.

Several years into the project we asked for a report. How were the researchers and compilers progressing with the tedious, laborious listing of topics in alphabetical order? They responded, "We have been through *Heaven* and *Hell*, past *Love* and *Lust*, and now we're working toward *Repentance.*"

The 750 headings for the Topical Guide were painfully rendered down from a list nearly twice that long. For there was a practical consideration: the book had to be of a size for everyday use.

There was a spirit of inspiration brooding over the work. Those working with the project talked often of how it was blessed. There were humbling spiritual experiences.

After more than seven years of quiet, intensive work, in 1979 the Latter-day Saint edition of the King James Bible came off the press. Already work was well under way on the Book of Mormon, the Doctrine and Covenants, and the Pearl of Great Price. Over the years manuscripts had come into our hands which made possible the correction of printers' errors that had crept into early editions of those scriptures.

The finished work would be seen by more than the sympathetic students and the devoted members of the Church. The cold, impartial eyes of the research scholars would study it, and the angry eyes of enemies and detractors would pore over it. It must be correct in every detail. Finally, after two more years, the books came from the press, the most accurate we have ever had.

Three months later, Derek Bowen, master editor of Bibles, passed away in England.

You should know also that by recent decision of the Brethren the Book of Mormon will henceforth bear the title *The Book of Mormon*, with the subtitle *Another Testament of Jesus Christ.*

Two Sticks One—A Crowning Achievement

The stick or record of Judah—the Old Testament and the New Testament—and the stick or record of Ephraim—the Book of Mormon, which is another testament of Jesus Christ—are now woven together in such a way that as you pore over one you are drawn to the other; as you learn from one you are enlightened by the other. They are indeed one in our hands. Ezekiel's prophecy now stands fulfilled.

With the passing of years, these scriptures will produce successive generations of faithful Christians who know the Lord Jesus Christ and are disposed to obey His will. The older generation has been raised without them, but there is another generation growing up. The revelations will be opened to them as to no previous generation in the history of the world. Into their hands now are placed the sticks of Joseph and of Judah. They will develop a gospel scholarship beyond that which their forebears could achieve. They will have the testimony that Jesus is the Christ and be competent to proclaim Him and to defend Him.

Without the inspired help of hundreds of dedicated workers it would have been impossible! Among them were scholars in Hebrew, Greek, Latin, and Old and New Testament studies. More than this, they are worthy men and women in whose lives the gospel of Jesus Christ is the dominating influence. Their work on this project, if they only knew it, may well be their greatest contribution in mortality.

As the generations roll on, this project will be regarded, in the perspective of history, as the crowning achievement in the administration of President Spencer W. Kimball.

As a very direct outgrowth of the scripture project, two new revelations were added to the Doctrine and Covenants, an event that had not occurred in over a hundred years. And before the books were closed, there came the glorious revelation on the priesthood, just in time for a declaration about it to be bound with the other revelations the Lord has given His Saints in this dispensation of the fulness of times.

Even all of this is but a beginning, for we have these publications only in English. Already work is well under way in Spanish, with the other languages to follow in the years ahead.

Concurrent with this publication project another great work was continuing. The entire curriculum of the Church was being restructured. All courses of study for children, youth, and adults were revised to center on the scriptures, on Jesus Christ. A veritable army of volunteer workers—many of them experts in writing, curriculum, instruction, and other related fields—worked for years to complete this task.

While we have been about the work of anchoring ourselves to the scriptures, others have been busily cutting themselves loose from them. They have been drifting downstream, interpreting and revising the scriptures to agree with the philosophies of men. We, on the other hand, have been struggling upstream against the same current. We are determined to reach the headwaters of divine communication and revelation, to have it, as the Doctrine and Covenants demands, "that every man might speak in the name of God the Lord, even the Savior of the world" (D&C 1:20).

There are Church-watchers, both in and out of the Church, who show great interest in what we do. They watch what they define as the power structure, the resources of the Church, the changes in organization, the political and social issues; and they draw conclusions from their watching. They write their observations and print them in publications and represent them to be accurate and objective reports of what is going on in the Church. In all of their watching and claiming, they have missed the most important of all the things that we have done in recent generations.

Some of them say that we have lost our way, that we are not Christians. Should they turn to that one thing in which they show the least interest and in which they have the least knowledge, the scriptures and the revelations, they would find in the Topical Guide fifty-eight categories of information about Jesus Christ; eighteen pages of small print, single-spaced, list literally thousands of scriptural references on the subject.

Informative Testimony of Jesus Christ

These references from the four volumes of scripture constitute the most comprehensive compilation of scriptural information on the mission and teachings of the Lord Jesus Christ that has ever been assembled in the history of the world.

The work affirms an acceptance of, a reverence for, and a testimony of the Lord Jesus Christ. Follow those references and you will open the door to whose church this is, what it teaches and by whose authority—all anchored to the sacred name of Jesus Christ, the Son of God, the Messiah, the Redeemer, our Lord.

I began by quoting Ezekiel, prophet of Judah. Two of those Old Testament verses show ten footnotes. One of the ten leads us to the Book of Mormon, which is another testament of Jesus Christ, where half a world away the prophet Lehi, of the lineage of Joseph, quoted this prophecy:

> Wherefore, the fruit of thy loins shall write; and the fruit of the loins of Judah shall write; and that which shall be written by the fruit of thy loins, and also that which shall be written by the fruit of the loins of Judah, shall grow together, unto the confounding of false doctrines and laying down of contentions, and establishing peace among the fruit of thy loins, and bringing them to the knowledge of their fathers in the latter days, and also to the knowledge of my covenants, saith the Lord (2 Nephi 3:12).

One footnote may seem a flimsy thread to tie the two together, but five of the ten footnotes lead us to the headings in the Topical Guide where 611 other references broaden our knowledge of this one subject and speak as voices from the dust.

Threads are wound into cords that bind together in our hands the sticks of Judah and of Ephraim—testaments of the Lord Jesus Christ.

I say again, these references constitute the most comprehensive compilation of scriptural information on the mission and teachings of the Lord Jesus Christ that has ever been assembled in the history of the world.

Do not mistake our reverent hesitation to speak glibly or too frequently of Him to mean that we do not know Him.

Our brethren of Judah knew Him in ancient times, our brethren of Ephraim also. He is no stranger to His Saints, to His prophets and Apostles now.

He lives. He is our Savior, our Redeemer, our Lord. Of Him I bear an apostolic witness, in the name of Jesus Christ, amen.

2

In the Spirit of Testimony

The *Deseret News* of 10 July 1956 printed a bulletin from the LDS Hospital on the condition of an eighteen-year-old girl who had been brought to the hospital six days earlier having survived nine days pinned under a car in Parley's Canyon, near Salt Lake City. The bulletin was, for a change, optimistic: "Attending physicians at the LDS Hospital said the girl's blood condition is so improved she likely will need no more transfusions. . . . Doctors said her diet has been increased to include potatoes, eggs, and puddings. She no longer requires intravenous feedings."

The injuries she had sustained in the accident were not of themselves the important factor. It was the lack of food and moisture that reduced her body to that poor condition. It was several days before the doctors gave much hope for her recovery.

It isn't easy to minister to one so starved. It was not a matter of just putting food before her. The food had to be carefully administered, for delicate balances could be upset, and her life was at

Address given at priesthood board meeting 19 February 1969.

stake. Doctors were extremely careful, for their very treatment might prove fatal. When she recovered, that was regarded as something of a miracle.

So it is with those around us who are spiritually undernourished, or starved. We refer to them as the lost sheep. We are called to minister to them. They are of all descriptions. Some have deficiencies of one kind or another that merely rob them of spiritual vigor. Others have so seriously starved themselves of spiritual things that we scarce can hope to save them.

Home Teacher Ministers to Undernourished

Responsibility for redemption of the lost sheep rests with the priesthood. The doing of it rests upon the home teacher. He is the priesthood representative charged with the responsibility to see that every member of the Church is properly nourished spiritually and does not suffer physical want. He it is who must see that the parents in the home are aware of the need to provide adequate spiritual sustenance for their children. And he is the one who can relate all Church agencies to the home, calling for just the right blend of spiritual nourishment to sustain those who are well and heal those who are undernourished.

We wonder why home teaching is not more successful than it is. Members who have been instructed often enough, and ought to *know*, still are listed among the lost sheep. If we are to redeem them we must know what kind of nourishment to administer, and when, and in what amounts. It is not a matter of just putting it before them.

What can improve our ability, as individuals or as organizations, to redeem the lost sheep? What "vitamin" sparks an appetite for spiritual things?

Feelings Must Be Engaged

In the April 1964 issue of the *Improvement Era* there appeared an article by Wilford B. Lee entitled "John Is Inactive . . . Why?" The author pointed out that knowledge does not necessarily control activity. Thus many know what they ought to do but fail to do it, even after encouragement from home teachers.

"There is a great body of evidence," Brother Lee wrote, "to indicate that, in moral behavior especially, people do not act in accordance with their knowledge." And he observed that one could hardly find an obese person who does not know that, if he is to reduce his weight, a part of what he must do is to reduce his intake of food. Can you imagine a medical doctor who uses cigarettes and does not know that smoking is detrimental to his health? Were you ever acquainted with a divorce of parents in which both of the parties didn't know full well that tragic effects would be visited upon their children? In such cases the persons know the right course but still fail to follow it.

As regards righteous behavior, then, to know intellectually is not enough. The *feelings* must be engaged. Nephi told his wayward brothers—lost sheep, if you will: "Ye are swift to do iniquity but slow to remember the Lord your God. Ye have seen an angel, and he spake unto you; yea, ye have heard his voice from time to time; and he hath spoken unto you in a still small voice, but ye were past *feeling*, that ye could not *feel* his words." (1 Nephi 17:45, italics added.)

Alma recognized what would redeem the lost sheep. He knew what the moving power was. In the eighth year of the reign of the judges he was heavily involved in secular affairs. But serious problems, remarkably similar to those we face, arose in the Church, and "the church began to fail in its progress." A major reason was that "the people of the church began to wax proud, because of their exceeding riches, . . . which they had obtained by their industry."

Alma was not the only one concerned. It was a source of worry to "the people whom Alma had consecrated to be teachers, and priests, and elders over the church." The blessing of prosperity somehow turned into "envyings, and strife, and malice, and persecutions, and pride." Fortunately, then as now, some members were faithful, "abasing themselves, . . . imparting their substance to the poor and the needy, feeding the hungry."

Faced with this situation in the Church, Alma withdrew from secular affairs. "And this he did that he himself might go forth among his people, . . . that he might preach the word of God unto them, to stir them up in remembrance of their duty, . . . seeing no way that he might reclaim them save it were in bearing down in pure testimony against them." (Alma 4:6, 7, 9, 10, 13, 19.)

Testimony Is the Moving Power

Testimony, then, is the moving power. Testimony is the redeeming force.

Programs will redeem only to the degree that they produce testimony. Elaborate programming will not hurt us if the Spirit is there, nor help us if it is not. To send priesthood home teachers to the lost sheep as a program is not enough. They must go in the spirit of testimony.

Since testimony is needed, all who hold offices in the Church ought to reach for it. If we know in the beginning that that is what we are trying to accomplish, we can come nearer to doing it. But we must know that it is tied to the scriptures—we must rely on the spirit of revelation. For "notwithstanding those things which are written, it always has been given to the elders of my church from the beginning, and ever shall be, to conduct all meetings as they are directed and guided by the Holy Spirit" (D&C 46:2).

At times we seem to do little better than our ancestors, who knew that iron was necessary for health, so they put a horseshoe in the well bucket. There is a better way.

There are two dimensions to testimony. The one, a *testimony we bear to them*, has power to lift and bless them. The other, infinitely more important, *the testimony they bear themselves*, has the power to redeem and exalt them. You might say they can get *a* testimony from what we say. *The* testimony comes when they themselves bear a witness of the truth and the Holy Ghost confirms it to them. James said, "Be ye doers of the word, and not hearers only" (James 1:22). And the Lord said, "If any man will do his will, he shall know of the doctrine" (John 7:17).

Give Opportunities to the Weak

If you who hold positions in the Church would redeem the lost sheep, see that the "vitamins" go to those with deficiencies and not merely to those who are nourished by regular, balanced diets.

Activity—the opportunity to serve and bear testimony—is like medicine. It will heal the spiritually sick. It will strengthen the spiritually weak. It is a most necessary ingredient in the redemption of the lost sheep. Yet there is a tendency, almost a programmed tendency, to give opportunities for growth to those who are already over-surfeited with activity. This kind of pattern, evident in our stakes and wards, may keep the lost sheep out.

When a home teacher brings a lost sheep to meetings, it is only a beginning of his being found. Where can he be used for his spiritual benefit? Actually, there aren't many places in which a leader can use a person who is struggling for worthiness. Unfortunately, it seems that those few situations in which we could use them—to offer prayers, to make brief responses, to bear testimony—are almost invariably reserved for the active: for the stake presidency, for the high council, for the bishopric, for the patriarch, for the auxiliary leaders. Indeed, we sometimes go to great lengths to import speakers and participants—to the loss of our hungry ones.

At a ward sacrament meeting I attended recently a sister had been invited to sing whose husband was not active in the Church. He was, however, at the meeting. The bishop wanted a very special program for this occasion. His first announcement was: "Brother X, my first counselor, will give the opening prayer." His second counselor gave the closing prayer.

How unfortunate, I thought. The three men in the bishopric struggle with such concern over the spiritually sick, then take the very medicine that would make those people well—activity, participation—and consume it themselves in front of the needy!

Some will say: "We must be careful with the weak among us. It is better not to call on them to pray or to bear testimony, for they will be frightened and repelled and will leave us." That is a myth! A commonly accepted one, but a myth nevertheless! I have asked bishops—hundreds of them—whether they could certify to such a happening in their personal experience. I have had very few affirmative responses—in fact all those bishops produced only one or two instances. So the risk is very small, whereas such an invitation may result in a lost sheep being reclaimed.

Several years ago I visited a stake presided over by a man of unusual efficiency and ability. Every detail of the stake conference had been scheduled. He had done the usual thing in assigning prayers from the selected circle of the stake presidency, the high council, the bishops, and the stake patriarch. Those brethren had not been notified, so we changed the assignment from those who deserved the honor to those who needed—desperately needed—the experience.

The president had a detailed agenda for the general sessions, and he mentioned that there were twenty minutes in one session that were not scheduled. I told him that we could call on some to respond who otherwise would not have the opportunity and needed the strengthening experience. He countered with the suggestion that he alert several able, prominent leaders to prepare for possible speaking assignments. "There will be many nonmembers present," he said. "We are used to having an organized and very polished conference performance. We have very able people in the stake. They will leave an excellent impression."

Twice again during our meeting he mentioned the schedule and pressed to have the stake's "best performers" called. "Why don't we save this time for those who need it most?" I said. His reaction was a disappointed, "Well, you are the General Authority."

Early Sunday morning he reminded me that there was still time to alert someone and thus leave the best impression.

The morning session was opened by the president with a polished and stirring address. Next we called on his second counselor. He was obviously flustered, and he began, "You can't believe a thing Brother Packer says." (We had previously indicated that both counselors would probably speak in the afternoon session.) We were to go to his home for the noon meal. He had known there would be time to go over his notes, so he had left them at home.

For want of his notes he turned to testimony, giving an inspiring account of an administration he had performed during the week. A brother, given up by his doctors, had been called from the very shadows of death by the power of the priesthood. I do not know what was on his notes, but surely it could not have compared in inspiration to the testimony he bore.

An elderly woman sat on the front row holding hands with a weathered-looking man. She looked a bit out of place in the fashionably dressed congregation—rather homespun by comparison. She looked as if she ought to talk in conference, and given the privilege she reported her mission. Fifty-two years before she had returned from the mission field, and since then she had never been invited to speak in Church. It was a touching and moving witness that she bore.

Others were called upon to speak, and near the close of the meeting the president suggested that I take the remainder of the time. "Have you had any inspiration?" I asked. He said that he kept thinking of the mayor. (The voters in that large city had elected a member of the Church to be mayor, and he was in attendance.) When I told him we could have a greeting from the mayor, he whispered that the man was not active in the Church. When I suggested that he call upon him anyway he resisted, saying flatly that he was not worthy to speak in that meeting. At my insistence, however, he called the man to the stand.

The mayor's father had been a pioneer of the Church in that region. He had served as bishop of one of the wards and had been succeeded by one of his sons—a twin to the mayor, as I recall. The mayor was the lost sheep. He came to the pulpit and spoke, to my surprise, with bitterness and with hostility. His talk began something like this: "I don't know why you called on me. I don't know why I am in church today. I don't belong in church. I have never fit in. I don't agree with the way the Church does things."

I confess that I began to worry, but he then paused and lowered his eyes to the pulpit. From then until his talk was over he did not look up. After hesitating, he continued: "I guess I just as well tell you. I quit smoking six weeks ago." Then, shaking his fist in a gesture over his head towards the congregation, he said, "If any of you think that's easy, you have never suffered the hell I have suffered in the last few weeks."

Then he just melted. "I know the gospel is true," he said. "I've always known it was true. I learned that from my mother as a boy.

"I know the Church isn't out of order," he confessed. "It's me that's out of order, and I've always known that, too."

Then he spoke, perhaps, for all of the lost sheep when he pleaded: "I know it's me that is wrong, and I want to come back. I have been trying to come back, but you won't let me!"

Of course we would let him come back, but somehow we hadn't let him know that. After the meeting the congregation flooded up—not to us but to him, to say, "Welcome home!"

On the way to the airport after conference the stake president said to me, "I've learned a lesson today."

Hoping to confirm it, I said, "If we had done what you wanted to do you would have called on this man's father, wouldn't you, or perhaps his brother, the bishop?"

He nodded in affirmation and said: "Either of them, given five minutes, would have presented a stirring fifteen- or twenty-minute sermon to the approval of all in attendance. But no lost sheep would have been reclaimed.''

All of us who lead in the wards and stakes must open the door to the lost sheep; stand aside to let them through. We must learn not to block the entrance. It is a narrow way. Sometimes we assume the clumsy posture of trying to pull them through the gate which we ourselves are blocking. Only when we have the spirit of lifting them, pushing them before us, seeing them elevated above us, do we have that spirit that will engender testimony.

I wonder if that is what the Lord meant when he said, ''They that be whole need not a physician, but they that are sick'' (Matthew 9:12).

I do not appeal for the lowering of standards. Just the opposite. More lost sheep will respond quicker to high standards than they will to low ones. There is therapeutic value in spiritual discipline.

Discipline is a form of love, an expression of it. It is necessary and powerful in people's lives.

When a toddler is playing near the road, we steer carefully around him. Few will stop and see him to safety: if necessary, discipline him. That is, unless it is our own child or grandchild. If we love them enough we will do it. To withhold discipline when it would contribute to spiritual growth is an evidence of lack of love and concern.

Spiritual discipline framed in love and confirmed with testimony will help redeem souls.

Take Opportunity to Bear Testimony

There are many situations in which Church programs can be spiritualized, many moments overlooked that are opportunities to testify. Let me give three examples.

First example:

Suppose that a stake priesthood executive committee is in session. Elsewhere in the building the stake Primary officers are assembled. The stake president asks Brother Ross of the high council, he being advisor to the Primary, to slip out of the meeting and see whether Sister Martin, the Primary president, has the name she would like cleared as her new second counselor. Brother Ross interrupts the Primary meeting briefly and gets the name that is to be cleared. He is about to leave the room when Sister Martin says, "Would you like to say anything to our Primary sisters?"

As sure as we are born, Brother Ross will say: "Oh, no, they are waiting for me in the high council room. You will have to excuse me." And he will slip away, missing the most choice opportunity to strengthen the Primary sisters that will come in many weeks.

Think how powerful it would be if he said: "Why, yes, there are two things, but I must be brief. First I want to thank you sisters for the dedicated and devoted service you give. We want you to know how grateful we are and that the Lord is pleased with you. Even more important, I want to assure you that the work in which we are engaged is the Lord's work. He does love His little children. He looks after them and those who help them, for He does live. I just want to leave that bit of testimony with you. Now if you will excuse me, please."

Thirty seconds—a testimony!

Second example:

A Sunday School teacher concludes a lesson—one perhaps led afield by the question of some unsettled and disturbed class member:

"It has been a challenging lesson today. We have not settled all of the issues raised, but as we conclude I want you to know there is one thing settled in my heart and soul. It is that the gospel of Jesus Christ is true. This is His church. Perhaps next week we can draw closer to the answers we seek. May the Lord bless you. See you next Sunday."

Twenty seconds—a testimony!

Third example:

The bishop concludes an interview—perhaps to sign a recommend, or any interview.

"It's good to visit with you, Brother Parks. I want to assure you that this is the Lord's work. That witness comes again and again as I serve in this calling. Thank you for coming tonight."

Ten seconds—a testimony!

The testimony of ward and stake and general leaders of the Church strengthens everyone who comes within their influence. Those who serve in the organizations are strengthened, and in turn they strengthen those who attend. Priesthood holders, who go out as home teachers, are strengthened, and they bear testimony to strengthen the members. The home teachers themselves have home teachers. Thus there is a cycle of strength and spiritual nourishment that can make each of us as an individual and the Church as an organization like a magnet, drawing more of the lost sheep into the fold.

New means of communication are being used. Wonderful, dedicated men, under call, are experimenting continually with new and better means of extending to all mankind the influence of testimony within the Church. At first we could be heard in but a single hall. Then that voice was extended across the world by radio. Now we can be both heard and seen live—on television. I hope the day is at hand when the message can be heard and seen and felt.

In our programming we must keep the "feel" of those who are in need. The mind will communicate with the mind, the heart with the heart, and the spirit with the spirit. What we feel they will feel. Somehow feeling must be kept in our work or we will not redeem the lost sheep.

Somehow as priesthood and auxiliary leaders we must remember how it is to be spiritually hungry and poor. Somehow we must remember—or imagine—what it is like to be unrepentant, rebellious, and unforgiving. We must pray fervently for a feeling for it, and pray for the gift to teach by the Spirit.

And there is the consolation that, as we seek to serve the Lord in serving them, others who are both physically and spiritually hungry may receive sustenance from what we do.

May the Lord bless all of us with an appreciation for the privilege of bearing testimony and with the desire to share it, I pray in the name of Jesus Christ, amen.

3

The Essence
of Education

In order to have the audience somewhat at ease, I make it a practice to begin a graduation address with these profound words:

> The month of June approaches, and soon through all the land
> The graduation speakers will tell us where we stand.
> We stand at Armageddon in the vanguard of the press.
> We're standing at the portals, at the gateway to success.
> We're standing on the threshold of careers, all brightly lit.
> And in the midst of all this standing, we sit and sit and sit.

The genius who wrote that entitled it "Oh, My Aching Baccalaureate!"

I thought that if you knew that I know that graduation speeches can be too long, you might relax and listen.

These assignments do not come easy for me, and I am painfully aware that after the tribute paid and the great honor that was

---

Address given at Weber College graduation 10 June 1983, at which time an honorary degree of Doctor of Humanities was conferred on Elder Packer.

bestowed upon me it would not do at all for me to give a dumb talk, nor a long one. As a graduate of Weber College I want very much to uphold the honor of our alma mater.

It is not uncommon for graduation speeches to be given *before*, but not really *to*, the graduates. A graduation exercise provides the platform for a speaker to address the public on such subjects as human rights or disarmament. It is a time, for instance, when a United States president may deliver a major foreign policy address.

While I know that it may be something of a departure, I intend to talk directly *to you*, the graduates. The rest of you may listen, or doze, as you please. What I say will not noticeably affect either the environment or the economy. But it could—I hope will—profoundly affect some individual graduate.

Weber State College is a very good school. The faculty holds 196 doctors' degrees and 146 masters' degrees. Unlike the honorary degrees conferred upon us tonight, those degrees were acquired in the old-fashioned way—they were earned.

Is Part of Your Education Neglected?

It would be foolish of me to try to repeat, less impressively and certainly in less detail, what your professors have already covered in classes. It is left, therefore, for me to concentrate on things that are not listed in the catalog of courses nor regarded as part of the curriculum. They are things which it is assumed everyone already knows or that somehow everyone will learn without having been taught them. I happen to believe that nothing receives less attention and is more neglected than the obvious.

And regardless of what your transcript of credit may say, one part of your education may have been neglected, leaving you developed only to a grade-school level. Now that you are graduating, you would do well to concentrate on those things that are scarcely touched upon in universities in our day.

For instance, you who have studied chemistry can mix a complicated formula without blowing up the chemistry lab. But have you learned to blend the ingredients of a happy marriage without having it blow up in your face?

You who have studied language can now construct a proper sentence and convey even the finest shades of meaning. But will you use that ability to sell unwitting customers something that they neither need nor can afford? Or will you promise, without quite saying so, great returns on investments that are actually worthless?

You who have studied accounting can keep complicated ledgers of principal and interest and increase. But do you intend to pay back your student loan?

You who have studied drama can write or direct a play, or interpret the lines in any script. But can you get your act together off-stage? Will your role in life be as a bumbling comedian, as a villain, or as the star of a self-made tragedy?

Others Not So Fortunate

I have talked to young people in sixty or seventy countries; and compared to the opportunities most of them enjoy, it surely must be said of you that you have had the opportunity for an excellent education. In addition to the excellent faculty, you have studied on a campus that is beautiful and you have had the use of an outstanding library. Many others are not so blessed.

A year or two ago I visited the University of Nanking. It had been one of the leading universities in the People's Republic of China, but during the Cultural Revolution everything that was traditional or Western was destroyed by the Red Guard, including the university libraries. I asked to visit the stacks. One would weep to think of what had been burned, compared to the meager collection of paperback books that now serve eager students.

On another occasion I visited a university in a large city in South America. I noticed a student sitting on the ground (there were no lawns on that campus) reading a manuscript. It was a ditto copy with purple ink, typical of a copying process used years ago. After a brief conversation he excused himself with the comment that he had to get back to his study. That worn stack of dirty, dog-eared paper was a textbook. He had borrowed it and could keep it only a short time.

Only a month ago I was going through customs in a large city in the Middle East. A 747 plane had landed just minutes before, and the passengers, perhaps four hundred of them, were ahead of us at passport control. They were all dressed alike in poorly fitting, baggy, wrinkled clothes. They had spent the night on the plane and were tired and sweaty. More than anything else, they looked like prisoners of war.

But they were not prisoners of war. They were from Pakistan and were obviously coming to work as laborers. They had come with hope. They would send their earnings back to wives and children and parents in a land where there is hunger and deprivation. Much of what they earned would go to agents who recruited them. The separation from their families would last for years.

One young man, perhaps thirty years old, came pushing his way to the front of the line. Other passengers were of course complaining. He stood next to me for a moment and I noticed he was holding his entry card up and pressing his thumb against the lower corner.

Then I understood—he was illiterate. He had been separated from his group while someone filled out the landing card for him. But it required a signature, which in his case would be a thumbprint because he did not know how to write his name. I thought of a wife and two or three children waiting at home; of the long separation; of the meager opportunities life would afford this man and his loved ones in Pakistan.

And then, interestingly enough, I thought of you, and of the talk I was to give you. I compared his opportunity with yours. Some of you are from the country he was to enter, some from the one he left. Your fortunes will be different indeed from his, because you have had the opportunity to attend school. Of course, only the future will reveal whether you received an education. The difference between being well schooled and well educated rests somehow in what you do with the knowledge you have gained.

Knowledge Not an End

I was acquainted with a Harvard professor of economics. He once told me that when he was a student in Germany someone asked him what he intended to do with the knowledge he was gaining. He said the question made him very angry. Why did he have to do anything with it? Was knowledge not worth acquiring for itself alone?

Somewhere in the economic difficulties we now suffer are the theories of the professor of economics who thought knowledge was an end in itself.

A number of years ago there was a student at Columbia University who was known as the "perennial student." He had been left an inheritance which stipulated that it should continue as long as he was engaged in collegiate study. Thereafter, the income was to go to a charity.

This man remained a student until he died. It was said that he had been granted every degree offered by Columbia University and had taken practically every course. No field of knowledge was foreign to him. He was probably more widely read than the best of his professors. He was described as the "epitome of erudition." But he could not possibly be described as educated. He fit the description of those spoken of in the scripture who are "ever learning, and never able to come to the knowledge of the truth" (2 Timothy 3:7). He was inherently selfish. What a pity! What a waste!

Treasures to Use for Mankind

I do not know who is the author of these very meaningful lines:

Today a professor, in a garden relaxing
Like Plato of old in the academy shade,
Spoke out in a manner I never had heard him,
And this is one of the things that he said:

Suppose that we state as a tenet of wisdom
That knowledge is not for delight of the mind,
Nor an end in itself, but a packet of treasure
To hold and employ for the good of mankind.

A torch or a candle is barren of meaning
Except it give light to men as they climb.
And theses and tomes are but impotent jumble
Unless they are tools in the building of time.

We scholars toil on with the zeal of a miner
For nuggets and nuggets, and one nugget more.
But scholars are needed to study the uses
Of all the great masses of data and lore.

And truly our tireless and endless researches
Need yoking with man's daily problems and strife.
For truth and beauty and virtue have value
Confirmed by their uses in practical life.

The diploma you now receive is not intrinsically worth anything. But it symbolizes knowledge that you have accumulated class by class and course by course over the last several years. That is an inestimable treasure. Road signs, newspapers, charts, graphs, bills and receipts, books of every kind, and entry cards as well are all yours at a glance. For the young man I met in customs, they will always be an obstacle and an embarrassment.

Your student loan is not the only debt you have to repay. Although you have earned it yourself, that diploma carries with it a very great responsibility indeed.

A year or two ago I was assigned to conduct the graduation at Brigham Young University. There was a large graduating class, much like we see here today. At those services it is the duty of the presiding officer, representing the Board of Trustees, to give parting counsel, together with a blessing, to the graduates.

I had carefully prepared my remarks. But something happened which made it advisable to take only a minute or two. So I slipped the carefully prepared talk into my briefcase in favor of a few off-the-cuff words of parting counsel. I mentioned opportunity and obligation, and I quoted a scripture. Actually, I misquoted it. The following week I received a most interesting letter from a woman who pointed out my error and told of an incident wherein she had misquoted the same verse.

What I had said was, "where much is given, much is expected." As she pointed out, the scripture, which is in both the Doctrine and Covenants and the New Testament, states: "Of him unto whom much is given much is required" (D&C 82:3; see also Luke 12:48).

There is a big difference, a very big difference indeed, between something that is expected and something that is *required.*

It is my conviction that of you who graduate tonight, much will be required. And, in the eternal scheme of things, if you do not give meaningful and unselfish service you will be judged as having been highly schooled but poorly educated.

Spiritual Education Is Often Neglected

Your years here at Weber College have filled your future with a world of opportunity. I wonder if there has been added along the way a sufficient sense of obligation. I wonder if in all of your

schooling you have come to realize that intrinsically that young illiterate father I met in an airport is worth quite as much as you are
worth. Although you have had the opportunity to attend school and
he has not, strangely enough it is possible that he will end up with
a better education. For it is not necessarily the education of the
intellect which is the crowning achievement in life. It is time you
learn, if you have not already, that there is a part of our nature, the
part we term spiritual, that needs training as well. It is the spiritual
part of our education that is most easily neglected. And conse-
quently we see many who are academic and intellectual giants but
morally are puny and stunted and diseased.

One often hears the nonsense that we can develop ourselves
spiritually simply by communing with nature, and also that no
consciously organized study is necessary. If that procedure works,
why did you not prepare for a career simply by reading widely or
by observing carefully? Why did you think it worth your while to
register at Weber College?

If only your intellect has been broadened in college, you will
not be happy. It is the training of the spirit that strengthens the
moral fiber of man. If you are immoral, you will create an immoral
world, you may even live in such a world already in your mind. If
you are not honest, you will make a dishonest world. If you are not
decent, you will not be happy. That will be true in spite of how
much you own or how prominent you become. Without a balance
between the intellectual and the spiritual we move through life
without achieving real success.

Yet it is the understanding of almost everyone that success, to
be complete, must include as essential ingredients a generous portion of both fame and fortune. The world seems to work on that
premise. But the premise is false. The Lord taught otherwise.

The Measure of Success

By the time you receive a college diploma you should have
learned that you need not either be rich or hold high position to be
completely successful and truly happy. In fact, if these things
come to you—and they may—true success must be achieved in
spite of them and not because of them.

It is remarkably difficult to teach this truth. If one who is not
well known, and not well compensated, claims that he has learned

for himself that neither fame nor fortune are essential to success, we tend to reject his statement as self-serving. What else could he say and not count himself a failure? On the other hand, if someone who has possession of fame or fortune asserts that neither matters to success or happiness, we suspect that his expression also is self-serving, even patronizing. Therefore we will not accept as reliable authorities either those who have fame and fortune or those who have not. We question that either can be an objective witness.

That leaves only one course open to us: trial and error, to learn for ourselves, by experience, about the relationship success bears to prominence and wealth or their opposites. Thus we struggle through life, perhaps missing both fame and fortune, to finally learn one day that one can, indeed, succeed without possessing either. Or we may, one day, have both and learn that neither has made us happy; that neither is basic to the recipe for true success and for complete happiness. That is a very slow way to learn. As Benjamin Franklin wrote in *Poor Richard's Almanac*, "Experience keeps a dear school, but fools will learn in no other."

It is true that it is possible to be both rich and famous and at the same time succeed spiritually. But the Lord warned of the difficulty of it when he talked of camels and needles.

Position and wealth, then, are no more essential to true happiness in mortality than their absence can prevent you from achieving it. Mortal life is a school, and most of the tests we undergo are multiple-choice tests.

If your growth in college has been solely intellectual, you may not have learned in the course of earning your diploma that the choice in life is not between fame and obscurity, nor is it between wealth and poverty. The choice is between good and evil, and that is a very different matter indeed. When we finally understand this lesson, thereafter our happiness will not be determined by material things. We may be happy without them or successful in spite of them.

As with success, our worth is not measured by renown or by what we own. And you may someday come to know that the poor young man I saw in an airport in the Middle East may receive higher grades on his transcript of credit in spite of his lack of schooling than you may receive because of your schooling.

Unless you *do* something with your schooling, in the eternal scheme of things it will end up to be as a burden on your back, not as wings on your heels. And the only way I know for you to ensure that it will be wings rather than a burden is to develop the spiritual part of your nature.

The crucial test of life, I repeat, does not center in the choice between fame and obscurity, nor between wealth and poverty. The greatest decision of life is between good and evil. Nor need we choose between developing our intellectual capacities and our spiritual capacities. The sensors which assist us to make correct choices are only incidentally academic or intellectual. They are primarily spiritual. With balanced attention to each you may have the best of both, and then you will be educated.

For now, your schooling is finished. Now you move into a future divided into the days and weeks and months ahead. Some of you stride boldly and recklessly forward. Others move with faltering, hesistant steps.

Some of you move forward with the steady confidence which bespeaks an educated soul. That confidence reveals a mind in which such words as *faith* and *spirit* and *church* and *prayer* are precious words; where decency and morality and honor are revered; where service is assumed as obligation.

Knowledge is depicted often as a lamp or as a torch, suggesting light. It has been said that a hero is one who walks the dark pathways of life setting torches along the way so that others may see; a saint is one who walks the dark pathways of life and is himself a light. On the matter of a heroism — and a sainthood — open to us all, an unidentified poet has written:

> We cannot all be heroes
> And thrill a hemisphere
> With some great, daring venture,
> Some deed that mocks at fear.
> But we can fill a lifetime
> With kindly acts, and true.
> For there's always noble service
> For noble souls to do.

May you each find your way to that kind of heroism, which is a mark of the educated soul.

4

"Feed My Sheep"

I want to talk to my young friends of the Aaronic Priesthood. I begin with a parable; and then I have a test for you.

"Intruders" at the Picnic

Imagine that our bishop has appointed you and me to plan a picnic for all of the ward members. It is to be the finest social in the history of the ward, and we are to spare no expense.

We reserve a beautiful picnic ground in the country. We are to have it all to ourselves; no outsiders will interfere with us.

The arrangements go very well, and when the day comes the weather is perfect. All is beautifully ready. The tables are in one long row. We even have tablecloths and china. You have never seen such a feast. The Relief Society and the Young Women have outdone themselves. The tables are laden with every kind of deli-

---

Address delivered at the priesthood meeting of general conference April 1984.

cious food: cantaloupe, watermelon, corn on the cob, fried chicken, hamburgers, cakes, pies—you get the picture.

We are seated, and the bishop calls upon the patriarch to bless the food. Every hungry youngster secretly hopes it will be a short prayer.

Then, just at that moment, there is an interruption. A noisy old car jerks into the picnic grounds and sputters to a stop close to us. We are upset. Didn't they see the Reserved signs?

A worried-looking man lifts the hood; a spout of steam comes out. One of our brethren, a mechanic, says, "That car isn't going anywhere until it is repaired."

Several children spill from the car. They are ragged and dirty and noisy. And then an anxious mother takes a box to that extra table nearby. It is mealtime. The children are hungry. She puts a few leftovers on the table. Then she nervously moves them about, trying to make it look like a meal for her hungry brood. But there is not enough.

We wait impatiently for them to quiet down so that we can have the blessing and enjoy our feast.

Then one of their little girls spies our table. She pulls her runny-nosed little brother over to us and pushes her head between you and me. We cringe aside, because they are very dirty. Then the little girl says, "Ummm, look at that. Ummm, ummm, I wonder what that tastes like."

Everyone is waiting. Why did they arrive just at that moment? Such an inconvenient time. Why must we interrupt what we are doing to bother with outsiders? Why couldn't they have stopped somewhere else? They are not clean! They are not like us. They just don't fit in.

Since the bishop has put us in charge, he expects us to handle these intruders. What should we do? Of course, this is only a parable. But now for the test. If it really happened, my young friends, what *would* you do?

I will give you three choices.

First, you could insist that the intruders keep their children quiet while we have the blessing. Thereafter we ignore them. After all, we reserved the place.

I doubt that you would do that. Could you choke down a feast before hungry children? Surely we are better than that! That is not the answer.

The next choice. There is that extra table. And we do have too much of some things. We could take a little of this and a little of that and lure the little children back to their own table. Then we could enjoy our feast without interruption. After all, we earned what we have. Did we not "obtain it by [our own] industry," as the Book of Mormon says? (See Alma 4:6.)

I hope you would not do that. There is a better answer. You already know what it is.

We should go out to them and invite them to come and join us. You could slide that way, and I could slide this way, and the little girl could sit between us. They could all fit in somewhere to share our feast. Afterwards, we will fix their car and provide something for their journey.

Could there be more pure enjoyment than seeing how much we could get those hungry children to eat? Could there be more satisfaction than to interrupt our festivities to help our mechanic fix their car?

Is that what you would do? Surely it is what you *should* do. But forgive me if I have a little doubt. Let me explain.

The Missionary Obligation

We, as members of the Church, have the fulness of the gospel. Every conceivable kind of spiritual nourishment is ours. Every part of the spiritual menu is included. It provides an unending supply of spiritual strength. Like the widow's cruse of oil, it is replenished as we use it and shall never fail (see 1 Kings 17:8-16).

And yet there are some people across the world and about us—our neighbors, our friends, some in our own families—who, spiritually speaking, are undernourished. Some of them are starving to death!

If we keep all our spiritual blessings to ourselves, it is not unlike feasting before those who are hungry.

We are to go out to them, and to invite them to join us. We are to be missionaries.

It does not matter if that interrupts your schooling or delays your career or your marriage—or basketball. Except those who have a serious health problem, every Latter-day Saint young man should answer the call to serve a mission.

Even mistakes and transgressions must not stand in the way. You should make yourself *worthy* to receive a call.

The early Apostles at first did not know that the gospel was for everyone, for the Gentiles as well as the Jews. Then Peter had a vision. He saw all kinds of creatures and was commanded to kill and to eat. But he refused, saying they were common and unclean. Then the voice said, "What God hath cleansed, that call not thou common." (See Acts 10:9–16.) That vision, and the experience he had immediately following it, convinced the Apostles of their duty. Thus began the great missionary work of all Christianity.

Almost any returned missionary will have a question: "If they are starving spiritually, why do they not accept what we have? Why do they slam the door on us and turn us away?"

One of my sons was serving in Australia and was thrown off a porch by a man who rejected his message. My son is big enough and strong enough that he had to be somewhat agreeable to what was happening or the man never could have done it.

Be patient if some will not eat when first invited. Remember, not all who are spiritually hungry will accept the gospel. Do you remember how reluctant you are to try any new food? Only after your mother urges you will you first take a tiny portion on the tip of a spoon to taste it to see if you like it.

Undernourished children must be carefully fed; so it is with the spiritually underfed. Some are so weakened by mischief and sin that to begin with they reject the rich food we offer. They must be fed carefully and gently.

Some are so near spiritual death that they must be spoonfed on the broth of fellowship, or nourished carefully on activities and programs. As the scriptures say, they must have milk before meat (see 1 Corinthians 3:2; D&C 19:22). But we must take care lest the only nourishment they receive thereafter is that broth.

But feed them we must. We are commanded to preach the gospel to every nation, kindred, tongue, and people. That message, my young friends, appears more than eighty times in the scriptures.

Poignant Experience in Japan

I did not serve a regular mission until my wife and I were called to preside in New England. When I was of missionary age, when I was your age, young men could not be called to the mission field.

It was World War II, and I spent four years in the military. But I did do missionary work; we did share the gospel. It was my privilege to baptize one of the first two Japanese to join the Church since the mission had been closed twenty-two years earlier. Brother Elliot Richards baptized Tatsui Sato. I baptized his wife, Chio. And the work in Japan was reopened. We baptized them in a swimming pool amid the rubble of a university that had been destroyed by bombs.

Shortly thereafter I boarded a train in Osaka for Yokohama and a ship that would take me home. Brother and Sister Sato came to the station to say good-bye. Many tears were shed as we bade one another farewell.

It was a very chilly night. The railroad station, what there was left of it, was very cold. Starving children were sleeping in the corners. That was a common sight in Japan in those days. The fortunate ones had a newspaper or a few old rags to fend off the cold.

On that train I slept restlessly. The berths were too short anyway. In the bleak, chilly hours of the dawn, the train stopped at a station along the way. I heard a tapping on the window and raised the blind. There on the platform stood a little boy tapping on the window with a tin can. I knew he was one of the orphans and a beggar; the tin can was the symbol of their suffering. Sometimes they carried a spoon as well, as if to say, "I am hungry; feed me."

He might have been six or seven years old. His little body was thin with starvation. He had on a thin, ragged shirt-like kimono, nothing else. His head was shingled with scabs. One side of his jaw was swollen—perhaps from an abscessed tooth. Around his head he had tied a filthy rag with a knot on top of his head—a pathetic gesture of treatment.

When I saw him and he saw that I was awake, he waved his can. He was begging. In pity, I thought, "How can I help him?" Then I remembered. I had money, Japanese money. I quickly groped for my clothing and found some yen notes in my pocket. I tried to open the window, but it was stuck. I slipped on my trousers and hurried to the end of the car. He stood outside expectantly. As I pushed at the resistant door, the train pulled away from the station. Through the dirty windows I could see him, holding that rusty tin can, with the dirty rag around his swollen jaw.

There I stood, an officer from a conquering army, heading home to a family and a future. There I stood, half-dressed, clutching some money which he had seen but which I could not get to him. I wanted to help him, but couldn't. The only comfort I draw is that I did want to help him.

That was thirty-eight years ago, but I can see him as clearly as if it were yesterday.

Perhaps I was scarred by that experience. If so, it is a battle scar, a worthy one, for which I bear no shame. It reminds me of my duty!

Young brethren, I can hear the voice of the Lord saying to each of us just as He said to Peter, "Feed my lambs. . . . Feed my sheep. . . . Feed my sheep." (See John 21:15–17.)

I have unbounded confidence and faith in you, our young brethren. You are the warriors of the Restoration. And in this spiritual battle you are to relieve the spiritual hunger and feed the sheep. It is your duty!

We have the fulness of the everlasting gospel. We have the obligation to share it with those who do not have it. God grant that we will honor that commission from the Lord and prepare ourselves and answer the call, I humbly pray, in the name of Jesus Christ, amen.

5

The Redemption
of the Dead

I have reason, my brothers and sisters, to feel very deeply about the subject that I have chosen for today, and to feel more than the usual need for your sustaining prayers because of its very sacred nature.

No Other Name

When the Lord was upon the earth He made it very clear that there was one way, and one way only, by which man may be saved. "I am the way, the truth, and the life: no man cometh unto the Father, but by me" (John 14:6). As we seek to proceed on that way, two things emerge as being firmly fixed. First, in His name rests the authority to secure the salvation of mankind, "for there is none other name under heaven given . . . whereby we must be saved" (Acts 4:12). And next, there is an essential ordinance —baptism—standing as a gate through which every soul must pass if he would obtain eternal life.

Address given at general conference October 1975.

The Lord was neither hesitant nor apologetic in proclaiming exclusive authority over those processes, all of them in total, by which we may return to the presence of our Heavenly Father. This ideal was clear in the minds of His Apostles also, and their preaching provided for one way, and one way only, for people to be saved.

Over the centuries men saw that many, indeed most, never found that way. This became very hard to explain. Perhaps they thought it was generous to conclude that there were other ways. So they tempered, or tampered with, doctrine.

This rigid emphasis on "one Lord and one baptism" was thought to be too restrictive, too exclusive, even though the Lord Himself had described the way as being narrow, for "strait is the gate, and narrow is the way, which leadeth unto life" (Matthew 7:14).

Since baptism is essential, there must be an urgent concern to carry the message of the gospel of Jesus Christ to every nation, kindred, tongue, and people. That came as a commandment from Him.

His true servants will be out to convert to the principles of the gospel all who hear, and they offer them that one baptism which He proclaimed as essential. The preaching of the gospel is evident to one degree or another in most Christian churches. Most of their members, however, are content to enjoy whatever they can gain from membership in their church without any real effort to see that others hear about it.

Missionary Effort Itself a Witness

The powerful missionary spirit and the vigorous missionary activity in The Church of Jesus Christ of Latter-day Saints becomes a very significant witness that the true gospel and the true authority are possessed in the Church. We accept the responsibility to preach the gospel to every person on earth. And if the question is asked, "You mean you are out to convert the entire world?" the answer is: "Yes. We will try to reach every living soul."

Some who measure that challenge quickly say, "Why, that's impossible! It cannot be done!"

To that we simply say, "Perhaps, but we shall do it anyway."

Against the insinuation that it cannot be done, we are willing to commit to this work every resource that can be righteously accumulated. And while our effort may seem modest when measured against the challenge, it is hard to ignore when measured against what is being accomplished, or even what is being attempted, elsewhere.

Presently we have over 21,000 missionaries serving in the field—and paying for the privilege. And that's only part of the effort. Now, I do not suggest that the number should be impressive, for we do not feel we are doing nearly as well as we should be. And more important than that number, any one of them would be evidence enough if the world knew the source of the individual conviction that each carries.

We ask no relief of the assignment to seek out every living soul, teach them the gospel, and offer them baptism. And we're not discouraged, for there is a great power in this work, and that can be verified by anyone who is sincerely inquiring.

What of Unbaptized Deceased?

Now, there is another characteristic that identifies the Lord's church and also has to do with baptism. There is a very provoking and very disturbing question about those who died without baptism. What about them? If there is none other name given under heaven whereby man must be saved (and that is true), and they have lived and died without even the invitation to accept it, where are they now?

That is hard to explain. It describes most of the human family.

There are several religions that are larger than most Christian denominations, and together those religions are larger than all of the Christian denominations combined. Their adherents for centuries have lived and died and never heard the word *baptism*. What is the answer for them?

That is a most disturbing question. What power would establish one Lord and one baptism and then allow it to happen that most of the human family never comes within its influence? With that question unanswered, the vast majority of the human family must be admitted to be lost, and against any reasonable application of the law of justice, or of mercy, either. How could Christianity itself be sustained?

When you find the true church you will find the answer to that disturbing question.

If a church has no answer for that, how can it lay claim to be the Church of Jesus Christ? He is not willing to write off the majority of the human family who were never baptized.

Those who admit in puzzled frustration that they have no answer to this cannot reasonably lay claim to authority to administer in the affairs of the Lord on the earth, or to oversee the work by which all mankind must be saved.

Since they had no answer concerning the fate of those who had not been baptized, Christians came to believe that baptism itself was not critical in importance, and that the name of Christ may not be all that essential. There must, they supposed, be other names whereby man could be saved.

Vicarious Ordinances Revealed

The answer to that puzzling challenge could not be invented by men, but was *revealed*. I emphasize the word *revealed*. Revelation too is an essential characteristic of His church. Communication with Him through revelation was established when the Church was established. It has not ceased and it is constant in the Church today.

As I address myself to the question of those who died without baptism, I do so with the deepest reverence, for it touches on a sacred work. Little known to the world, we move obediently forward in a work that is marvelous in its prospects, transcendent above what man might have dreamed of, supernal, inspired, and true. In it lies the answer.

In the earliest days of the Church the Prophet Joseph Smith was given direction through revelation that work should commence on the building of a temple, akin to the temples that had been constructed anciently. Ordinance work to be performed there for the salvation of mankind was revealed.

Then another ancient scripture, ignored or overlooked by the Christian world in general, was understood and moved into significant prominence: "Else what shall they do which are baptized for the dead, if the dead rise not at all? why are they then baptized for the dead?" (1 Corinthians 15:29.)

Here, then, was the answer. With proper authority an individual could be baptized for and in behalf of someone who had died without ever having the opportunity. In the spirit world that individual would then accept or reject the baptism, according to his or her own desire.

This work came as a great affirmation of something very basic that the Christian world now only partly believes, and that is that there is life after death. Mortal death is no more an ending than birth was a beginning. The great work of redemption goes on beyond the veil as well as here in mortality.

The Lord said, "Verily, verily, I say unto you, The hour is coming, and now is, when the dead shall hear the voice of the Son of God: and they that hear shall live" (John 5:25).

On October 3, 1918, President Joseph F. Smith was pondering on the scriptures, including this one from Peter: "For this cause was the gospel preached also to them that are dead, that they might be judged according to men in the flesh, but live according to God in the spirit" (1 Peter 4:6).

There was opened to him a marvelous vision. In it he saw the concourses of the righteous. And he saw Christ ministering among them. Then he saw those who had not had the opportunity, and those who had not been valiant. And he saw the work for their redemption. I quote from his record of this vision: "I perceived that the Lord went not in person among the wicked and the disobedient who had rejected the truth, to teach them: but behold, from among the righteous, he organized his forces and appointed messengers, clothed with power and authority, and commissioned them to go forth and carry the light of the gospel to them that were in darkness, even to all the spirits of men; and thus was the gospel preached to the dead" (D&C 138:29–30).

We have been authorized to perform baptisms vicariously so that when those who have passed on hear the gospel preached and desire to accept it, that essential ordinance will have been performed. They need not ask for any exemption from that essential ordinance. Indeed, the Lord Himself was not exempted from it.

Here and now, then, we move to accomplish the work to which we are assigned. We are busily engaged in that kind of baptism. We gather the records of our kindred dead—indeed, the records of the entire human family; and in sacred temples in baptismal fonts designed as those were anciently, we perform these sacred ordinances.

"Strange," one may say. It *is* passing strange. It is transcendent and supernal. The very nature of the work testifies that Jesus

Christ is our Lord, that baptism is essential, that He taught the truth.

And so the question may be asked, "You mean you are out to provide baptism for all who have ever lived?"

And the answer is simply, "Yes." For we have been commanded to do so.

"You mean for the entire human family? Why, that is impossible! If the preaching of the gospel to all who are living is a formidable challenge, then the vicarious work for all who have ever lived is impossible indeed."

To that we say, "Perhaps, but we shall do it anyway."

And once again we certify that we are not discouraged. We ask no relief of the assignment, no excuse from fulfilling it. Our effort today is modest indeed when viewed against the challenge. But since nothing is being done for them elsewhere, our accomplishments, we have come to know, have been pleasing to the Lord.

The Work Goes Forward

Already we have collected hundreds of millions of names, and the work goes forward in the temples and will go on in other temples that will be built. We do not suggest that the size of the effort should be impressive, for we are not doing nearly as well as we should be.

Those who thoughtfully consider the work inquire about those names that cannot be collected. "What about those for whom no record was ever kept? Surely you will fail there. There is no way you can search out those names."

To this I simply observe, "You have forgotten revelation." Already we have been directed to many records through that process. Revelation comes to individual members as they are led to discover their family records in ways that are miraculous indeed. And there is a feeling of inspiration attending this work that can be found in no other. When we have done all that we can do, we shall be given the rest. The way will be opened up.

Every Latter-day Saint is responsible for this work. Without this work, the saving ordinances of the gospel would apply to so few who have ever lived that it could not be claimed to be true.

There is another benefit from this work that relates to the living. It has to do with family life and the eternal preservation of it. It has to do with that which we hold most sacred and dear — the association with our loved ones in our own family circle.

Something of the spirit of this can be sensed as I quote from a letter from my own family records. The letter is dated 17 January 1889, Safford, Graham County, in Arizona. It concerns my great-grandfather Jonathan Taylor Packer, who was the first of our line in the Church and who died a few days after the letter was written to the family by a daughter-in-law.

After describing the distress and difficulty he had suffered for several weeks, she wrote:

> But I will do all I can for him for I consider it my duty. I will do for him as I would like someone to do for my dear mother, for I am afraid I shall never see her again in this world.

And then she wrote this:

> Your father says for you all to be faithful to the principles of the gospel and asks the blessings of Abraham, Isaac, and Jacob upon you all, and bids you all good-bye until he meets you in the morning of the resurrection.
>
> Well, Martha, I can't hardly see the lines for tears, so I will stop writing.
>
> From your loving sister, Mary Ann Packer.

I know that I shall see this great-grandfather beyond the veil, and my grandfather, and my father. And I know that I shall there also meet those of my ancestors who lived when the fulness of the gospel was not upon the earth; those who lived and died without ever hearing the name of Jesus Christ, without ever having the invitation to be baptized.

I say that no point of doctrine sets this church apart from the other claimants as this one does. Save for it, we would, with all of the others, have to accept the clarity with which the New Testament declares baptism to be essential and then admit that most of the human family could never have it.

But we have the revelations. We have those sacred ordinances. The revelation that places upon us the obligation for this baptism for the dead is section 128 in the Doctrine and Covenants. I should like to read two or three of the closing verses of that section.

> Brethren, shall we not go on in so great a cause? Go forward and not backward. Courage, brethren; and on, on to the victory! Let your hearts rejoice, and be exceedingly glad. Let the earth break forth into singing. Let the dead speak forth anthems of eternal praise to the King Immanuel, who hath ordained, before the world was, that which would enable us to redeem them out of their prison. . . .
>
> Let the mountains shout for joy, and all ye valleys cry aloud; and all ye seas and dry lands tell the wonders of your Eternal King! And ye rivers, and brooks, and rills, flow down with gladness. Let the woods and all the trees of the field praise the Lord; and ye solid rocks weep for joy! . . .
>
> Let us, therefore, as a church and a people, and as Latter-day Saints, offer unto the Lord an offering in righteousness; and let us present in his holy temple . . . a book containing the records of our dead, which shall be worthy of all acceptation. (D&C 128: 22–24.)

I bear witness that this work is true; that God lives; that Jesus is the Christ; that there is on this earth today a prophet of God to lead modern Israel in this great obligation. I know that the Lord lives and that He broods anxiously over the work for the redemption of the dead. In the name of Jesus Christ, amen.

II

Inspiration

6

To Young Women and Men

This is a worldwide church. I once received a clipping from a newspaper in India reporting something I had said to young people at this pulpit. Among those who now listen, or who may later read what we say, are young men and women, in many lands, struggling through those wonderful, worrisome teenage years. I meet teenagers all over the world, in perhaps seventy countries by now. I have stayed in the homes where you live—from tiny houses propped up on poles in the jungle to luxury city apartments.

I am about fifty years farther down the road of life than you are, but my memory is pretty good and I haven't forgotten entirely how it felt to be where you are. And my children and grandchildren renew my memory of how it feels to be a teenager.

Some years ago my wife and I stopped at a small restaurant. The young woman who served our meal was courteous but very sober. When she handed me the check, I said, "Can you tell us which road we take to get out of town?" Suddenly she burst into

Address given at general conference April 1989.

tears and said, "Mister, I don't even know how I got into this town."

I have wished more than once that we could have gone to a table in the corner and talked. Perhaps we could have helped her.

Teenage Wishes

Teenagers, even young men, sometimes feel like bursting into tears and saying, "Mister, I don't even know how I got here." You wonder *who* you are and *why* you are and how you got to *where* you are.

I know that you sometimes feel that life isn't fair; you wonder why you can't have things that others have. You even wonder why you can't *be* somebody else and exchange your body with someone who appears to be more beautiful or handsome or talented, or brighter or stronger or thinner; or why you can't change personalities with someone who is not so shy or blundering or frightened as you are.

Sometimes you wonder why you can't trade your parents for some better ones. No need to apologize—they sometimes wish they could trade you for someone easier to live with.

But parents and grandparents make allowances for those feelings. After all, we are just teenagers who have evened out a few of our frustrations so that they don't show as much as they did when we were your age. And someday, soon enough, *you* are going to be *us!*

A Different World

I wish we could promise you that the world will be safer and easier for you than it was for us. But we cannot make that promise, for just the opposite is true.

There are temptations beckoning to you that were not there when we were teenagers. AIDS had not been invented when we were young, and drugs were something a doctor prescribed. We knew about opium from reading mysteries, but steroids, pills, and crack and all the rest belonged to future imaginations.

Modesty was not mocked then. Morality and courtesy were fostered in books and films as much as their opposites are today.

Perversion was not talked about, much less endorsed as a life-style. What was shunned then as pornographic you see now on prime-time television.

Your challenge is *much* greater than was ours. Few of us would trade places with you. Frankly, we are quite relieved that we are not back where you are. Few of us would be equal to it.

But, oh, what a wonderful time to be young! You have knowledge of many more things than we needed to have. It is my conviction that your generation is better and stronger than was ours— better in many ways! I have faith that you young men and young women can meet the world on its own terms and conquer it!

The Black Knight

Alfred, Lord Tennyson told of Gareth, a prince and a knight of King Arthur's round table, and of his quest. The fair Lady Lyonors had been stolen away by the horrible black knight, who held her in his castle. Many young knights tried to rescue her but failed. They returned defeated and broken, with tales of the awesome power of the black knight; they begged Gareth not to go.

But Gareth went to the castle with the drawbridge, the tower, and the window where "Lady Lyonors wrung her hands and wept." Then, "high on a night-black horse, in night-black arms, with white breastbone, and barren ribs of Death," a laughing skull engraved upon his helmet, "in the half-light—thro' the dim dawn—advanced the monster," more awesome, more terrible even than Gareth had been told. ("Gareth and Lynette," *Idylls of the King*, in *The Complete Poetical Works of Alfred, Lord Tennyson* [Cambridge, Mass.: Riverside Press, 1898], p. 332.)

The black knight lowered his lance and thundered forward. Gareth, who had been defeated in more than one tournament, sensed his terrible fate. Every logic and emotion shouted, "Flee for your life!" But he could not turn away. Not, that is, and keep his honor. Gareth lowered his lance and met the charge.

And then, to his surprise, Gareth unseated the black knight and tore his helmet away. There in that black armor with the bones engraven on it sat a little boy who began to cry and beg for mercy.

Young women, young men, no matter how many tournaments you lose along the way, no matter how monstrous your challenges may be, if you will learn a few simple lessons it can be with you as it was with Gareth on that bridge before the castle of the black knight.

Of Royal Birth

Gareth was only a prince. You are more than that. You are a child of God. He is the father of your spirit. Spiritually you are of noble birth, the offspring of the King of Heaven. Fix that truth in your mind and hold to it. However many generations in your mortal ancestry, no matter what race or people you represent, the pedigree of your spirit can be written on a single line. You are a child of God!

You are a dual being, a spirit clothed in a mortal body. Your body is the instrument of your mind and the foundation of your character. Take nothing into your body which may harm it or disturb the functions of your mind and spirit. Anything that is addictive is dangerous.

Within your body is the power to beget life, to share in creation. The only legitimate expression of that power is within the covenant of marriage. The worthy use of it is the very key to your happiness. Do not use the power prematurely, not with anyone. The misuse of it cannot be made right by making it popular.

Your spirit operates through your mind, but cultivating your intellect is not enough. Reason alone will neither protect nor redeem you. Reason nourished by faith can do both.

The Dark Side

A warning: There is a dark side to spiritual things. In a moment of curiosity or reckless bravado some teenagers have been tempted to toy with Satan worship. Don't you ever do that! Don't associate with those who do! You have no idea of the danger! And there are other foolish games and activities that are on that dark side. Leave them alone!

There is a courage far greater than Gareth needed to face the black knight. It is the courage to run away from unworthy things when you will be mocked for doing so. That courage is laced with wisdom. We had to gain it from experience; you need it now.

You have an alarm system built into both body and spirit. In your body it is pain; in your spirit it is guilt—or spiritual pain. While neither pain nor guilt is pleasant, and an excess of either can be destructive, both are a protection, for they sound the alarm "Don't do that again!"

Be grateful for both. If the nerve endings in your hands were altered so that you couldn't feel pain, you might put them in fire or machinery and destroy them. In your teenage heart of hearts, you know right from wrong (see 2 Nephi 2:5). Learn to pay attention to that spiritual voice of warning within you. Even then you will not get by without some mistakes.

Forgiveness

Those who make one serious mistake tend to add another by assuming that it is then too late for them. It is never too late! Never!

While your temptations are greater than were ours, that will be considered in the judgments of the Lord. He said that "his mercies [are suited] according to the conditions of the children of men" (D&C 46:15). That is only just.

A great contribution to Christian doctrine is the explanation in the Book of Mormon of how *justice* and *mercy* and *repentance* and *forgiveness* work together to erase transgressions (see Alma 42).

The discouraging idea that a mistake (or even a series of them) makes it everlastingly too late does not come from the Lord. He has said that *if* we will repent, not only will He forgive us our transgressions but He will also forget them, will remember our sins no more (see Isaiah 43:25; Hebrews 8:12; 10:17; D&C 58:42; Alma 36:19). Repentance is like soap; it can wash sin away. Ground-in dirt may take the strong detergent of discipline to get the stains out, but out they will come.

Never Give Up

Teenagers also sometimes think: "What's the use? The world will soon be blown all apart and come to an end." That feeling comes from fear, not from faith. No one knows the hour or the day (see D&C 49:7), but the end cannot come until all of the purposes of the Lord are fulfilled. Everything that I have learned from the revelations and from life convinces me that there is time and to spare for you to carefully prepare for a long life.

One day you will cope with teenage children of your own. That will serve you right. Later, you will spoil your grandchildren, and they in turn will spoil theirs. If an earlier end should happen to be in store for someone, that is more reason to do things right.

However limited your body may be, it is a precious gift.

One of you may be well-born and well-formed while another is not. In either case there is a testing. That is what mortality is all about. The poorly born may lack self-esteem, or the well-born may be infected with pride. Pride is the most deadly spiritual virus. In the eternal scheme of things, who is to say which is the more favored?

Note carefully these words from the Book of Mormon: "If men come unto me I will show unto them their weakness. I give unto men weakness that they may be humble; and my grace is sufficient for all men that humble themselves before me; for if they humble themselves before me, and have faith in me, then will I make weak things become strong unto them." (Ether 12:27.)

There may be more justice in who we are and what we have or do not have than we ever suppose.

You are a *child* of God!

What a wonderful time to be young. You will see events in your lifetime that will test your courage and extend your faith. If you will face the sunlight of truth, the shadows of discouragement and sin and error will fall behind you. You must never give up! It is never too late! There is no knight in black armor with such power as you may have if you live righteously.

The Lord calls to you:

> Wherefore, lift up your hearts and rejoice, and gird up your loins, and take upon you my whole armor, that ye may be able to withstand the evil day, having done all, that ye may be able to stand.
>
> Stand, therefore, having your loins girt about with truth, having on the breastplate of righteousness, and your feet shod with the preparation of the gospel of peace, which I have sent mine angels to commit unto you;

Taking the shield of faith wherewith ye shall be able to quench all the fiery darts of the wicked;

And take the helmet of salvation, and the sword of my Spirit, which I will pour out upon you, and my word which I reveal unto you, and be agreed as touching all things whatsoever ye ask of me, and be faithful until I come, and ye shall be caught up, that where I am ye shall be also. (D&C 27:15–18.)

God bless you young women and young men who struggle through the worrisome teenage years. Some of you may not yet have found yourselves, but you are *not* lost, for Jesus is the Christ, the Son of God, our Savior and Redeemer. The gospel has been revealed and restored. Of Him I bear witness as I pray His blessings upon you, our youth, in the name of Jesus Christ, amen.

7

The Country
with a Conscience

When my wife and I lived in New England we visited two historic sites as often as we could. Each inspired a deep feeling of reverence. The first, the birthplace of the Prophet Joseph Smith at South Royalton, Vermont; the other, the Old North Bridge at Concord, Massachusetts, where the never-ending struggle for independence began.

At Concord you follow the battle lane through the trees toward the bridge. A few yards in on the left is a small marker that is missed by most who go there. It marks the grave of two British soldiers. The small plaque reads:

> They came three thousand miles and died
> To keep the past upon the throne;
> Unheard, beyond the ocean tide,
> Their English mother made her moan.
>
> —James Russell Lowell

Address given at American Freedom Festival, Provo, Utah, 25 June 1989.

From this distance it does not offend one's patriotism to feel some deep compassion for those who then were the enemy. Time rearranges our prejudices, and enemies become allies.

But it takes time for feelings to mellow. One early American historian describing the Battle of Bunker Hill said, "Three times in the face of the withering fire, the cowardly British charged up the hill."

Closer to the bridge is the memorial shaft. The monument was dedicated in 1837. Ralph Waldo Emerson, who lived in the neighborhood, wrote his famous "Concord Hymn" for the occasion. Across the bridge where the farmers made their stand is the statue of the Minuteman, cast from old cannons—a colonial farmer depicted leaving his plow, musket in hand. It was dedicated in 1875. President Ulysses S. Grant, his cabinet, and the governors from all New England were present. Emerson's words are engraved on the base of the statue. Let me recite them for you. They are well worth memorizing.

Concord Hymn

By the rude bridge that arched the flood,
　　Their flag to April's breeze unfurled,
Here once the embattled farmers stood,
　　And fired the shot heard round the world.

The foe long since in silence slept;
　　Alike the conqueror silent sleeps;
And Time the ruined bridge has swept
　　Down the dark stream which seaward creeps.

On this green bank, by this soft stream,
　　We set today a votive stone;
That memory may their deed redeem,
　　When, like our sires, our sons are gone.

Spirit, that made these heroes dare
　　To die, and leave their children free,
Bid Time and Nature gently spare
　　The shaft we raise to them and thee.

—Ralph Waldo Emerson

Historical Greatness of Rank and File

George Washington was not at Concord Bridge, nor anyone else you can name. Those there were the anonymous rank and file of the colonists, who wore no uniforms, were untrained for combat, and carried nondescript weapons never intended for military action.

At the dedication of the Minuteman statue, George William Curtis said of them:

> The minute-man of the Revolution!—he was the old, the middle-aged, and the young. He was Captain Miles of Concord, who said that he went to battle as he went to church. He was Captain Davis of Acton, who reproved his men for jesting on the march. He was Deacon Josiah Haynes of Sudbury, eighty years old, who marched with his company to the South Bridge at Concord, then joined in the hot pursuit to Lexington, and fell as gloriously as Warren at Bunker Hill. [We don't remember Warren, either.] He was James Hayward of Acton, twenty-two years old, foremost in that deadly race from Concord to Charlestown, who raised his piece at the same moment with a British soldier, each exclaiming, "You are a dead man!" The Briton dropped, shot through the heart. James Hayward fell mortally wounded. "Father," he said, "I started with forty balls; I have three left. I never did such a day's work before. Tell mother not to mourn too much; and tell her whom I love more than my mother, that I am not sorry I turned out."
>
> This was the minute-man of the Revolution, the rural citizen trained in the common school, the church, and the townmeeting; who carried a bayonet that thought, and whose gun, loaded with a principle, brought down, not a man, but a system." (Charles Eliot Norton, ed., *Orations and Addresses of George William Curtis* [New York: Harper & Brothers, 1894].)

However anonymous each may be, it is always on the rank and file of humankind that the great moments in history rest. It was true then and it is true now.

Let me tell you of two whose names you have never before heard.

Peter Francisco

No one knows for sure where Peter Francisco came from. It is thought that he may have been kidnapped from the island of

Terceira, in the Azores, by Portuguese sailors who hoped to sell him in the American colonies as an indentured servant. If that was the plan something went wrong with it, because they abandoned him on the wharf at Hopewell, Virginia, a few miles downriver from Richmond. He was five years old.

Peter was taken into the home of Judge Anthony Winston, an uncle of Patrick Henry's. Peter was present when the famous "Give me liberty or give me death" speech was given. It did something to the boy. He was sixteen years old and a strapping six feet six inches when he joined Company Nine of the Virginia Tenth Regiment on 10 October 1776.

His first fight was the ill-fated Battle of Brandywine Creek. There he was wounded in the leg and removed to a Moravian farmhouse for treatment. General Lafayette was there being treated for a bullet wound. The general asked the boy if he could do something for him. Peter requested a sword big enough to match his physical stature. The general sent him one. It was five feet long.

Peter fought at Germantown and suffered through Valley Forge. At Monmouth he took a musket ball in his thigh. At the British stronghold at Stony Point he was the second man over the wall and fought on despite a nine-inch bayonet slash across his abdomen.

At nineteen he returned home with a musket ball in one of his legs. It would cause him pain for the rest of his life. Within a year he had re-enlisted and was fighting with the Virginia militia in the South. At Camden, South Carolina, the militia was defeated. Peter rescued a cannon and a colonel from behind enemy lines.

At Guilford Courthouse a British soldier stabbed through the calf of Peter's leg with a bayonet. Later another pierced his other leg at the knee, slicing all the way to the hip bone before Peter fell from his horse. He stayed conscious long enough to crawl to a tree. He was then twenty-one.

Near the end of the war he emerged from a tavern at Burkeville, Virginia, to face nine British soldiers who were scavenging for supplies. Peter was completely unarmed. While some of them looted the tavern, two soldiers held him at sword point. One of them took an interest in Peter's silver knee-buckles. Presently the soldier was dead and Peter held the sword. Six British survivors fled to the advance guard of Tarleton's Legion. The entire guard, four hundred strong, retreated, not knowing that the "ambush" was only one man.

There is more, much more, but that should suffice. Question: Why isn't Peter Francisco remembered? Answer: Because he wasn't a general, even an officer. He was offered a battlefield commission but had to refuse—literacy was required for a commission. Peter Francisco could neither read nor write.

Peter lived to raise a family and died 16 January 1830, when he was about seventy years old.

Hannah Hendee

On 16 October 1780, about the time that Peter was routing the British at the Burkeville tavern, Robert Havens was awakened by the barking of a neighbor's dog; something was after the sheep. Partially clothed, he left his house near the White River in South Royalton, Vermont, and ascended the hill. He found the sheep safe. He stood pensively looking back as the first light of dawn touched his frontier home. Something was wrong!

As he turned to retrace his steps, he saw a large company of Indians move from the forest and push in the front door of his home. Two teenage boys who had been aroused to help with the sheep were getting dressed. One was his son Daniel Havens. The other, Thomas Pimber, was courting a neighbor girl and had stayed overnight with the Havens family.

The boys burst through the back door and ran for their lives. Daniel stumbled as he reached the stream, rolled down the bank under a log, and was not discovered. Thomas Pimber was not so fortunate. In a few minutes the Indians were roaring with delight. His scalp had a double cowlick. Cut in two, it would fetch a double bounty from the British.

The Indians—three hundred of them from Canada—and a few Tories were commanded by a British captain named Horton. The British had offered the Indians eight dollars each for live captive men, something less for boys, and a lesser amount for scalps. The British had placed no bounty on women and girls, who were therefore immune to captivity and subject to something less than death.

During that long-forgotten burning of South Royalton, Vermont, the Indians moved downriver capturing the men and boys, killing those who resisted. They killed all the livestock and burned the houses and barns holding the harvest upon which the colonists depended for survival during the long New England winter.

Some distance downstream, the Hendee family had been warned. The husband set out on foot to warn others further downstream. Hannah Hendee grabbed her seven-year-old son, Michael, and a younger daughter and ran for the woods. Just when she thought she had reached safety a band of Indians stepped from the shadows and wrested her boy from her. One of them spoke English. She demanded to know what they were going to do to her boy. The Indian replied, "Make a soldier of him."

As the Indians dragged her sobbing boy away, she made her way toward the road along the river carrying her little girl, who screamed in panic for her mother to keep the Indians away.

Near the river she met Captain Horton and asked what they intended to do with the little boys. She was told that they would be marched to Canada with the men. She said the youngsters could not endure such a march, and was told, "In that case, they will be killed."

She headed down the road toward Lebanon, sixteen miles away, carrying her little girl. She had not gone far when she was filled with a surge of uncommon resolve, a fierce determination. They should not keep her little boy!

She returned upriver and found the British and the Indians gathering their captives on the opposite bank. She started across and would have drowned had not an old Indian helped her to shore.

Oblivious of the danger, she demanded her little boy. Captain Horton said he could not control the Indians; it was none of his concern what they did. She threatened him: "You are their commander, and they *must* and will obey you. The curse will fall upon *you* for whatever crime *they* may commit, and all the innocent blood they shall here shed will be found in your skirts when the secrets of men's hearts are made known, and it will cry for vengeance upon your head!"

When her little son was brought in she took him by the hand and refused to let go. An Indian threatened her with a cutlass and jerked her son away. She defiantly took him back and said that she would follow them every step of the way to Canada, she would never give up, they would not have her little boy!

Finally, intimidated by her determination, Captain Horton told her to take her son and leave. He could face an army of men, but not a mother driven by the strongest of emotions. She had gone but a few rods when she was made to return. Captain Horton said she must wait in camp until all the captives were assembled and the march north began.

During the day other little boys were brought into camp. Desperately they clung to Mrs. Hendee. With uncommon courage she interceded for them as vigorously as she had for her own.

Finally, when the captives were assembled for the long march to Canada, Mrs. Hendee somehow crossed the river with her daughter and nine small boys: her son, Michael, Roswell Parkurst, Andrew and Sheldon Durkey, Joseph Rix, Rufus Fish and his brother, Nathaniel Evans, and Daniel Downer. Two of them she carried across. The others waded through the water with their arms around each other's necks, clinging to her skirts. As the cold October night closed in, Mrs. Hendee huddled in the woods with the soaking-wet little brood she had rescued from certain death.

One of the boys, Daniel Downer, "received such an affright from the horrid crew, that he was ever afterwards unable to take care of himself, wholly unfit for business and lived for many years, wandering from place to place, a solemn, tho' silent witness of the distress and horror of that dreadful scene." (Evelyn Wood Lovejoy, *History of Royalton, Vermont* [Burlington, Vermont: Free Press Printing Co., 1911].)

> They talk about a woman's sphere,
> As though it has a limit;
>
> There's not a place in earth or heaven,
> There's not a task to mankind given,
>
> There's not a blessing nor a woe,
> There's not a whispered yes or no,
>
> There's not a life, or death, or birth,
> That has a feather's weight of worth . . .
>
> Without a woman in it.
>
> — Author unknown

Inspired by the Cause

Surely neither the famous Patrick Henry, who demanded liberty or death, nor the revered Nathan Hale, who regretted that he had but one life to give for his country, offered more than did

Hannah Hendee, the long-forgotten mother from South Royalton, Vermont. Mrs. Hendee was at war, inspired by the best of all causes, armed with nothing more than a clear conscience, justified by the highest principles of morality.

War is a terrible, terrible thing, but there are times when the God of Heaven justifies a people in taking up arms. The Book of Mormon tells of Nephites locked in battle against a stronger enemy army who "did fight like dragons."

> Nevertheless [the record says], the Nephites were inspired by a better cause, for they were not fighting for monarchy nor power but they were fighting for their homes and their liberties, their wives and their children, and their all, yea, for their rites of worship and their church.
>
> And they were doing that which they felt was the duty which they owed to their God; for the Lord had said unto them, and also unto their fathers, that: Inasmuch as ye are not guilty of the first offense, neither the second, ye shall not suffer yourselves to be slain by the hands of your enemies.
>
> And again, the Lord has said that: Ye shall defend your families even unto bloodshed. Therefore for this cause were the Nephites contending with the Lamanites, to defend themselves, and their families, and their lands, their country, and their rights, and their religion. (Alma 43:45–47.)

Since that fateful day at Concord Bridge, few generations have passed in this land without a call to arms. Threats to our independence have recurred with persistent regularity.

Only twenty-one years passed between the armistice in 1918, which ended World War I, and September 1939, when World War II began! Who was it said, "We learn from history that we learn nothing from history"?

With little hesitation, this nation has responded to threats to freedom with military action. We have fought not only to protect our own independence but also to secure or protect it for other nations.

Sustained by a courage that comes only from a moral people, we have fought for our homes and our families, our lands, our country, our rights, and our religion. "Chains," President David O. McKay said, "are worse than bayonets" (Conference Report, April 1955, p. 24).

While Americans were never to a man "Simon Pure" and there have always been some of us bad enough not to deserve the title of good, moral Christian people, there have always been enough of us who have been good enough to deserve it.

Balance of Decency Shifts

Strength that comes from decency, from morality, is the one, the essential ingredient required for the preservation of freedom, indeed for the preservation of humankind. And there is reason to believe that we are losing it.

Something changed. Perhaps for the first time since Concord Bridge that balance of decency and morality is shifting past the center. The balance, which measures the morality of all of us put together, is slowly tipping in the wrong, fatal direction. These lines written to describe another time and place seem to fit our circumstance now.

> That which they would never yield
> To military might,
> They threw away unwittingly
> When evil came by night
>
> And scattered tares among the grain.
> They did not rouse to see
> Their fundamental moral strength
> In mortal jeopardy.
>
> —"Ancestral Home," by
> Boyd K. Packer, from Donna S. Packer,
> *On Footings from the Past*
> (Salt Lake City: Bookcraft, 1988), p. 401.

The war in Vietnam did something to us. We had the military might—the arms, the ammunition, the manpower, the planes and ships and instruments of war undreamed of in the past. But we could not conquer!

What happened did not happen at Danang or Saigon. It only surfaced there. It happened first in and to the universities of America. It happened when agnostics and atheists were protected in teaching their philosophy of religion in public institutions of higher learning. Because they claim affiliation with no church, the principle of separation of church and state is supposed not to apply to them. They are free to teach their faithless philosophy at public expense, to shake—even destroy—the faith of their students. Meanwhile teachers of faith are restrained and churches are kept off campus.

What happened, happened in and to the schools and the churches, to the towns and the cities; it happened in the homes and in the hearts of the American people.

Some terrible things occurred in Vietnam. Our men had no stomach for it when they were doing it and could not get over it after it was done. Many fought without the conviction that what they were doing had a fundamental moral purpose.

Vietnam was different from the atomic bombs on Nagasaki and Hiroshima at the end of World War II. At that time, because of the slaughter occurring each day and the certainty of a horrible increase in casualties on *both* sides in the event of an invasion of Japan, it had been argued, not without substance, that the loss of life on both sides would be less should the war be brought to an end by the use of the bomb. Even then, something was lost to humanity when that occurred, because the rank and file of humanity suffered.

It was different in the war in Korea as well, for there we had our motives more securely in place. And what was to happen later to the moral fabric of our nation had not happened then.

Weakening of Moral Fiber

Something has happened to our collective conscience. Countries have a conscience, just as people do. Something in our national conscience became unsettled. In the end, a clouded conscience cannot conquer. In the end, a clear conscience cannot be defeated.

Something is weakening the moral fiber of the American people. We have always had couples live together without marriage, but we have not honored it as an acceptable life-style. We have always had children born out of wedlock, but we have never made it to be respectable. And we have never before regarded babies, whether conceived in or out of wedlock, to be an inconvenience and destroyed them by the thousands through abortion; and this while barren couples yearn for a child to raise.

We have always had some who followed a life of perversion, but we have never before pushed through legislation to protect that way of life lest we offend the rights of an individual. We have never been this "liberated" before.

We have always had those who were guilty of criminal acts, but we have not put the rights of the accused above the rights of the victim.

If one single soul does not wish to listen for a moment to a public prayer—one which does not offend, which even pleases the majority—we are told we must now eliminate prayer completely from all public life.

We have always had addictive drugs, but not in the varieties we have now and not widely sold near public schools, even elementary schools. When perversion and addiction are justified as the expression of individual rights and call up a pestilence which threatens even the innocent, must the right of privacy preclude even individual testing to help find out where it is moving? What kind of personal freedom is this, anyway?

Individual and Collective Rights

Did our young men give their lives for this? We have always held the rights of the individual to be sovereign. But we have never before placed the collective rights of the majority in subjugation to the individual rights of any single citizen.

Any virtue, pressed to an extreme, becomes a vice; thrift becomes stinginess, generosity becomes wastefulness, self-confidence becomes pride, humility becomes weakness, and on and on. Individual rights as an ideal cannot endure except there be respect for the agency of others. There is no true freedom without responsibility. Freedom without restraint becomes tyranny of a new and fatal kind.

Freedom certainly cannot exist under a system where the citizens are stripped of individuality and pressed into the classless society by a despotic state, where men and women are compelled to exist as faceless worker bees. That is slavery!

Neither can freedom long survive in a society where the rights of the individual are fanatically promoted regardless of what happens to society itself. The rights of the individual—the ideal, the virtue—when pressed to the extreme, like other virtues will presently become a vice. Unless they ensure some balance, activists, lawyers, legislators, judges, and courts who think they are protecting individual freedom are in fact fabricating a new and subtle and sinister kind of dictatorship.

We have a present example.

A symbol is an object that represents something which, though equally real, is not tangible. The flag is a symbol.

> When Freedom from her mountain height,
> Unfurled her standard to the air,
> She tore the azure robe of night,
> And set the stars of glory there;
> She mingled with its gorgeous dyes
> The milky baldric of the skies,
> And striped its pure, celestial white
> With streakings of the morning light.
> Then from his mansion in the sun
> She called her eagle bearer down,
> And gave into his mighty hand
> The symbol of her chosen land.
>
> —Joseph Rodman Drake, in John Bartlett,
> *Familiar Quotations* (Boston: Little,
> Brown and Company, 1968), p. 578.

To destroy that symbol is to reject what it represents.

The burning of the flag is an act which in itself becomes symbolic. It symbolizes the rejection of the Pledge of Allegiance. The Bill of Rights guarantees freedom of speech. Speech is made up of spoken or printed words. Words are words are words. Acts are acts are acts.

The willful destruction of the flag that belongs to all of us is the act of an extremist. A court decision legalizing the destruction of it to protect the rights of one protester is equally extreme.

The rights of the individual, though God-given, cannot be absolute, simply because there are many individuals. Did not God himself counsel us to be temperate in all things? (Alma 7:23; 38:10; D&C 12:8.)

Freedom Requires a Virtuous Citizenry

Freedom cannot survive in the face of this strange new despotism. But it can survive in a sensible society where extremes are pulled back into balance. We call that democracy. It is worth preserving. It is now in an ominous kind of danger.

The Book of Mormon says something about that.

> Choose you by the voice of this people, judges, that ye may be judged according to the laws which have been given you by our fathers, which are correct, and which were given them by the hand of the Lord.
>
> Now it is not common that the voice of the people desireth anything contrary to that which is right; but it is common for the lesser part of the people to desire that which is not right; therefore this shall ye observe and make it your law—to do your business by the voice of the people.
>
> And if the time comes that the voice of the people doth choose iniquity, then is the time that the judgments of God will come upon you; yea, then is the time he will visit you with great destruction even as he has hitherto visited this land. (Mosiah 29:25–27.)

The Book of Mormon warns us as well to be alert during times of peace and prosperity:

> Yea, and we may see at the very time when he doth prosper his people, yea, in the increase of their fields, their flocks and their herds, and in gold, and in silver, and in all manner of precious things of every kind and art; sparing their lives, and delivering them out of the hands of their enemies; softening the hearts of their enemies that they should not declare wars against them; yea, and in fine, doing all things for the welfare and happiness of his people; yea, then is the time that they do harden their hearts, and do forget the Lord their God, and do trample under their feet the Holy One—yea, and this because of their ease, and their exceedingly great prosperity.
>
> And thus we see that except the Lord doth chasten his people with many afflictions, yea, except he doth visit them with death and with terror, and with famine and with all manner of pestilence, they will not remember him. (Helaman 12:2–3.)

There needs to be enough of us who have faith enough and who are moral enough to desire that which is right. Virtues, like love and liberty and patriotism, do not exist in general, they exist in particular. If morality exists at all, it exists in the individual heart and mind of the ordinary citizen. Such virtues cannot be isolated in any other place; not in the rocks or in the water, not in trees or air, not in animals or birds. If it exists at all, it exists in the human heart. Morality flourishes when the rank and file are free. It flourishes where a conscience is clear, where men have faith in God and are obedient to the restraints he has set upon human conduct.

There is a light, a "true Light, which lighteth every man that cometh into the world" (John 1:9). This Light of Christ is the ingredient which binds the whole human family together and forms something of a universal conscience. There is nothing that is right that we cannot achieve if our individual and our national conscience is clear.

Live Ordinary, Decent Lives

Now what are we to do? Let me tell you:

Just go home and be decent, Sunday-go-to-meeting people. Teach your children decency and honor, cooperation and tolerance, citizenship and patriotism. Teach them to be good. Teach them to have a clear conscience. Then we will produce a generation who will know what to do and have the courage to do it.

Eighty-year-old Deacon Josiah Haynes, who fell at Concord, and twenty-two-year-old James Hayward, whose last words to the girl he loved more than his mother were, "I'm not sorry I turned out," both had conviction and the courage to die for it. Peter Francisco in Virginia, Hannah Hendee in Vermont—both lived for it.

You live for it! Just be decent. Take care of your family, you yourself. Don't abandon that responsibility to the government, and don't let them take it from you. Go where virtue and morality and clear consciences are fostered. Go to church, do your part, pay your tithes and offerings, say your prayers, read the scriptures. Be a citizen, vote; in fact, pray and then vote. Then, when the crisis comes—and come it will—you and all the rest of us will know what is right and be willing to do what is right.

I see something else happening, something good. I see a resurgence of faith and decency. I see a restless public saying, "Hey now, we're getting close to the limit of some things!" I see the rank and file joining to express a collective will. I hear them saying: "We've had enough of extremes. We want balanced, common, garden-variety democracy."

It has been prophesied that the Constitution of the United States will hang by a thread and that the elders of Israel will step forth to save it (Brigham Young, *Journal History*, 4 July 1854; *Church News*, 15 December 1948). In my mind that does not require a few heroes in public office steering some saving legislation through the halls of Congress, neither some brilliant military leaders rallying our defense against an invading army. In my mind, it could well be brought about by the rank and file of men and women of faith who revere the Constitution and believe that the strength of democracy rests in the ordinary family and in each member of it.

That saving strength rests in ordinary fathers and mothers who do not neglect the spiritual development of their children. It rests in fathers and mothers who will send their sons and daughters to the four corners of the earth to teach that if we will follow in His word, "then [we will be his] disciples indeed; and [we] shall know the truth, and the truth shall make [us] free" (John 8:31–32).

Patrick and Nathan, we need you! George and Abraham, we need you! We need your heroic kind of patriotism! Josiah and James and Peter and Hannah, we need you most of all. We need you right where you are, in ordinary towns living in ordinary homes, going to ordinary jobs, sending your children to ordinary schools, and taking them to ordinary churches to worship God. That will secure to us the moral fiber from which will come the extraordinary patriotism and the extraordinary faith to keep us free.

8

The Secret of Service

Much of the past year we have spent presiding over the New England Mission. I can't resist quoting a few lines from Robert Frost. Coming from New England to the many varieties of good weather we have seen here today, these lines seem so appropriate:

> The sun was warm but the wind was chill,
> You know how it is with an April day
> When the sun is out and the wind is still,
> You're one month on in the middle of May.
> But if you so much as dare to speak,
> A cloud comes over the sunlit arch,
> A wind comes off a frozen peak,
> And you're two months back in the middle of March.
>
> —From "Two Tramps in Mudtime"

Address given at general conference April 1966.

New England is beautiful in many ways:

> Oh, beautiful for pilgrim feet,
> Whose stern, impassioned stress
> A thoroughfare of freedom beat
> Across the wilderness!
>
> —Katherine Lee Bates,
> "America the Beautiful"

Something is said about New England's being the cradle of liberty. It is more than that. It is the birthplace of prophets of God. Joseph Smith was born there, Brigham Young, Wilford Woodruff, and many others. Joseph Smith twice preached there from door to door.

Dedication—The Secret of Our "Success"

Today our elders set foot on the same granite cobblestones, tap the same knockers on the same doors to bear the selfsame witness.

People see them come, two by two—teaching truth, leaving blessings. Because they are but striplings, nonmembers do not see them as servants of the Lord, authorized to represent The Church of Jesus Christ of Latter-day Saints—by His own declaration "the only true and living church upon the face of the whole earth, with which I, the Lord, am well pleased" (D&C 1:30).

This dedicated service of the missionaries is most appealing to nonmembers. Last week I sat at lunch with two executives of a national service organization. One of them solicited: "Will you spend an evening with us to explain how your volunteer program works? We depend to a large measure on volunteer help, and we need to know the secret of your success."

If there is a secret to our success, it is poorly kept. The whole purpose of this conference and of our missionary effort is to tell it—over and over and over again.

A prominent minister recently reflected on why their people would not serve. "Our ministers are dedicated. Why will our people not respond?" The thing he does not understand is that the response to such a call does not depend on the dedication and conviction of the minister or the one making the call, but rather upon the dedication and conviction of the one who answers it.

Members' Response to Calls

In The Church of Jesus Christ of Latter-day Saints there is no professional clergy, as there commonly is in the other churches. Perhaps more significant than this, there is no laity. All members of the Church are subject to call to render service and carry on the activities of the Church. The miracle is, the members respond!

On one occasion I was in the office of President Henry D. Moyle when he placed a call. After greeting the man at the other end, he said: "I wonder if your business affairs would bring you into Salt Lake City sometime in the near future? I would like to meet with you and your wife, for I have a matter of some importance that I would like to discuss with you."

Though it was many miles away, that man suddenly remembered that his business would bring him to Salt Lake City the very next morning. I was there when President Moyle announced to this man that he had been called to preside over one of the missions of the Church.

"Now," he said, "we don't want to rush you into this decision. Call me in a day or two, as soon as you are able to make a determination as to your feelings concerning the call."

The man looked at his wife and she looked at him, and without a word there was that silent conversation between husband and wife, and that gentle, almost imperceptible nod. The husband turned back to President Moyle and said: "Well, President, what is there to say? What could we tell you in a few days that we couldn't tell you now? We have been called. What answer is there? Of course, we will respond to the call."

Then President Moyle said gently: "Well, if you feel that way about it, actually there is some urgency about this matter. I wonder if you could be prepared to leave on the thirteenth of March."

The man gulped, for that date was just eleven days away. He glanced at his wife. There was another silent conversation. And he said, "Yes, President, we can meet that appointment."

"What about your business?" asked the President. "What about your grain elevator? What about your livestock? What about your other holdings?"

"I don't know," said the man. "But we will make arrangements. Somehow all of those things will be all right."

Such is the great miracle that we see repeated day after day. These men, each with his wife and family, leave their private affairs settled as best they can with relatives or partners. They respond to the call, giving up political preference, opportunities for promotions and advancements in their careers, opportunities to enlarge their holdings and increase their wealth.

One of the marvelous testimonies we witness regularly is the generosity of nonmember employers. They not only permit but encourage men who may be their key executive officers to respond to such calls and reassure them with this farewell: "We do not understand it, but we compliment you on your dedication. We assure you that you can return with full status."

The generosity of such men, though not members of the Church, will not go unheeded. To you, our friends, who have been thus generous, we say that you are within the scope of our prayers, and blessings will accrue to your benefit.

Perhaps the most remarkable thing about the men and women who serve is their willingness to pay for the privilege. "Bring ye all the tithes into the storehouse, that there may be meat in mine house, and prove me now herewith, saith the Lord of hosts, if I will not open you the windows of heaven, and pour you out a blessing, that there shall not be room enough to receive it" (Malachi 3:10).

Without any dunners or any billing or any system of collections, ten percent of their increase is generously donated. Indeed, this is just the beginning. There is a fast offering to sustain the poor; there are building funds; there are donations of every kind. Such giving robs them of selfishness. It is one thing to give lip service; it is another to order one's life.

These are men and women who are "in the world" but "not of the world." They are Saints—Latter-day Saints—and there are hundreds of thousands of them. The test, of course, is not in numbers only. To know the so-called "secret" one must see within the heart of the individual.

A Personal Witness

It is no light thing to open one's heart and expose the most tender and delicate feelings. I hesitatingly do so only from the feeling that it may help someone, that it may illustrate, that you may understand that the gospel has practical application in everyday life; but most of all, because it is Easter.

Just more than a year ago my mother passed away, a lovely trim little mother of eleven children about whom I have spoken before at this pulpit. Her parents emigrated from the old country, and she grew up speaking Danish.

Two years ago she contracted a fatal malady. Fortunately she was under the care of a doctor who was like a son; his ministering to her showed such a reverence. She faced the experience all too common among us: the gradual weakening and erosion of her capacities, accompanied by increasing pain. At this time one of my brothers in company with the patriarch gave her a blessing, as authorized under the revelation that specifies that "the elders of the church, two or more, shall be called, and shall pray for and lay their hands upon them in my name; and if they die they shall die unto me, and if they live they shall live unto me" (D&C 42:44).

In a marvelous way she was released from pain and could rest comfortably, except when moved about. She faced the long ordeal of the decline.

One Friday afternoon at my desk, while I was working on correspondence, it suddenly occurred to me that my wife and I should go and visit Mother. It was a very strong impression. We made the trip that very day.

We found Mother about the same as she had been on a number of previous visits. She seemed more appreciative than usual for our visit. She then whispered over and over again the single word *tomorrow*. Finally I understood and said, "Mother, is tomorrow the day?"

She smiled a radiant smile that brightened the face of this weakened little lady. "Yes," she said.

"Mother, are you sure?"

"Oh, yes," she said. "I am sure."

I then asked if she would like to have a blessing. "That would be good," she said.

That evening the brothers came, as they usually did, and the six of us administered to her. The spirit of inspiration was present, and the words of the blessing held a sacred assurance to our family.

I was under the necessity of meeting a conference appointment in Panguitch the following day, and hesitated; but finally I felt that I must be about the ministry to which I had been called. The doctor assured us that there was no change in Mother's condition, and it was suggested that I call the home on Sunday evening when I returned.

"Oh, no," I said. "I'll check with you tomorrow."

On Saturday, the tomorrow about which she spoke, I called before leaving. The doctor had been there, and everything was as before. Upon arriving at my destination I called again and received the same assurance. After the first meeting I placed another call and was informed that Mother had slept peacefully away, surrounded by her family. The last words she was heard to speak were "Ira, Ira," the name of my father, who by six years had preceded her in death.

This, then, is the secret: In a thousand quiet, spiritual ways, that witness comes. The gospel of Jesus Christ is true. I bear solemn witness that Jesus is the Christ. I know, and she knew, that He is the resurrection and the life and that, as He said, "he that believeth in me, though he were dead, yet shall he live: and whosoever liveth and believeth in me shall never die" (John 11:25–26).

In the name of Jesus Christ, amen.

9

Atonement, Agency, Accountability

The Lord had come from Gethsemane; before Him was His crucifixion. At the moment of betrayal, Peter drew his sword against Malchus, a servant of the high priest. Jesus said: "Put up again thy sword into his place. . . . Thinkest thou that I cannot now pray to my Father, and he shall presently give me more than twelve legions of angels?" (Matthew 26:52–53.)

"I Lay Down My Life"

During all of the taunting, the abuse, the scourging, and the final torture of crucifixion, the Lord remained silent and submissive. Except, that is, for one moment of intense drama which reveals the very essence of Christian doctrine.

That moment came during the trial. Pilate, now afraid, said to Jesus: "Speakest thou not unto me? knowest thou not that I have

---

Address given at general conference April 1988.

power to crucify thee, and have power to release thee?'' (John 19:10.)

One can only imagine the quiet majesty when the Lord spoke. "Thou couldest have no power at all against me, except it were given thee from above" (John 19:11).

What happened thereafter did not come because Pilate had power to impose it, but because the Lord had the will to accept it. "I lay down my life," the Lord said, "that I might take it again. No man taketh it from me, but I lay it down of myself. I have power to lay it down, and I have power to take it again." (John 10:17–18.)

Before the Crucifixion and afterward, many men have willingly given their lives in selfless acts of heroism. But none faced what the Christ endured. Upon Him was the burden of all human transgression, all human guilt.

Atonement

And hanging in the balance was the Atonement. Through His willing act, mercy and justice could be reconciled, eternal law sustained, and that mediation achieved without which mortal man could not be redeemed.

He, by choice, accepted the penalty for all mankind for the sum total of all wickedness and depravity; for brutality, immorality, perversion, and corruption; for addiction; for the killings and torture and terror—for all of it that ever had been or ever would be enacted upon this earth.

In choosing He faced the awesome power of the evil one, who was not confined to flesh nor subject to mortal pain. That was Gethsemane!

How the Atonement was wrought we do not know. No mortal watched as evil turned away and hid in shame before the light of that pure being.

All wickedness could not quench that light. When what was done was done, the ransom had been paid. Both death and hell forsook their claim on all who would repent. Men at last were free. Then every soul who ever lived could choose to touch that light and be redeemed.

By this infinite sacrifice, through this atonement of Christ, all mankind may be saved by obedience to the laws and ordinances of the gospel.

Atonement is really three words: *at-one-ment*, meaning to set at one, one with God; to reconcile, to conciliate, to expiate.

But did you know that the word *atonement* appears only once in the English New Testament? Only once! I quote from Paul's letter to the Romans: "Christ died for us. . . . For if . . . we were reconciled to God by the death of his Son, much more, being reconciled, we shall be saved by his life. And not only so, but we also joy in God through our Lord Jesus Christ, by whom we have now received the *atonement.*" (Romans 5:8, 10–11, italics added.)

Precious Things Removed—and Restored

Only that once does the word *atonement* appear in the English New Testament. *Atonement,* of all words! It was not an unknown word, for it had been used much in the Old Testament in connection with the law of Moses, but once only in the New Testament. I find that to be remarkable.

I know of only one explanation. For that we turn to the Book of Mormon.

Nephi testified that the Bible once "contained the fulness of the gospel of the Lord, of whom the twelve apostles bear record," and that "after [the words] go forth by the hand of the twelve apostles of the Lamb, from the Jews unto the Gentiles, thou seest the formation of that great and abominable church, which is most abominable above all other churches; for behold, they have taken away from the gospel of the Lamb many parts which are plain and most precious; and also many covenants of the Lord have they taken away" (1 Nephi 13:24, 26).

Jacob defined the great and abominable church in these words: "Wherefore, he that fighteth against Zion, both Jew and Gentile, both bond and free, both male and female, shall perish; for they are they who are the whore of all the earth; for they who are not for me are against me, saith our God" (2 Nephi 10:16).

Nephi said, "Because of the many plain and precious things which have been taken out of the book, . . . an exceedingly great many do stumble, yea, insomuch that Satan hath great power over them" (1 Nephi 13:29). He then prophesied that the precious things would be restored (see 1 Nephi 13:34–35).

And they were restored. In the Book of Mormon the word *atone* in form and tense appears fifty-five times. I quote but one verse from Alma: "And now, the plan of mercy could not be brought about except an *atonement* should be made; therefore God himself *atoneth* for the sins of the world, to bring about the plan of mercy, to appease the demands of justice, that God might be a perfect, just God, and a merciful God also" (Alma 42:15, italics added).

Only once in the New Testament—fifty-five times in the Book of Mormon. What better witness that the Book of Mormon is indeed another testament of Jesus Christ?

And that is not all. The words *atone, atonement, atoneth* appear in the Doctrine and Covenants eleven times and in the Pearl of Great Price three. Sixty-nine references of transcendent importance. And that is not all! Hundreds of other verses help explain it.

Agency, Choice, and the Fall

The cost of the Atonement was borne by the Lord without compulsion, for agency is a sovereign principle. According to the plan, agency must be honored. It was so from the beginning, from Eden. "The Lord said unto Enoch: Behold these thy brethren; they are the workmanship of mine own hands, and I gave unto them their knowledge, in the day I created them; and in the Garden of Eden, gave I unto man his agency" (Moses 7:32).

Whatever else happened in Eden, in his supreme moment of testing Adam made a choice.

After the Lord commanded Adam and Eve to multiply and replenish the earth and commanded them *not* to partake of the tree of knowledge of good and evil, He said: "Nevertheless, thou mayest choose for thyself, for it is given unto thee; but, remember that I forbid it, for in the day thou eatest thereof thou shalt surely die" (Moses 3:17).

There was too much at issue to introduce man into mortality by force. That would contravene the very law essential to the plan. The plan provided that each spirit child of God would receive a mortal body and each would be tested. Adam saw that it must be so and made his choice. "Adam fell that men might be; and men are, that they might have joy" (2 Nephi 2:25).

Adam and Eve ventured forth to multiply and replenish the earth as they had been commanded to do. The creation of their bodies in the image of God, as a separate creation, was crucial to the plan. Their subsequent fall was essential if the condition of mortality was to exist and the plan proceed.

Jacob described what would happen to our bodies and our spirits except an atonement, an infinite atonement, were made. We should, he said, have become "like unto [the devil]" (see 2 Nephi 9:7–9).

I seldom use the word *absolute.* It seldom fits. I use it now — twice. Because of the Fall, the Atonement was absolutely essential for resurrection to proceed and overcome mortal death.

The Atonement was absolutely essential as the means for men to cleanse themselves from sin and overcome the second death, which is the spiritual death, which is separation from our Father in Heaven. For the scriptures tell us — seven times they tell us — that no unclean thing may enter the presence of God.

Those scriptural words "Thou mayest choose for thyself, for it is given unto thee" (Moses 3:17) introduced Adam and Eve and their posterity to all the risks of mortality. In mortality men are free to choose, and each choice begets a consequence. The choice Adam made energized the law of justice, which required that the penalty for disobedience would be death.

But those words spoken at the trial, "Thou couldest have no power at all against me, except it were given thee from above" (John 19:11), proved that mercy was of equal rank. A redeemer was sent to pay the debt and set men free. That was the plan.

Punishment and Repentance

Alma's son Corianton thought it unfair that penalties must follow sin, that there need be punishment. In a profound lesson Alma taught the plan of redemption to his son, and so to us. He spoke of the Atonement and said, "Now, repentance could not come unto men except there were a punishment" (Alma 42:16).

If punishment is the price repentance asks, it comes at bargain price. Consequences, even painful ones, protect us. So simple a thing as a child's cry of pain when his finger touches fire can teach us that. Except for the pain, the child might be consumed.

I readily confess that I would find no peace, neither happiness nor safety, in a world without repentance. I do not know what I should do if there were no way for me to erase my mistakes. The agony would be more than I could bear. It may be otherwise with you, but not with me.

An atonement was made. Ever and always it offers amnesty from transgression and from death if we will but repent. Repentance is the escape clause in it all. Repentance is the key with which we can unlock the prison from inside. We hold that key within our hands, and agency is ours to use it.

How supernally precious freedom is; how consummately valuable is the agency of man!

Lucifer in clever ways manipulates our choices, deceiving us about sin and consequences. He, and his angels with him, tempt us to be unworthy, even wicked. But he cannot—in all eternity he cannot, with all his power he cannot—completely destroy us; not without our own consent. Had agency come to man without the Atonement, it would have been a fatal gift.

Not Chance but Choice

We are taught in Genesis, in Moses, in Abraham, in the Book of Mormon, and in the endowment that man's mortal body was made in the image of God in a separate creation. Had the Creation come in a different way, there could have been no Fall.

If men were merely animals, then logic favors freedom without accountability.

How well I know that among learned men are those who look down at animals and stones to find the origin of man. They do not look inside themselves to find the spirit there. They train themselves to measure things by time, by thousands and by millions, and say these animals called men all came by chance. And this they are free to do, for agency is theirs.

But agency is ours as well. We look up, and in the universe we see the handiwork of God and measure things by epochs, by eons, by dispensations, by eternities. The many things we do not know we take on faith.

But this we know! It was all planned before the world was. Events from the Creation to the final, winding-up scene are not based on *chance*; they are based on *choice!* It was planned that way.

This we know! This simple truth! Had there been no Creation, no Fall, there would have been no need for any Atonement, neither a Redeemer to mediate for us. Then Christ need not have been.

Passover and Sacrament

At Gethsemane and Golgotha the Savior's blood was shed. Centuries earlier the Passover had been introduced as a symbol and a type of things to come. It was an ordinance to be kept forever (see Exodus 12).

When the plague of death was decreed upon Egypt, each Israelite family was commanded to take a lamb—firstborn, male, without blemish. This paschal lamb was to be slain without any of its bones being broken, its blood being used to mark the doorway of the home. The Lord promised that the angel of death would *pass over* the homes so marked and not slay those inside. They were saved by the blood of the lamb.

After the crucifixion of the Lord, the law of sacrifice required no more shedding of blood. For that was done, as Paul taught the Hebrews, "once for all, . . . one sacrifice for sins for ever" (Hebrews 10:10, 12). The sacrifice thenceforth was to be a broken heart and a contrite spirit—repentance.

And the Passover would be commemorated forever as the sacrament, in which we renew our covenant of baptism and partake in remembrance of the body of the Lamb of God, and of His blood, which was shed for us.

It is no small thing that this symbol reappears in the Word of Wisdom. Beyond the promise that obedient Saints in this generation will receive health and great treasures of knowledge is this: "I, the Lord, give unto them a promise, that the destroying angel shall pass by them, as the children of Israel, and not slay them" (D&C 89:21).

I cannot with composure tell you how I feel about the Atonement. It touches the deepest emotion of gratitude and obligation. My soul reaches after Him who wrought it, this Christ, our Savior of whom I am a witness. I testify of Him. He is our Lord, our Redeemer, our advocate with the Father. He ransomed us with His blood.

Humbly I lay claim upon the atonement of Christ. I find no shame in kneeling down in worship of our Father and His Son. For *agency* is mine, and this I *choose* to do!

In the name of Jesus Christ, amen.

10

The Only True Church

We believe that a man must [not could be or might be, but must] be called of God, by prophecy, and by the laying on of hands by those who are in authority, to preach the gospel and administer in the ordinances thereof" (Articles of Faith 1:5). In this manner we receive our commissions to move forward.

Today we have all participated in the sustaining of Elder M. Russell Ballard as a new member of the Quorum of the Twelve Apostles. I'm sure Brother Bruce R. McConkie, with whom Brother Ballard worked on a daily basis in missionary work, is rejoicing this day in what has transpired.

I think the world little understands the significance of this sacred priesthood body. I join my brethren in welcoming you, Brother Ballard, to this sacred brotherhood.

In a former day it was Peter, James, John, Andrew, Philip, Bartholomew, and the others. And in just as real and literal a way the same office, the same calling, the same sacred relationship with

---

Address given at general conference October 1985.

the Lord exists today. In our day it is Spencer, Marion, and Gordon, Ezra and Howard and Thomas and the others, with the same obligation, the same sustaining power to see this work move forward.

I feel humble that it was my privilege with you to raise my hand on this sacred occasion.

In the few moments allotted me I desire to encourage you who feel inadequate when someone rejects one or another of the fundamental doctrines of the gospel.

The Lord said that "every man might speak in the name of God the Lord, even the Savior of the world" (D&C 1:20). So humble men and women, and even young people, not professionally trained for the ministry, carry on the work of the Lord—many of us with little more than the spiritual conviction that it is true. Surely we must appear at times to be very amateurish when compared to the professional clergy of other churches.

The Only-True-Church Challenge

One doctrine presents a particular challenge. It is our firm conviction that The Church of Jesus Christ of Latter-day Saints is, as the revelations state, "the only true and living church upon the face of the whole earth" (D&C 1:30). This doctrine often generates resistance and repels the casual investigator. Some have said, "We want nothing to do with anyone who makes so presumptuous a claim as that."

The early Latter-day Saints were bitterly persecuted for holding to this doctrine. They were the butt of many clever stories. We, of course, are not free from that today.

Should we not, then, make one accommodation and set this doctrine aside? Would it not be better to have more accept what would be left of the gospel than the relatively few who are converted now?

Our missionaries sift through thousands to find one convert. Our harvest may seem impressive, but we are but gleaners. As the scriptures have foretold, we gather "one of a city, and two of a family" (Jeremiah 3:14).

Some have recommended that we confine ourselves strictly to evidences of the gospel, happy family life, temperate living, and so on.

Could we not use the words *better* or *best?* The word *only* really isn't the most appealing way to begin a discussion of the gospel.

If we thought only in terms of diplomacy or popularity, surely we should change our course. But we must hold tightly to it even though it causes some to turn away. It is little wonder that our missionaries are sometimes thought to be overbearing, even when they are most courteous.

If our main desire is to be accepted and approved, surely we will feel uncomfortable when others reject the gospel.

Feeling Comfortable with Rich and Poor

I recall an experience from pilot training in World War II. Air cadets were posted to colleges for ground training. I was in a group assigned to Washington State University at Pullman. Eight of us who had never met were assigned to the same room. The first evening we introduced ourselves.

The first to speak came from a wealthy family in the East. He described the private schools he had attended. He said that each summer his family had "gone on the Continent." I had no way of knowing that meant they had traveled to Europe.

The father of the next had been governor of Ohio and at that time was in the president's cabinet.

And so it went. I was younger than most, and it was my first time away from home. Each of the others had attended college; I had not. In fact, there was nothing to distinguish me at all.

When finally I got the courage to speak, I said: "I come from a little town in Utah that you have never heard of. I come from a large family, eleven children. My father is a mechanic and runs a little garage." I said that my great-grandfather had joined the Church and come West with the pioneers.

To my surprise and relief, I was accepted. My faith and my obscurity were not a penalty.

From then until now I have never felt uncomfortable among people of wealth or achievement, of high station or low. Nor have I been ashamed of my heritage or of the Church, nor have I felt the need to apologize for any of its doctrines, even those I could not defend to the satisfaction of everyone who might ask.

The Lord's Plain Words

Inevitably (and properly) the "true church" doctrine emerges very early in any serious discussion of the gospel. For there is no better place to start such a discussion than with the First Vision; and there, in that very first conversation with man in this dispensation, the Lord presented this doctrine in unmistakable clarity.

Joseph Smith sought answer to the question "which of all the sects was right . . . and which should [he] join" (Joseph Smith—History 1:18). Surely he supposed that somewhere the "right" church was to be found. A simple direction to it would end his search. He could then join that church, live the tenets it proclaimed, and that would be that.

But that was not to be. In response to his humble prayer the Father and the Son appeared to him. When he gained possession of himself so as to be able to speak, he asked "which of all the sects was right, that [he] might know which to join" (Joseph Smith—History 1:18).

He recorded this:

> I was answered that I must join none of them, for they were all wrong; and the Personage who addressed me said that all their creeds were an abomination in his sight; that those professors were all corrupt; that: "they draw near to me with their lips, but their hearts are far from me, they teach for doctrines the commandments of men, having a form of godliness, but they deny the power thereof."
> He again forbade me to join with any of them. (Joseph Smith—History 1:19–20.)

That is very blunt language. Little wonder that when Joseph Smith repeated it, the troubles began.

If ever he was tempted to disregard those words, he could reflect that they were sustained in subsequent revelations. A little more than a year after the Church was organized, the first section of the Doctrine and Covenants was revealed. In it the Lord said that the Book of Mormon was given in order that his servants "might have power to lay the foundation of this church, and to bring it forth out of obscurity and out of darkness, *the only true and living church upon the face of the whole earth*, with which I, the Lord, am well pleased, speaking unto the church collectively and not individually'' (D&C 1:30, italics added).

After making it clear that he was ''speaking unto the church collectively and not individually,'' the Lord warned, ''I the Lord cannot look upon sin with the least degree of allowance'' (D&C 1:31).

We know there are decent, respectable, humble people in many churches, Christian and otherwise. In turn, sadly enough, there are so-called Latter-day Saints who by comparison are not as worthy, for they do not keep their covenants.

Doctrine Is Logical and True

But it is not a matter of comparing individuals. We are not baptized collectively, nor will we be judged collectively. Good conduct without the ordinances of the gospel will neither redeem nor exalt mankind; covenants and the ordinances are essential. We are required to teach the doctrines, even the unpopular ones. Yield on this only-true-church doctrine and you cannot justify the Restoration. The doctrine is true, it is logical; the opposite position is not.

A few weeks ago I was returning from the East with President Hinckley. We conversed with a passenger who said something to the effect that all churches lead to heaven. How often have you heard that—the parallel-path-to-heaven philosophy?

Those who believe this say that one church is not really better than another, but just different. Eventually the paths will converge. A person is therefore quite as safe in any church as in any other.

While this seems to be very generous, it just cannot be true.

I find it so interesting that those who condemn us reject the parallel-path philosophy themselves when it comes to non-Christian religions. For if they do not, they have no reason to accept the Lord as our Redeemer or regard the Atonement as essential. And what could they do with His statement that ''he that believeth and is baptized shall be saved; but he that believeth not shall be damned''? (Mark 16:16.)

While the converging-path idea is very appealing, it really is not reasonable. Suppose schools were operated on that philosophy, with each discipline a separate path leading to the same diploma. No matter whether those enrolled studied or not, passed the tests or not, all would be given the same diploma—the one of their choice. Without qualifying, one could choose the diploma of an attorney, an engineer, a medical doctor. Surely you would not submit yourself to surgery under the hands of a graduate of that kind of school!

But it does not work that way. It cannot work that way—not in education, not in spiritual matters. There are essential ordinances just as there are required courses. There are prescribed standards of worthiness. If we resist them, avoid them, or fail them, we will not enter in with those who complete the course.

Do you realize that the notion that all churches are equal presupposes that the *true* church of Jesus Christ actually does not exist anywhere? Now, others may insist that *this* is not the true church. That is their privilege. But to claim that the true church does not exist anywhere, that it does not even *need* to exist, is to deny the scriptures. The New Testament teaches of "one Lord, one faith, one baptism" and speaks of [all coming] in the unity of the faith" (Ephesians 4:5, 13), and of a "restitution of all things, which God hath spoken by the mouth of all his holy prophets since the world began" (Acts 3:21).

We Latter-day Saints did not invent the doctrine of the only true church. It came from the Lord. Whatever perception others have of us, however presumptuous we appear to be, whatever criticism is directed to us, we must teach it to all who will listen.

Church Must Stand Independent

The Lord commanded the Latter-day Saints that "notwithstanding the tribulation which shall descend upon you," the Church must "stand independent above all other creatures beneath the celestial world" (D&C 78:14). In obedience we remain independent. While we cooperate with others to reach mutual objectives, we do it in our own way. We cannot recognize the ordinances performed in other churches. We cannot exchange baptisms, a practice which has become commonplace in the Christian world. We do not join associations of clergy or councils of churches. We keep our distance from the ecumenical movements. The restored gospel is the means by which Christians must ultimately be united.

We do not claim that other Christian churches have no truth. The Lord described them as having "a form of godliness." Converts to the Church may bring with them all the truth they possess —and have it added upon.

We are not free to alter this fundamental doctrine of the gospel, not even in the face of the tribulation prophesied in the revelation I have quoted (D&C 78). Popularity and the approval of the world perhaps must remain ever beyond our reach.

Bear Witness and Be at Peace

Some years ago, at a time when a Church member's campaign for national office was creating much interest, I was invited to speak to a group at Harvard University. Both faculty members and students were to be present. I, of course, hoped that the gospel message would be accepted and that the meeting would end in a harmony of views. As I prayed that this might result, there came to me the strong impression that this petition would not be granted. I determined that, however preposterous talk about angels and golden plates and restoration might be to my audience, I would teach the truth with quiet confidence, for I have a testimony of the truth. If some must come from the meeting unsettled and disturbed, it would not be *me*. Let *them* be disturbed, if they would.

It was as the Spirit foretold. Some in the group shook their heads in amazement, even cynical amusement, that anyone could believe such things. But I was at peace. I had taught the truth, and they could accept it or reject it, as they pleased.

There is always the hope, and often it is true, that in a group one person with an open mind may admit one simple thought: "Could it possibly be true?" Combine that thought with sincere prayer and one more soul enters a private sacred grove to find the answer to the question, "Which of all the churches is true, and which should I join?"

As I grow in age and experience, I grow ever *less* concerned over whether others agree with us. I grow ever *more* concerned that they understand us. If they do understand, they have their agency and can accept or reject the gospel as they please.

It is not an easy thing for us to defend the position that bothers so many others. But, brethren and sisters, never be ashamed of the gospel of Jesus Christ. Never apologize for the sacred doctrines of the gospel. Never feel inadequate and unsettled because you cannot explain them to the satisfaction of all who might inquire of you. Do not be ill at ease or uncomfortable because you can give little more than your conviction.

Be assured that, if you will explain what you know and testify of what you feel, you may plant a seed that will one day grow and blossom into a testimony of the gospel of Jesus Christ.

I bear testimony that The Church of Jesus Christ of Latter-day Saints is, as the Lord declared, the only true and living church upon the face of the earth; that with it he is well pleased, speaking of the Church collectively; and that if individually we are humble and faithful we can stand approved of him.

If we can stand without shame, without hesitancy, without embarrassment, without reservation, to bear witness that the gospel has been restored, that there are prophets and Apostles upon the earth, that the truth is available for all mankind—if we can do this the Lord's Spirit will be with us. And that assurance can be affirmed to others. Of that I bear witness in the name of Jesus Christ, amen.

III
Caution

11

Steady As She Goes

There is a mariner's command, given usually by the captain to the helmsman, that embodies my message to you this morning. It is a command; but it becomes an expression of direction and reassurance, particularly when a vessel is set on course in difficult times. The expression is "Steady as she goes." Those of you who have served on ships, particularly in times of stress and difficulty, have heard that reassuring command, "Steady as she goes."

"Like the Present Period"

Charles Dickens opened his classic historical novel *A Tale of Two Cities* with this long sentence:

> It was the best of times, it was the worst of times, it was the age of wisdom, it was the age of foolishness, it was the epoch of belief, it was the epoch of incredulity, it was the season of Light, it

Address given to Brigham Young University student body 7 January 1969.

was the season of Darkness, it was the spring of hope, it was the winter of despair, we had everything before us, we had nothing before us, we were all going direct to Heaven, we were all going direct the other way—in short, the period was so far like the present period, that some of its noisiest authorities insisted on its being received, for good or for evil, in the superlative degree of comparison only. . . . It was the year of Our Lord one thousand seven hundred and seventy-five.

Across the world in that year there was unrest, dissension, disorder, violence, insurrection, and revolution. It was indeed a "period . . . like the present period."

We live in such a time. Your voyage on the sea of life now heads into troubled waters. During this school year we have already ridden out a squall or two. Storm clouds gather ominously overhead. Perhaps they will pass over, but perhaps we must face into the storm and ride them out. You will be participants in—at least witnesses to—trying and important events in the history of the world and the history of the Church.

Thank God that you were born in this era! Be grateful that you are alive and have the happy opportunity, the priceless, happy opportunity, of arriving at early maturity in this momentous, adventuresome time.

I have several suggestions for you—positive hints on navigation—each in keeping with my conviction that this is the best, the very best, time to be sailing toward maturity.

A Good Beginning

First, please know that your voyage has a good beginning. While no one of you is so well endowed as to be overly impressed with your own potential, no one of you is so unendowed that you don't have an adequate beginning—particularly spiritually, which is where the test will come.

You may wish to compare your beginning with another. A few weeks ago I was traveling in The Netherlands with President Peter Dalebout. As we drove into Rotterdam along the Rhine River I commented on the barges moving upstream loaded with sand and rock and timber. President Dalebout mentioned that as a boy he had lived on a barge. And then he related this touching story:

When he was eight, his father was in America trying to get means to bring the family over here. His mother did her best to keep several children fed and clothed. They were in difficult if not desperate circumstances. Because of their impoverished way of living they contracted tuberculosis. When one member of the family was cured, he would be reinfected from another who had the disease. Two sisters died.

One night, after the boy was asleep, an uncle whom he had never seen stopped to visit. He worked on a barge going up and down the Rhine. It almost never stopped at this little community, but that night it did. The uncle had come to see the family. Peter's mother sobbed out her concern for the lives of her children, and her brother generously thought of a way that he could help. "I can take the boy with me," he said. "He will be all right on the barge." So that night, while the boy was still asleep, his uncle carried him to a rowboat, along with the few meager items of clothing he possessed, and took him aboard the barge.

Peter was awakened the next morning by the motion of the barge. Puzzled and frightened, he began to cry. A woman he had never seen came into the cabin to comfort him and said: "I am your Aunt Elizabeth. You are going to live with us now." He cried most of the time for the first two weeks.

Then one day, as he changed clothing, he felt in his pockets and to his surprise found a dime. Now, a dime in the Netherlands, which contains a profile of Queen Wilhelmina, is a very small coin, much smaller than our own ten-cent piece. He wept for joy when he found the coin, for he knew then that his mother loved him. His mother just didn't have a dime to spare for anything, yet she must have put that in his pocket; it was a message to him. The coin was almost worn through between his little fingers. He looked at it so often that somehow he became sure that the picture on the coin was of his mother. It was eighteen months later when, robust in health, he was returned to his family—a family united in hopeless poverty.

It is an interesting account, the story of how he found his way through life—how he finally came to own a large steel plant in Los Angeles, how he came to possess substantial wealth, but, more important, how he became capable and worthy to be called of the Lord to return to his homeland and preside over the Church mission there.

Power to Control

No one of you has a less promising beginning than President Dalebout had; so we say, move ahead, steady as she goes. You have great power for good, power to control your course.

In that regard, here is a lesson drawn from a little girl who reported to her mother that her brother was setting traps for birds. She didn't like it at all.

"He won't catch any birds in his trap, will he, Mother?" she asked. "I have prayed about it and asked Heavenly Father to protect the birds. He won't catch anything, will he, Mother?" Becoming more positive, she said, "I *know* he won't catch anything, because I have prayed about it."

The mother asked, "How can you be sure he won't catch anything?"

Then came a meaningful addition: "He won't catch anything because, after I said my prayers, I went out and kicked that old trap all to pieces."

I think no editorializing on that is necessary.

Live Now, Be Settled

The next suggestion I have for you is to learn to live fully and righteously *now*. If there are storms and uncertainties on the course ahead, look to the present.

I learned a lesson while serving in the military during World War II. A group of us was sent overseas to the Pacific, and while we were en route to our assignment the Japanese surrendered. The war was over, and we were diverted to a replacement depot on Leyte in the Philippines. From there we moved to Manila, then to Clark Field. No one seemed to know what to do with us. We would be in one place a short time and then be shipped to another place. It was miserable!

At some time during this experience I heard a lesson relating to the pioneers. It emphasized the theme that they built permanently wherever they were. In Kirtland, in Missouri, in Nauvoo, they settled down; they built fine, substantial homes and strong communities. When the storms broke over them, they were exiled and had to move from place to place. Each time, they built in the new location as well and as permanently as they could. When they moved to these Utah valleys they built the best they possibly could with the materials and resources available to them. Many of them had hardly finished building their homes when they were called to colonize other places in the Great Basin. There they followed the same pattern; they settled down and built substantially.

After hearing that lesson I rebelled against my own circumstances. For months we had been living out of our duffel bags —pushed here and there, never knowing how long we would be staying, never unpacking, living from hour to hour and day to day, always waiting for the next assignment. I decided I would thereafter have no part of that spirit; if the pioneers could settle down, so could I. That day I unpacked and settled in as comfortably as possible and began to act like a permanent resident. Before long we moved again. The day we arrived at the new destination I unpacked and settled down.

This change of approach meant the difference between misery and happiness. And it was a great lesson. It is one we all ought to draw from our forefathers. My wife and I have lived that way since. This ideal has contributed to our security in marriage and to our happiness and stability as a family.

I meet so many people who are "en route," anxious to finish their present task so that they may begin to live, yet nervous about the uncertainties and the storm clouds ahead. Don't be that way; settle down. Here in school look forward, but remember that life is *today*. Settle into your studies, particularly settle into your ward assignments, your spiritual growth. Settle down permanently where you are. Relax, enjoy it, even though as students you know you will not be here very long. The *future* is not your challenge, nor will it ever be. The *present* is your challenge; so remember, set your course steady as she goes.

Be You

Now, be glad that you live in stormy, troubled times, and be glad that you are you. Never, never wish that you were someone else. You *are* you. Accept that. You will always be you.

You may complain about your lot in life. Your social or economic inheritance may not be to your desire. You may think yourself limited mentally (we probably don't use 15 percent of our mental capacity). You may not like the body you are inhabiting—but remember that ultimately it may be perfected. You are you—a separate, individual intelligence. You are a spirit inhabiting a body: "And the spirit and the body are the soul of man" (D&C 88:15). Sometimes we make an appraisal of ourselves in comparison with another and foolishly wish we were somebody else. Never do that. Thank the Lord for who you are and what you may become. "As man is, God once was; as God is, man may become" (Lorenzo Snow).

The measure of success will be neither fame nor fortune nor wealth. I am sure there are those here—particularly I am thinking of faculty members who are not known widely beyond the classrooms where they teach—who live in almost complete obscurity yet whose names are spoken reverently on the lips of angels as the spiritual aristocracy on earth. Now stand steady. Be *you*. Steady as she goes.

Use Spiritual Powers

As the squalls hit us, there are those aboard who lack faith. Some are embarrassed and fearful. They question the course we are on, pointing nervously to the clouds and criticizing the captain and the crew. "Change course, change course," they plead. Some grow mutinous, and a few abandon ship to be set adrift in the endless expanse of eternity, perhaps lost in the darkness and the depths. Steady as you go, lest you be washed overboard.

As you sail through stormy issues, be wise in your judgments. Make sure you use all of your powers, particularly your spiritual powers, to resolve the touchy issues before you. Some things are not as they seem to be.

On that point, let me share with you one other experience.

Several years ago I was a member of a city council and also a member of a stake high council. Late one Monday night, I was going home from a high council meeting. While I was traveling through the business district on a street without traffic, suddenly I found that behind me was a police car with a red light flashing. The officer said that I had been going forty-five miles an hour in a thirty-five-mile-an-hour zone. I couldn't contest it—I wasn't paying that much attention. The streets were deserted, and I was probably going as fast as he said. Since it was his duty, he made out a ticket. I was embarrassed, and irritated at myself because there were a number of places where I could have put the money that would go for the fine. (We squandered a good deal on food and clothing and things like that.)

Early the next morning, wanting to get the matter settled, I went to the city judge. He chuckled at my embarrassment and asked a question: "Well, what do you want to do with it?" It was a meaningful question. As a city councilor, I was in charge of the city judge. He had recently asked for new furniture for his office, and I was in the process of seeing his request through the council. Well, this was one of those moments of temptation. I finally answered that he must treat me as he would any other citizen. He was a bit reluctant, but said, "All right, ten dollars. A dollar a mile for each mile of excess speed." That was the going rate. I took the good-natured ribbing from the city treasurer and paid the fine, and that was that.

Two nights later I attended a city council session. It was an open meeting with a number of delegations present, including a representative from the press. When each of the councilors made his report, the one in charge of the police department announced that he had fired one of the patrolmen. It was the man who had issued me the ticket. When the mayor asked the reason for the dismissal, the councilor said, "Oh, he was always arresting the wrong people." What the councilor had meant was that his rookie policeman just didn't seem to be able to catch the idea of what he should do when on patrol duty at night. Someone could be hot-rodding through the cemetery at night pushing over the headstones, or could be running along the curbing clipping off newly planted trees, while the policeman was parked on a little-traveled street waiting for an unsuspecting motorist.

I had nothing to do with his dismissal, knew nothing about it, may even have objected to it had I known about it sooner. But do you think that you could ever convince that man that I didn't have him fired? The circumstantial evidence was too convincing. Monday night he gave a ticket to a city councilor. Wednesday morning he was dismissed from the police force for "arresting the wrong people." Can you see his surprise and the trial of his faith when I was called as one of the General Authorities of the Church? Can you hear him saying, "Well, I remember him—he had my job because I gave him a ticket."

Now, the lesson is to all of us. The circumstantial evidence was in error. Any one of us can be easily misled save we have inspiration and save we are steady on course. We can be washed overboard or diverted and destroyed in the storms.

Seaworthy Craft, Celestial Radar

I do not doubt that we sail into troubled waters. There are storms to ride out, there are reefs and shoals to negotiate ere we reach port. "The heavens shall be darkened, and a veil of darkness shall cover the earth; and the heavens shall shake, and also the earth; and great tribulations shall be among the children of men, but my people will I preserve" (Moses 7:61). Our craft has weathered storms and navigated dangerous channels before, and found safe passage. It is seaworthy. Steady as she goes.

What a glorious time to be alive! What a marvelous age to live in! Thank the Lord for the privilege of living in an adventuresome day of challenge. There is celestial radar—revelation from God—guiding us. There is an inspired captain, a prophet of God, leading us.

I want to bear witness to you, my young friends, that The Church of Jesus Christ of Latter-day Saints is on the right course. It is led by inspiration, and I say to you, to all of us, "Steady as she goes." I bear witness that Jesus is the Christ. The gospel of Jesus Christ is true. It was formulated for strength and direction in stormy times. Steady as she goes.

I leave for your contemplation these words about another storm.

> And there arose a great storm of wind, and the waves beat into the ship, so that it was now full.
> . . . And they awake him, and say unto him, Master, carest thou not that we perish?
> And he arose, and rebuked the wind, and said unto the sea, Peace, be still. And the wind ceased, and there was a great calm. (Mark 4:37–39.)

In the name of Jesus Christ, amen.

12

The Mantle Is Far, Far Greater Than the Intellect

The fact that I speak quite directly on a most important subject will, I hope, be regarded as something of a tribute to you who are our loyal, devoted, and inspired associates.

I have come to believe that it is the tendency for many members of the Church who spend a great deal of time in academic research to begin to judge the Church—its doctrine, organization, and leadership, present and past—by the principles of their own profession. Ofttimes this is done unwittingly, and some of it, perhaps, is not harmful.

It is an easy thing for a man with extensive academic training to measure the Church using as his standard the principles he has been taught in his professional training. In my mind it ought to be the other way around. A member of the Church ought always, particularly if he is pursuing extensive academic studies, to judge the professions of man against the revealed word of the Lord.

Address given to the Fifth Annual Church Educational System Religious Educators' Symposium 22 August 1981.

Academic Disciplines and Dangers

Many disciplines are subject to this danger. Over the years I have seen many members of the Church lose their testimonies and yield their faith as the price for academic achievement. Many others have been sorely tested. Let me illustrate.

During my last year as one of the supervisors of seminaries and institutes of religion, a seminary teacher went to a large university in the East to complete a doctorate in counseling and guidance. The ranking authority in that field was there and quickly took an interest in this personable, clean-cut, very intelligent young Latter-day Saint.

Our teacher attracted attention as he moved through the course work with comparative ease, and his future looked bright indeed—that is, until he came to the dissertation. He chose to study the ward bishop as a counselor.

At that time I was called as one of the General Authorities, and I helped him obtain authorization to interview and send question-naires to a cross-section of bishops.

In the dissertation he described the calling and ordination of a bishop; he described the power of discernment, the right of a bishop to receive revelation, and his right to spiritual guidance. His doctoral committee did not understand this. They felt it had no place in a scholarly paper and insisted that he take it out.

He came to see me. I read his dissertation and suggested that he satisfy their concern by introducing the discussion on spiritual matters with a statement such as "the Latter-day Saints believe the bishop has spiritual power," or "they claim that there is inspiration from God attending the bishop in his calling."

But the committee denied him even this. It was obvious that they would be quite embarrassed to have this ingredient included in a scholarly dissertation. It is as Paul said: "The natural man receiveth not the things of the Spirit of God: for they are foolishness unto him: neither can he know them, because they are spiritually discerned" (1 Corinthians 2:14).

The teacher was reminded of his very great potential and was told that with some little accommodation—specifically, leaving out all the spiritual references—his dissertation would be published and his reputation established. They predicted that he would become an authority in the field.

He was tempted. Perhaps, once established, he could then insert this spiritual ingredient back into his work. Then, as an established authority, he could *really* help the Church.

But something stood in the way: his faith, his integrity. So he just did the best he could with his dissertation. It did not contain enough of the Spirit to satisfy him and contained too much of it to have been fully accepted by his worldly professors. But he received his degree.

His dissertation is not truly the scholarly document it might have been, because the most essential ingredient is missing. Revelation is so central a part of a bishop's experience in counseling that any study which ignores it cannot be regarded as a scholarly work.

He returned to the modest income and the relative obscurity of the Church Educational System.

I talked to this teacher a day or two ago. We talked about the dissertation and the fact that it was never published. He has been a *great* influence among the youth of the Church. He did the right thing. He summed up his experience in this way: "The mantle is far, far greater than the intellect; the priesthood is the guiding power." His statement becomes the title for this talk and embodies what I hope to convey to you.

I must not be too critical of those professors. They do not know of the things of the Spirit. One can understand their position. It is another thing, however, when we consider members of the Church, particularly those who hold the priesthood and have made covenants in the temple. Many do not do as my associate did; rather, they capitulate, cross over the line, and forsake the things of the Spirit. Thereafter, they judge the Church, the doctrine, and the leadership by the standards of their academic profession.

Teaching and Writing Church History

This problem has affected some of those who have taught and have written about the history of the Church. These professors say of themselves that religious faith has little influence on Mormon scholars. They say this because, obviously, they are not simply Latter-day Saints but are also intellectuals trained, for the most part, in secular institutions. They would that some historians who are Latter-day Saints write history as they were taught in graduate school rather than as Mormons.

If we are not careful, very careful, and if we are not wise, very wise, we first leave out of our professional study the things of the Spirit. The next step soon follows: we leave the spiritual things out of our lives.

I want to read to you a most significant statement by President Joseph F. Smith, a statement that you would do well to keep in mind in your teaching and research, and one which will serve as somewhat of a text for my remarks to you:

> It has not been by the wisdom of man that this people have been directed in their course until the present; it has been by the wisdom of Him who is above man and whose knowledge is greater than that of man, and whose power is above the power of man. . . . The hand of the Lord may not be visible to all. There may be many who can not discern the workings of God's will in the progress and development of this great latter-day work, *but there are those who see in every hour and in every moment of the existence of the Church, from its beginning until now, the overruling, almighty hand of Him who sent His only Begotten Son to the world to become a sacrifice for the sin of the world.* (In Conference Report, April 1904, p. 2, italics added.)

If we do not keep this constantly in mind—that the Lord directs this Church—we may lose our way in the world of intellectual and scholarly research.

You seminary teachers and some of you institute and BYU men will be teaching the history of the Church this school year. This is an unparalleled opportunity in the lives of your students to increase their faith and testimony of the divinity of this work. Your objective should be that they will see the hand of the Lord in every hour and every moment of the Church from its beginning till now.

As one who has taken the journey a number of times, I offer four cautions before you begin.

First Caution

There is no such thing as an accurate, objective history of the Church without consideration of the spiritual powers that attend this work.

There is no such thing as a scholarly, objective study of the office of bishop without consideration of spiritual guidance, of discernment, and of revelation. That would not be scholarship. Accordingly I repeat, there is no such thing as an accurate or objective history of the Church which ignores the Spirit. You might as well try to write the biography of Mendelssohn without hearing or mentioning his music, or write the life of Rembrandt without mentioning light or canvas or color.

If someone who knew very little about music should write a biography of Mendelssohn, one who had been trained to have a feeling for music would recognize that very quickly. That reader would not be many pages into the manuscript before he would know that a most essential ingredient had been left out.

Mendelssohn no doubt would emerge as an ordinary man, perhaps not an impressive man at all. That which makes him most worth remembering would be gone. Without it he would appear, at best, eccentric. Certainly, controversy would develop over why a biography at all. Whoever should read the biography would not know, really know, Mendelssohn at all—even though the biographer might have invested exhaustive research in his project and might have been accurate in every other detail.

And if you viewed Rembrandt only in black and white, you would miss most of his inspiration.

Those of us who are extensively engaged in researching the wisdom of man, including those who write and those who teach Church history, are not immune from these dangers. I have walked that road of scholarly research and study and know something of the dangers. If anything, we are more vulnerable than those in some of the other disciplines. Church history can be so interesting and so inspiring as to be a very powerful tool indeed for building faith. If not properly written or properly taught it may be a faith destroyer.

President Brigham Young admonished Karl G. Maeser not to teach even the times tables without the Spirit of the Lord. How much more essential is that Spirit in the research, the writing, and the teaching of Church history!

If we who research, write, and teach the history of the Church ignore the spiritual on the pretext that the world may not understand it, our work will not be objective. And if, for the same reason, we keep it quite secular, we will produce a history that is not accurate and not scholarly—this in spite of the extent of research or the nature of the individual statements or the incidents which are included as part of it, and notwithstanding the training or scholarly reputation of the one who writes or teaches it. We would end up with a history that left out the one most essential ingredient.

Those who have the Spirit can recognize very quickly whether something is missing in a written Church history—this in spite of the fact that the author may be a highly trained historian and the reader is not. And, I might add, we have been getting a great deal of experience in this regard in the past few years.

President Wilford Woodruff warned: "I will here say God has inspired me to keep a Journal and History of this Church, and *I warn the future Historians to give Credence to my History of this Church and Kingdom;* for my Testimony is true, and the truth of its record will be manifest in the world to Come." (Journal of Wilford Woodruff, 6 July 1877, Historical Department, The Church of Jesus Christ of Latter-day Saints; italics added. Spelling and punctuation have been standardized.)

Second Caution

There is a temptation for the writer or the teacher of Church history to want to tell everything, whether or not it is worthy or faith-promoting.

Some things that are true are not very useful.

Historians seem to take great pride in publishing something new, particularly if it illustrates a weakness or mistake of a prominent historical figure. For some reason, historians and novelists seem to savor such things. If it related to a living person it would come under the heading of gossip. History can be as misleading as gossip and much more difficult—often impossible—to verify.

The writer or the teacher who has an exaggerated loyalty to the theory that everything must be told is laying a foundation for his own judgment. He should not complain if one day he himself receives as he has given. Perhaps that is what is contemplated in having one's sins preached from the housetops.

Some time ago a historian gave a lecture to an audience of college students on one of the past Presidents of the Church. It seemed to be his purpose to show that that President was a man subject to the foibles of men. He introduced many so-called facts that put that President in a very unfavorable light, particularly when they were taken out of the context of the historical period in which he lived.

Anyone who was not previously acquainted with this historical figure (particularly anyone not mature) must have come away very negatively affected. Those who were unsteady in their convictions surely must have had their faith weakened or destroyed.

I began teaching seminary under Abel S. Rich, principal. He was the second seminary teacher employed by the Church, and a man of maturity, wisdom, and experience. Among the lessons I learned from him was this: When I want to know about a man, I seek out those who know him best. I do not go to his enemies but to his friends. He would not confide in his enemy. You could not know the innermost thoughts of his heart by consulting those who would injure him.

We are teachers and should know the importance of the principle of prerequisites. It is easily illustrated with the subject of chemistry. No responsible chemist would advise, and no reputable school would permit, a beginning student to register for advanced chemistry without a knowledge of the fundamental principles of chemistry. The advanced course would be a destructive mistake, even for a very brilliant beginning student. Even that brilliant student would need some knowledge of the elements, of atoms and molecules, of electrons, of valence, of compounds and properties. To let a student proceed without the knowledge of fundamentals would surely destroy his interest in, and his future with, the field of chemistry.

The same point may be made with reference to so-called sex education. There are many things that are factual, even elevating, about this subject. There are other aspects of this subject that are so perverted and ugly that it does little good to talk of them at all. Some things cannot be safely taught to little children or to those who are not eligible by virtue of age or maturity or authorizing ordinance to understand them.

Teaching prematurely or at the wrong time some things that are true can invite sorrow and heartbreak instead of the joy intended to accompany learning.

What is true with these two subjects is, if anything, doubly true in the field of religion. The scriptures teach emphatically that we must give milk before meat. The Lord made it very clear that some things are to be given only to those who are worthy.

It matters very much not only *what* we are told but *when* we are told it. Be careful that you build faith rather than destroy it.

President William E. Berrett has told us how grateful he is that a testimony that the past leaders of the Church were prophets of God was firmly fixed in his mind *before* he was exposed to some of the so-called facts that historians have put in their published writings.

This principle of prerequisites is so fundamental to all education that I have never been quite able to understand why historians are so willing to ignore it. And if those outside the Church have little to guide them but the tenets of their profession, those inside the Church should know better.

Some historians write and speak as though their only readers or listeners are mature, experienced historians. They write and speak to a very narrow audience. Unfortunately, many of the things they tell one another are not uplifting, go far beyond the audience they may have intended, and destroy faith.

What that historian did with the reputation of the President of the Church was not worth doing. He seemed determined to convince everyone that the *prophet* was a *man.* We knew that already. All of the prophets and all of the Apostles have been men. It would have been much more worthwhile for him to convince us that the *man* was a *prophet,* a fact quite as true as the fact that he was a man.

He has taken something away from the memory of a prophet. He has destroyed faith. I remind you of the truth Shakespeare taught, ironically spoken by Iago:

> Who steals my purse steals trash; 'tis something, nothing;
> 'Twas mine, 'tis his, and has been slave to thousands;
> But he that filches from me my good name
> Robs me of that which not enriches him,
> And makes me poor indeed.
> —*Othello*, act 3, sc. 3, lines 157–61

The sad thing is that in years past this historian may have taken great interest in those who led the Church, and desired to draw close to them. But instead of following that long, steep, discouraging, and occasionally dangerous path to spiritual achievement, instead of going up to where they were, he devised a way of collecting mistakes and weaknesses and limitations to compare with his own. In that sense he has attempted to bring a historical figure down to his level and in that way feel close to him and perhaps justify his own weaknesses.

I agree with President Stephen L Richards, who stated:

> If a man of history has secured over the years a high place in the esteem of his countrymen and fellow men and has become imbedded in their affections, it has seemingly become a pleasing pastime for researchers and scholars to delve into the past of such a man, discover, it may be, some of his weaknesses, and then write a book exposing hitherto unpublished alleged factual findings, all of which tends to rob the historic character of the idealistic esteem and veneration in which he may have been held through the years.
>
> This "debunking," we are told, is in the interest of realism, that the facts should be known. If an historic character has made a great contribution to country and society, and if his name and his deeds have been used over the generations to foster high ideals of character and service, what good is to be accomplished by digging out of the past and exploiting weaknesses, which perhaps a generous contemporary public forgave and subdued? (*Where Is Wisdom?* [Salt Lake City: Deseret Book Co., 1955], p. 155.)

That historian or scholar who delights in pointing out the weakness and frailties of present or past leaders destroys faith. A destroyer of faith—particularly one within the Church, and more particularly one who is employed specifically to build faith—places himself in great spiritual jeopardy. He is serving the wrong master, and unless he repents he will not be among the faithful in the eternities.

One who chooses to follow the tenets of his profession, regardless of how they may injure the Church or destroy the faith of those not ready for "advanced history," is himself in spiritual jeopardy. If that one is a member of the Church, he has broken his covenants and will be accountable. After all of the tomorrows of mortality have been finished, he will not stand where he might have stood.

I recall a conversation with President Henry D. Moyle. We were driving back from Arizona and were talking about a man who destroyed the faith of young people from the vantage point of a teaching position. Someone asked President Moyle why this man was still a member of the Church when he did things like that. "He is not a member of the Church," President Moyle answered firmly. Another replied that he had not heard of his excommunication. "He has excommunicated himself," President Moyle responded. "He has cut himself off from the Spirit of God. Whether or not we get around to holding a court doesn't matter that much; he has cut himself off from the Spirit of the Lord."

Third Caution

In an effort to be objective, impartial, and scholarly, a writer or a teacher may unwittingly be giving equal time to the adversary.

Someone told of the man who entitled his book *An Unbiased History of the Civil War from the Southern Point of View*. While we chuckle at that, there is something to be said about presenting Church history from the viewpoint of those who have righteously lived it. The idea that we must be neutral and argue quite as much in favor of the adversary as we do in favor of righteousness is neither reasonable nor safe.

In the Church we are not neutral. We are one-sided. There is a war going on, and we are engaged in it. It is the war between good and evil, and we are belligerents defending the good. We are therefore obliged to give preference to and protect all that is represented in the gospel of Jesus Christ, and we have made covenants to do it.

Some of our scholars establish for themselves a posture of neutrality. They call it "sympathetic detachment." Historians are particularly wont to do that. If they make a complimentary statement about the Church, they seem to have to counter it with something that is uncomplimentary.

Some of them, since they are members of the Church, are quite embarrassed with the thought that they might be accused of being partial. They care very much what the world thinks and are very careful to include in their writings criticism of the Church leaders of the past.

They particularly strive to be acclaimed as historians as measured by the world's standard. They would do well to read Lehi's vision of the iron rod and ponder verses 24–28.

And it came to pass that I beheld others pressing forward, and they came forth and caught hold of the end of the rod of iron; and they did press forward through the mist of darkness, clinging to the rod of iron, even until they did come forth and partake of the fruit of the tree.

And *after* they had partaken of the fruit of the tree they did cast their eyes about as if they were ashamed. [Notice the word *after*. He is talking of those who are partakers of the goodness of God — of Church members.]

And I also cast my eyes round about, and beheld, on the other side of the river of water, a great and spacious building; and it stood as it were in the air, high above the earth.

And it was filled with people, both old and young, both male and female; and their manner of dress was exceedingly fine; and they were in the attitude of mocking and pointing their fingers towards those who had come at and were partaking of the fruit.

And *after* they had tasted of the fruit they were ashamed, because of those that were scoffing at them; and they fell away into forbidden paths and were lost. (1 Nephi 8:24–28, italics added.)

And I want to say in all seriousness that there is a limit to the patience of the Lord with respect to those who are under covenant to bless and protect His Church and kingdom upon the earth but do not do it.

Particularly are we in danger if we are out to make a name for ourselves, if our

hearts are set so much upon the things of this world, and aspire to the honors of men, that [we] do not learn this one lesson—

That the rights of the priesthood are inseparably connected with the powers of heaven, and that the powers of heaven cannot be controlled nor handled only upon the principles of righteousness.

That they may be conferred upon us, it is true; but when we undertake to cover our sins, or to gratify our pride, our vain ambition, or to exercise control or dominion or compulsion upon the souls of the children of men, in any degree of unrighteousness, behold, the heavens withdraw themselves; the Spirit of the Lord is grieved; and when it is withdrawn, Amen to the priesthood or the authority of that man.

Behold, ere he is aware, he is left unto himself, to kick against the pricks, to persecute the saints, and to fight against God. (D&C 121:35–38.)

There is much in the scriptures and in our Church literature to convince us that we are at war with the adversary. We are not obliged as a church, nor are we as members obliged, to accommodate the enemy in this war.

President Joseph Fielding Smith pointed out that it would be a foolish general who would give the enemy access to all his intelligence. It is neither expected nor necessary for us to accommodate those who seek to retrieve references from our sources, distort them, and use them against us.

Suppose that a well-managed business corporation is threatened by takeover from another corporation. Suppose that the corporation bent on the takeover is determined to drain off all the other company's assets and then dissolve it. You can rest assured that the threatened company would hire legal counsel to protect itself.

Can you imagine that attorney, under contract to protect the company, having fixed in his mind that he must not really take sides, that he must be impartial?

Suppose that when the records of the company he has been employed to protect are opened for him to prepare his brief he collects evidence and passes some of it to the attorneys of the enemy company. His own firm may then be in great jeopardy because of his disloyal conduct.

Do you not recognize a breach of ethics, integrity, or morality?

I think you can see the point I am making. Those of you who are employed by the Church have a special responsibility to build faith, not destroy it. If you do not do that, but in fact accommodate the enemy, who is the destroyer of faith, you become in that sense a traitor to the cause you have made covenants to protect.

Those who in the name of academic freedom or so-called honesty have carefully purged their work of any religious faith ought not to expect to be accommodated in their researches or to be paid by the Church to do it.

Rest assured, also, that you will get little truth, and less benefit, from those who steal documents or those who deal in stolen goods. There have always been, and are among us today, those who seek entrance to restricted libraries and files in order to secretly copy material and steal it away in hopes of finding some detail that has not as yet been published—this in order that they may sell it for money, or profit in some way from its publication, or inflate an ego by being the first to publish it.

In some cases the motive is to destroy faith, if they can, and the Church, if they are able. The Church will move forward, and their efforts will be of little moment. But such conduct does not go unnoticed in the eternal scheme of things.

We should not be ashamed to be committed, to be converted, to be biased in favor of the Lord.

Elder Joseph Fielding Smith pointed out the fallacy of trying to work both sides of the street: "You may as well say that the Book of Mormon is not true because it does not give credence to the story the Lamanites told of the Nephites" (*Utah Genealogical and Historical Magazine*, April 1925, p. 55).

A number of years ago, professors from Harvard University who were members of the Church invited me to lunch over at the Harvard Business School faculty dining room. They wanted to know if I would join them in participating in a new publication; they wanted me to contribute to it.

They were generous in their compliments, saying that because I had a doctorate a number of people in the Church would listen to me, and, being a General Authority (at that time I was an Assistant to the Twelve), I could have some very useful influence.

I listened to them very attentively but indicated at the close of the conversation that I would not join them. I asked to be excused from responding to their request. When they asked why, I told them this: "When your associates announced the project, they described how useful it would be to the Church—a niche that needed to be filled. And then the spokesman said, 'We are all active and faithful members of the Church; *however*, . . .' "

I told my two hosts that if the announcement had read, "We are all active and faithful members of the Church; *therefore*, . . ." I would have joined their organization. I had serious questions about a "however" organization. I have little worry over a "therefore" organization.

That *however* meant that they put a condition upon their Church membership and their faith. It meant that they put something else first. It meant that they were to judge the Church and gospel and the leaders of it against their own backgrounds and training. It meant that their commitment was partial, and partial commitment is not enough to qualify one for full spiritual light.

I would not contribute to publications, nor would I belong to organizations, that by spirit or inclination are faith-destroying. There are plenty of scholars in the world determined to find all secular truth. There are so few of us, relatively speaking, striving to convey the spiritual truths, who are protecting the Church. We cannot safely be neutral.

Many years ago Elder John A. Widtsoe made reference to a foolish teacher in the Mutual Improvement Association who sponsored some debate with the intent of improving the abilities of the young members of the Church. He chose as a subject, "Resolved: Joseph Smith was a prophet of God." Unfortunately, the con side won.

The youngsters speaking in favor of the proposition were not as clever and their arguments were not as carefully prepared as those of the opposing side. The fact that Joseph Smith remained a prophet after the debate was over did not protect some of the participants from suffering the destruction of their faith and thereafter conducting their lives as though Joseph Smith were not a prophet and as though the church he founded and the gospel he restored were not true.

Fourth Caution

The final caution concerns the idea that so long as something is already in print, so long as it is available from another source, there is nothing out of order in using it in writing or speaking or teaching.

Surely you can see the fallacy in that.

I have on occasion been disappointed when I have read in writings of those who are supposed to be worthy members of the Church statements that tend to belittle or degrade the Church or past leaders of the Church. When I have commented on my disappointment at seeing such things in print, the answer has been, "It was printed before, and it's available, and therefore I saw no reason not to publish it again."

You do not do well to see that such writing is disseminated. It may be read by those not mature enough for "advanced history," and a testimony in seedling stage may be crushed.

Several years ago President Ezra Taft Benson spoke to you and said:

It has come to our attention that some of our teachers, particularly in our university programs, are purchasing writings from known apostates . . . in an effort to become informed about certain points of view or to glean from their research. You must realize that when you purchase their writings or subscribe to their periodicals, you help sustain their cause. We would hope that their writings not be on your seminary or institute or personal bookshelves. We are entrusting you to represent the Lord and the First Presidency to your students, not the views of the detractors of the Church. ("The Gospel Teacher and His Message" [address delivered to Church Educational System personnel, 17 September 1976], p. 12.)

I endorse that counsel to you.

Remember: When you see the bitter apostate, you do not see only an absence of light; you see also the presence of darkness.

Do not spread disease germs!

I learned a great lesson years ago when I interviewed a young man in the mission home. He was disqualified from serving a mission. He confessed to a transgression that you would think would never enter the mind of a normal human being.

"Where on earth did you ever get an idea to do something like that?" I asked.

To my great surprise he said, "From my bishop."

He said the bishop in the interview had asked, "Have you ever done this? Have you ever done that? Have you ever done this other?" and described in detail things that the young man had never thought of. They preyed upon his mind until, under perverse inspiration, the opportunity presented itself, and he fell.

Don't perpetuate the unworthy, the unsavory, or the sensational.

Some things that are in print go out of print, and the old statement "good riddance to bad rubbish" might apply.

Elder G. Homer Durham of the First Quorum of the Seventy told of counsel he had received from one of his professors who was an eminent historian: "You don't write [and, I might add, you don't teach] history out of the garbage pails."

Mormon gave an excellent rule for historians to follow:

For behold, the Spirit of Christ is given to every man, that he may know good from evil; wherefore, I show unto you the way to judge; for every thing which inviteth to do good, and to persuade to believe in Christ, is sent forth by the power and gift of Christ; wherefore ye may know with a perfect knowledge it is of God.

But whatsoever thing persuadeth men to do evil, and believe not in Christ, and deny him, and serve not God, then ye may know with a perfect knowledge it is of the devil; for after this manner doth the devil work, for he persuadeth no man to do good, no, not one; neither do his angels; neither do they who subject themselves unto him. (Moroni 7:16–17.)

It makes a great deal of difference whether we regard mortality as the conclusion and fulfillment of our existence or as a preparation for an eternal existence as well.

Those are the cautions I give to you who teach and write Church history.

Qualifications Are Spiritual

There are qualifications to teach or to write the history of this church. If one is lacking in any one of these qualifications, one cannot properly teach the history of the Church.

I will state these qualifications in the form of questions so that you can assess your own qualifications.

Do you believe that God the Father and His Son Jesus Christ personally appeared to the boy prophet, Joseph Smith Jr., in the year 1820?

Do you have personal witness that the Father and the Son appeared in all their glory and stood above that young man and instructed him according to the testimony that he gave to the world in his published history?

Do you know that the Prophet Joseph Smith's testimony is true because you have received a spiritual witness of its truth?

Do you believe that the church that was restored through him is, in the Lord's words, "the only true and living church upon the face of the whole earth, with which I, the Lord, am well pleased" (D&C 1:30)? Do you know by the Holy Ghost that this is *the* Church of Jesus Christ of Latter-day Saints restored by heavenly messengers in this modern era; that the Church constitutes the kingdom of God on the earth, not just an institution fabricated by human agency?

Do you believe that the successors to the Prophet Joseph Smith were and are prophets, seers, and revelators; that revelation from heaven directs the decisions, policies, and pronouncements that come from the headquarters of the Church? Have you come to the settled conviction, by the Spirit, that these prophets truly represent the Lord?

Now, you obviously noted that I did not talk about academic qualifications. Facts, understanding, and scholarship can be attained by personal study and essential course work. The three qualifications I have named come by the Spirit, to the individual. You can't receive them by secular training or study, by academic inquiry, or by scientific investigation.

I repeat: If there is a deficiency in any of these areas, then, regardless of what other training an individual possesses, he cannot comprehend and write or teach the true history of this Church. The things of God are understood only by one who possesses the Spirit of God.

The Brethren Need Your Support

Now, what about that historian who defamed the early Presidents of the Church and may well have weakened or destroyed faith in the process? What about other members of the Church who have in their writings or in their teaching been guilty of something similar?

I want to say something that may surprise you. I know of a man who did something quite as destructive as that who later became the prophet of the Church. I refer to Alma the Younger. I learned about him from reading the Book of Mormon, which in reality is a very reliable history of the Church in ancient times.

You are acquainted with the record of Alma as a young man. He followed his father, the prophet Alma, about, and ridiculed what his father preached. He was, in that period of his life, a destroyer of faith. Then came a turning point.

Because his father had prayed for it, he came to himself. He changed. He became one of the great men in religious history.

I want to say something to that historian and to others who may have placed higher value on intellect than upon the mantle.

The Brethren then and now are men, very ordinary men, who have come for the most part from very humble beginnings. We need your help. We desperately need it! We cannot research and organize the history of the Church. We do not have the time to do it. And we do not have the training that you possess. But we do know the Spirit and how essential a part of our history it is. Ours is the duty to organize the Church, to set it in order, to confer the keys of authority, to perform the ordinances, to watch the borders of the kingdom, and to carry burdens, heavy burdens, for others and for ourselves that you can know little about.

Do you know how inadequate we really are compared to the callings we have received? Can you feel in a measure the weight, the overwhelming weight, of responsibility that is ours? If you look for inadequacy and imperfections, you can find them quite easily. But you may not feel as we feel the enormous weight of responsibility associated with the callings that have come to us. We are not free to do some of the things that scholars think would be so reasonable, for the Lord will not permit us to do them, and it is His church. He presides over it.

Forgiveness, Inspiration, Sacrifice

There is another part of the ongoing history of the Church that you may not be acquainted with. Perhaps I can illustrate it for you.

A few years ago it was my sad privilege to accompany President Kimball, then President of the Twelve, to a distant stake to replace a stake leader who had been excommunicated for a transgression. Our hearts went out to this good man who had done such an unworthy thing. His sorrow and anguish and suffering brought to my mind the phrase "gall of bitterness."

Thereafter, on intermittent occasions, I would receive a call from President Kimball: "Have you heard from this brother? How is he doing? Have you been in touch with him?" After Brother Kimball became President of the Church, the calls did not cease. They increased in frequency.

One day I received a call from the President. "I have been thinking of this brother. Do you think it is too soon to have him baptized?'' (Always a question, never a command.) I responded with my feelings, and he said, "Why don't you see if he could come here to see you? If you feel good about it after an interview, we could proceed."

A short time later, I arrived very early at the office. As I left my car I saw President Kimball enter his. He rolled down the window to greet me, and I told him I had good news about our brother. "He was baptized last night," I said.

He motioned for me to get into the car and sit beside him and asked me to tell him all about it. I told him of the interview and that I had concluded by telling our brother very plainly that his baptism must not be a signal that his priesthood blessings would be restored in the foreseeable future. I told him that it would be a long, long time before that would happen.

President Kimball patted me on the knee in a gentle gesture of correction and said, "Well, maybe not so long . . ." Soon thereafter the intermittent phone calls began again.

I want to tell you of another lesson I received. Many years ago, when I was a new General Authority and not very experienced, I was called to the office of the First Counselor in the First Presidency. "We find you are going to the West Coast for conference this weekend. We wonder if you would leave a day or so early to help with a problem at a mission headquarters in another city."

A missionary had confessed to transgression, and the mission president was reluctant to take action. I was instructed to see that a court was convened and that the missionary was excommunicated.

I went, and I interviewed the elder at great length. I then went to a park to think and pray about it. It was an unusual case, most unusual. After two hours, I telephoned the member of the First Presidency from a pay telephone and told him a little of what I had learned and of how I felt about the matter. He asked what I wanted to do. Hesitantly I told him I wanted to delay, to take no action now. Then I said, "But, President, tell me to do it, again, and I will do it."

His voice came over the telephone and seemed like thunder to me: "Don't you go against the voice of the Spirit!"

I had learned a great lesson, and I have never forgotten it. The inspiration greatly affected the outcome when final action was taken.

Do not yield your faith in payment for an advanced degree or for the recognition and acclaim of the world. Do not turn away from the Lord nor from His Church nor from His servants. You are needed—oh, how you are needed!

It may be that you will lay your scholarly reputation and the acclaim of your colleagues in the world as a sacrifice upon the altar of service. They may never understand the things of the Spirit as you have a right to do. They may not regard you as an authority or as a scholar. And just remember, when the test came to Abraham he didn't really have to sacrifice Isaac. He just had to be willing to.

A Faith-Building Example

Now a final lesson from Church history, one that illustrates the kind of thing from the past that builds faith and increases testimony.

William W. Phelps had been a trusted associate of the Prophet Joseph Smith. Then, in an hour of crisis when the Prophet needed him most, he turned against him and joined the apostates and oppressors who sought the Prophet's life.

Later, Brother Phelps came to himself. He repented of what he had done and wrote to the Prophet Joseph Smith, asking for his forgiveness. I want to read you the letter the Prophet Joseph wrote to Brother Phelps in reply.

I confess also that many times I have moaned in agony when I have thought of the many incidents of this kind that researchers have discovered when they have pored over the records of our history but have left them out of their writings for fear these would be regarded as not worthy of a scholarly review.

Now the letter.

> Dear Brother Phelps: . . .
> You may in some measure realize what my feelings, as well as Elder Rigdon's and Brother Hyrum's were, when we read your letter—truly our hearts were melted into tenderness and compassion when we ascertained your resolves, &c. I can assure you I feel a disposition to act on your case in a manner that will meet the approbation of Jehovah (whose servant I am), and agreeable to the principles of truth and righteousness which have been revealed; and inasmuch as long-suffering, patience, and mercy have ever

characterized the dealings of our heavenly Father towards the humble and penitent, I feel disposed to copy the example, cherish the same principles, and by so doing be a savior of my fellow men.

It is true, that we have suffered much in consequence of your behavior—the cup of gall, already full enough for mortals to drink, was indeed filled to overflowing when you turned against us. One with whom we had oft taken sweet counsel together, and enjoyed many refreshing seasons from the Lord—"had it been an enemy, we could have borne it." . . .

However, the cup has been drunk, the will of our Father has been done, and we are yet alive, for which we thank the Lord. And having been delivered from the hands of wicked men by the mercy of our God, we say it is your privilege to be delivered from the powers of the adversary, be brought into the liberty of God's dear children, and again take your stand among the Saints of the Most High, and by diligence, humility, and love unfeigned, commend yourself to our God, and your God, and to the Church of Jesus Christ.

Believing your confession to be real, and your repentance genuine, I shall be happy once again to give you the right hand of fellowship, and rejoice over the returning prodigal. . . .

"Come on, dear brother, since the war is past,
For friends at first, are friends again at last."
Yours as ever,
Joseph Smith, Jun.

(*History of the Church* 4:162–64.)

Brother Phelps did return to full fellowship. He was a writer of hymns. The one we sang to open this meeting, "Praise to the Man," was written by Brother Phelps, as were "O God, the Eternal Father," "Now Let Us Rejoice," "Gently Raise the Sacred Strain," "The Spirit of God Like a Fire"—to mention but a few.

Oh, how great the loss to the Church if Brother Phelps had not returned! And how great would have been the tragedy for him!

When I read about our Brethren of the past, I am overwhelmed with humility. Consider the Prophet Joseph Smith and the little opportunity he had for formal schooling. Read the letters written in his own hand, and you will know that he could not spell correctly. Oh, how grateful he must have been for a scribe! I have wept when I have contemplated what they accomplished with what little they had. I sense how grateful they were to those who stood by them.

Teach and Write by the Spirit

To you who may have lost your way we say, Come back! We know how that can happen; we have walked that path of research and study. Come and help us—you with your scholarship and your training, you with your bright, intelligent minds, you with your experience and with your academic degrees.

How grateful we are today for the many members who have special gifts and special training that they devote to the building up of the church and kingdom of God and to the protecting of it.

May God bless you who so faithfully compile and teach the history of the Church and build the faith of those you teach. I bear witness that the gospel is true. The Church is His church. I pray that you may be inspired as you write and as you teach. May His Spirit be with you in rich abundance.

As you take your students over the trails of Church history in this dispensation, yours is the privilege to help them to see the miracle of the Restoration, the mantle that belongs to His servants, and to "see in every hour and in every moment of the existence of the Church . . . the overruling, almighty hand of [God]" (Joseph F. Smith, in Conference Report, April 1904, p. 2).

As you write and as you teach Church history under the influence of His Spirit, one day you will come to know that you were not only spectators but a central part of it, for you are His Saints.

This testimony I leave, with my blessings, in the name of Jesus Christ, amen.

13

A Call to the Christian Clergy

I feel subdued in spirit, brethren and sisters, as we come near the closing moments of this great conference. There is the promise that "when a man speaketh with the power of the Holy Ghost the power of the Holy Ghost carrieth it unto the hearts of the children of men" (2 Nephi 33:1). Because there are some here visiting with us as guests about whom I care deeply, I pray for an interest in your faith and prayers as I direct my remarks to them.

It has been our privilege over the past two years in the mission field to become acquainted with clergymen from a number of Christian churches. We find them to be good men—sincere, honest in their dedication to the ministry that they have chosen. It is to you "men of the cloth," as you term yourselves, that I speak.

Would you be offended if I called you "our brethren"? This term, commonly used in the Church, is a title of dignity and honor, and I address you thusly in respect for your ministerial assignment.

Address given at general conference April 1967.

Please understand the spirit in which I speak. It is with humility and without arrogance that I call to your attention a matter of significant spiritual importance in the spirit of what might be termed a call to the Christian clergy.

Something Missing from Christian Church

In conversation several of you have opened your hearts and given expression to your solemn feelings concerning the Christian Church at large; the feeling that something is out of order that wants to be put in order. Not so much, as you have said, that the clergy is not desirous of moving people to good works, but rather that there is something missing.

Your youth have become unresponsive, and although you have introduced innovations into the worship services—jazz combos, poetic reading, interpretive dancing, all thought to be appealing to youth—nevertheless they are drawn away and grow up without faith.

One reads with serious reflection the words of the prophet Amos: "Behold, the days come, saith the Lord God, that I will send a famine in the land, not a famine of bread, nor a thirst for water, but of hearing the words of the Lord: and they shall wander from sea to sea, and from the north even to the east, they shall run to and fro to seek the word of the Lord, and shall not find it. In that day shall the fair virgins and young men faint for thirst." (Amos 8:11–13.)

I testify that such a spiritual famine is upon the world. And as moral fiber is weakened, forces of darkness grow in courage. Evil has unclothed itself and walks the street in brazen impudence—defiant, frightening, persuasive.

In recognition of this you point out with nervous realization that the churches are not fulfilling their obligation to mankind; and you find yourselves reaching out to one another, hoping to draw close together, to stand shoulder to shoulder, sensing that in unity there may be strength.

You have told me of your councils—local, regional, national, and worldwide—in which you devote yourselves to the spirit of ecumenism. These are ecumenical councils in which you labor industriously to bring into one the whole of Christianity.

In all of this you see us, The Church of Jesus Christ of Latter-day Saints, standing apart, not participating. We are not in the councils. And not only this, but you find us sending missionaries among your parishioners, pleading with them to hear the message of the gospel of Jesus Christ and bearing witness that He lives.

Why, you ask, will we not support the great ecumenical movement? Why do we absent ourselves from councils called in the name of Christian unity?

It is in answer to this question, to you and to the wandering youth in the Church, that we yearn with prayerful, fervent desire that you may feel the spirit in which we speak.

Our brethren, we declare that councils alone will not bring unity. The efforts of men only, regardless of how well-intentioned, will not call it forth. No more will be accomplished through uninspired reorganization and attempted unification of the Christian churches than has been accomplished through uninspired separation of them.

It was when men denied the gift of the Spirit and failed to heed the inspirations from the Lord and the promptings of the Holy Ghost that they strayed from the gospel of Jesus Christ and began to contend one with another and to protest one against the other.

The very concern—the recognition of the need to be put together again, the very feeling that something is out of order that wants to be put in order, indeed, the very reason for which the ecumenical councils are being called—is evidence that the division was wrong in the first place, and even apostate in its dimensions.

There is indeed a need for unity. But we would be mistaken to assume that each of the multiplicity of Christian churches is part of the so-called "body of Christ" (one church representing the arm, another the leg, another the head, and so on), and that putting them all together would make the full "body of Christ."

They are not component parts, but are imperfect and distorted copies of the whole. To pretend that bringing them together would constitute bringing into one whole all that is essential for the salvation of mankind would be to mislead one another.

You have no doubt on many occasions read these words in the Gospel of John: "If ye love me, keep my commandments. And I will pray the Father, and he shall give you another Comforter, that he may abide with you for ever; even the Spirit of truth; whom the world cannot receive, because it seeth him not, neither knoweth him: but ye know him; for he dwelleth with you, and shall be in you. I will not leave you comfortless: I will come to you." (John 14:15–18.)

In no age in the history of the world were people more in need of that spiritual comforter.

Is it unreasonable to ask you — you who are by disposition such seekers after truth that you have chosen the ministry — to set aside for a moment self-interest, prejudice, even concern over the source of your livelihood, and to openly and honestly and prayerfully consider that there may be an answer provided by the Lord that cannot be arrived at in ecumenical councils? "For my thoughts are not your thoughts, neither are your ways my ways, saith the Lord. For as the heavens are higher than the earth, so are my ways higher than your ways, and my thoughts than your thoughts." (Isaiah 55:8–9.)

Are you so illiberal that you could not admit at least as a thought that God may have chosen not to restructure, nor to repair, nor to renovate, nor even to reunite the churches?

Restoration Is the Answer

Mankind is not left alone. There is the answer to the problem of Christian unity, but it is not a reuniting nor a renovation. It is a *restoration*.

The Lord's way was certified to man on 6 April 1830, when there was organized The Church of Jesus Christ of Latter-day Saints. The Father and the Son had appeared. The heavens were opened!

Angelic messengers restored the priesthood by ordination. God once again spoke through His prophet. A council of twelve Apostles was called. And the organization, with proper authority, was restored as it had been first established by Jesus Christ.

It is not an easy way we offer. It is not easy to change, particularly when we come to see in a new light the path we have walked.

A naturalist one day knelt in the Scottish highlands with his magnifying glass focused upon some blossoms of the heather until, as he afterwards confessed, he lost track of time. Suddenly he glanced over his shoulder and found an old highland shepherd watching. I suppose he was somewhat embarrassed, but without saying a word he plucked the heather bell and handed it with the magnifying glass to the shepherd.

The old man put the instrument to his eyes and peered at the heather bell. He was silent for a while; then, handing back the flower and the instrument, he said slowly: "Ay, man, I wish ye no had shown me that."

"Why?" asked the naturalist.

"Because these rude feet have trodden so many of them."

It is not easy to change.

In this conference you have heard quotations from the Book of Mormon.

Some have been offended that anyone would assume that the Bible was incomplete or that there needed to be more. They have, indeed, said, "A Bible! A Bible! We have got a Bible, and there cannot be any more Bible." (2 Nephi 29:3.)

Nonetheless we are inescapably faced with the fact that with the Bible only, well-intentioned men, as worthy as you today, with centuries of opportunity to seek their end, have devised such a multiplicity of churches that even the ecumenical movement seems hopeless to unite them. And if the present trend continues, the Bible itself will be repudiated by the churches.

Our brethren, as you look for that "missing something," consider these words spoken by a Book of Mormon prophet:

> And Christ hath said: If ye will have faith in me ye shall have power to do whatsoever thing is expedient in me.
>
> And he hath said: Repent all ye ends of the earth, and come unto me, and be baptized in my name, and have faith in me, that ye may be saved.
>
> And now, my beloved brethren, if this be the case that these things are true which I have spoken unto you, and God will show unto you, with power and great glory at the last day, that they are true, and if they are true has the day of miracles ceased?
>
> Or have angels ceased to appear unto the children of men? Or has he withheld the power of the Holy Ghost from them? Or will he, so long as time shall last, or the earth shall stand, or there shall be one man upon the face thereof to be saved?
>
> Behold I say unto you, Nay; for it is by faith that miracles are wrought; and it is by faith that angels appear and minister unto men; wherefore, if these things have ceased wo be unto the children of men, for it is because of unbelief, and all is vain.

For no man can be saved, according to the words of Christ, save they shall have faith in his name; wherefore, if these things have ceased, then has faith ceased also; and awful is the state of man, for they are as though there had been no redemption made.

But behold, my beloved brethren, I judge better things of you, for I judge that ye have faith in Christ because of your meekness; for if ye have not faith in him then ye are not fit to be numbered among the people of his church. (Moroni 7:33–39.)

"What today's world must have," said President J. Reuben Clark, "if humanity is to go on climbing upward, is men—those wearing the cloth as well as the laity—who know that God lives and that Jesus is the Christ; men that, having this knowledge, have also the intellectual honesty not only to *admit* but to *proclaim* it; who have further the moral courage and the sterling character to live the righteous lives this knowledge demands. This knowledge must be a living, burning knowledge of God and Christ."

Our brethren, we bear testimony that The Church of Jesus Christ of Latter-day Saints is the Lord's church upon the earth, by His own declaration the only true and living church upon the face of the whole earth with which He, the Lord, is well pleased.

One hundred thirty-seven years ago, in anticipation of the dilemma that man would face, the problem of Christian unity was answered with the organization of the Lord's church, the restoration of the gospel of Jesus Christ, presided over by a prophet of God, having the apostolic power and authority and all the organization as it had existed in the primitive Church.

I bear you my witness that I know that the gospel of Jesus Christ is true, that it is the power of God unto salvation, and that all who will may come and receive by baptism the saving ordinances of the Church and know of a certainty in their own heart of the truth of the message of this gospel. In the name of Jesus Christ, amen.

14

"From Such Turn Away"

Brethren and sisters, I had in mind speaking on another subject today. During the last few days, however, I have had pressing upon me—by inspiration as I believe—the feeling that I should present some counsel on another subject.

Leadership Authority Received and Perceived

I have here in my hand a most interesting document. Let me quote from it:

> To whom it may concern:
> This certifies that Parley P. Pratt, has been received into the church of the Latter Day saints, . . . and has been ordained an elder according to the rules and regulations of said church, and is duly authorized to preach the gospel, agreeably to the authority of that office.

Address given at general conference April 1985.

Given by the direction of a conference of the elders of said church, assembled in Kirtland, Geauga County, Ohio, this 26th day of April, in the year of our Lord one thousand, eight hundred, and thirty-five.

Signed Joseph Smith Jr., Chairman

Oliver Cowdery, Clerk

(Parley P. Pratt Collection, Archives of The Church of Jesus Christ of Latter-day Saints, Salt Lake City.)

So that you may sense the significance of this document, I quote from Section 42 of the Doctrine and Covenants:

I say unto you, that it shall not be given to any one to go forth to preach my gospel, or to build up my church, except *he be ordained by some one who has authority, and it is known to the church that he has authority and has been regularly ordained by the heads of the church* (D&C 42:11, italics added).

I read that elder's certificate to show that from the beginning of the Church very careful procedures of authorization have been followed. It is important that every member of the Church understand that.

The Apostle Paul wrote to Timothy of perilous times and apostasy to come in the last days. He listed the many evils that would be abroad in those perilous times—such things as false accusers, despisers of those that are good, and traitors—and he warned, "From such turn away." He continued: "Evil men and seducers shall wax worse and worse, deceiving, and being deceived. But continue thou in the things which thou hast learned and hast been assured of, *knowing of whom thou hast learned them.*" (2 Timothy 3:1-5, 13-14, italics added.)

That phrase, *knowing of whom thou hast learned them,* has great significance.

Paul taught that a knowledge of the scriptures was our immunization against these evils.

Repeating the Lord's words, from Doctrine and Covenants 42:

Again I say unto you, that it shall not be given to any one to go forth to preach my gospel, or to build up my church, except

(1) *he be ordained by some one who has authority,*

and

(2) *it is known to the church that he has authority and has been regularly ordained by the heads of the church.*

The Church will always be led by those who have been called by the regularly ordained heads of the Church.

Now, this does not prevent any member from sharing the gospel in a missionary attitude; that is their duty. There are duties, such as home teaching, and ordinances, such as blessing the sick, which go with the priesthood, and no special setting apart is required for their performance. But for any and every office there is care to see that anyone given authority receives it from one who has authority and it is *known to the Church* that he has authority.

We sometimes puzzle others with the many titles we have in the Church. They wonder why we have so many presidents. We have presidents in stakes and missions and quorums and women's auxiliaries. Each is sustained by the appropriate congregation before he or she is ordained or set apart, and a record is kept of that action. Bishops receive a certificate of ordination. So do stake and mission presidents and elders and high priests. It is known to the Church that they have authority.

In company with Elder Gene R. Cook and the mission president I once traveled in a remote region on the Altiplano, or high plain, in Bolivia. We had traveled much of the day in a four-wheel-drive vehicle. We had crossed an arm of Lake Titicaca on an ancient ferry. We followed mountain roads first built by the ancient Incan Indians.

At one point we had to build a stone ramp to emerge from a riverbed which formed something of a road in the dry season. I found that lifting stones at an altitude of more than thirteen thousand feet is no small task.

We came eventually to our destination, Huacuyo. It is really not a village so much as houses scattered about the mountains, as high, I suppose, as people live anywhere on earth. There we found what we were seeking—a little adobe-and-stone chapel. The few Saints in the region had built it themselves with no help from the Church.

The distance and the forbidding terrain made this, I'm sure, as remote from Church headquarters as any place on earth.

The chapel had a dirt floor and rude hand-hewn benches. The interior walls had been whitewashed. Hanging on the front wall

were three pictures: the President of the Church and his two counselors—the First Presidency.

I repeat the words of Paul: "Continue thou in the things which
thou hast learned . . . , knowing of whom thou hast learned them."

Even in that remote little branch the members could identify
those who held the keys of authority.

It is not unusual to see pictures of the General Authorities in
Church buildings across the world. These pictures appear in
Church publications. Whenever there is a change, new pictures
appear. Now, with the sustaining of a new Presiding Bishopric and
the calling of other Brethren, their pictures will appear in Church
magazines and eventually in chapels across the world.

Those who know me well know that I very much dislike to see
pictures of me displayed. But I endure that, as do the other Brethren, for very good reason. There is purpose in members of the
Church everywhere in the world being able to identify the general
and local authorities. In that way they can know of whom they
learn.

A few years ago Sister Packer and I were returning to Salt Lake
City from New Zealand. We left Auckland at midnight and landed
in Papeete in Tahiti, where we waited for a connecting flight. Just
before dawn, a plane landed. It was not the one we were to board,
and we did not know its route; it was just an airliner landing on
that small island in the South Pacific in the wee hours of a Monday
morning.

I told my wife, "I will know someone on that plane." I stood
near the gate, and as the passengers disembarked, four of them,
none of whom I had met before, approached me. "Are you Brother
Packer?" And near the end of the line was one man I knew.

The point is this: It is manifestly impossible—whether in
Huacuyo, Bolivia; Tierra del Fuego, Argentina; Kemi, Finland;
Vava'u in Tonga; or anywhere else on earth—for an impostor to
present himself as a member of the Quorum of the Twelve
Apostles and not be detected by the members as one who has not
been regularly ordained by the leaders of the Church.

Turn Away from False Claimants

There are those who claim authority from some secret ordinations of the past. Even now some claim special revealed authority

to lead or to teach the people. Occasionally they use the names of members of the First Presidency or of the Twelve or of the Seventy and imply some special approval of what they teach. But there have been too many names presented, too many sustaining votes taken, too many ordinations and settings apart performed before too many witnesses, too many certificates prepared, and too many pictures published in too many places for any Church member to be deceived as to who holds proper authority. Claims of special revelation or secret authority from the Lord or from the Brethren are false on the face of them and really are utter nonsense!

The Lord has never operated in that way. These things were not done in a corner (see Acts 26:26); there is light on every official call and every authorized ordination, and it has always been that way.

Now, the priesthood is structured so that ordinary men and women and youth are called to work in the Church. Surely we must appear at times to be very amateurish when compared to the highly schooled clergy of other churches. The very nature of the priesthood allows for a great variety in the gospel knowledge of members struggling to learn as they serve. Hence at any given time a member may not understand one point of doctrine, or another may have a misconception, or may even believe something is true that in fact is false.

There is not much danger in that. That is an inevitable part of learning the gospel. No member of the Church should be embarrassed at the need to repent of a false notion he or she might have believed. Such ideas are corrected as one grows in light and knowledge.

It is not the *belief* in a false notion that is the problem; it is the *teaching* of it to others. In the Church we have the agency to believe whatever we want to believe about whatever we want to believe. But we are not authorized to teach something to others as truth unless in fact it is true.

If someone approaches you individually, or invites you to very private meetings, claiming to have some special calling, whatever you do, follow Paul's counsel: "From such turn away."

Such people may claim not only special callings but also special revelations. They may even claim visions and visitations. But where, pray tell me, can they claim the sustaining vote of the membership? In the revelation on organization and Church government given in 1830, the Lord said: "No person is to be ordained to any office in this church, where there is a regularly organized branch of the same, without the vote of that church" (D&C 20:65).

There is another area wherein caution means safety. There are some who, motivated by one influence or another, seek through writing and publishing criticisms and interpretations of doctrine to make the gospel more acceptable to the so-called thinking people of the world. They would do well to read very thoughtfully the parable of the tree of life in the eighth chapter of 1 Nephi, and to ponder very soberly verse 28: "And *after* they had tasted of the fruit [meaning after they were members of the Church] they were ashamed, because of those that were scoffing at them; and they fell away into forbidden paths and were lost" (italics added).

If their spirits are pure and their motives worthy, they will do no harm either to themselves or to others. If not, we would all do well to follow Paul's admonition and "from such turn away."

I saw something else on the wall of that little chapel in Huacuyo. It was a rudely printed poster. I could not hold back the tears as I read the heading "preparacion para ser estaca"—preparation for stakehood.

There followed a list of qualifications for a stake of Zion. A stake of Zion, there in the remotest village atop the Andes Mountains? Oh, yes! That will be one day. And when it comes, one of us will be there to give authority to the leaders. When a stake of Zion is organized anywhere on earth, a man sitting on this stand must be there to confer the keys of presidency. Only from those who *have the authority* and *it is known to the Church that they have authority* can they receive them.

Members Can Have Witness of the Spirit

There is yet a further witness. Any seeking soul—any member—has the right to know by the gift of the Spirit about the call of our leaders.

On one occasion I was organizing a new stake on Upolu Island in Samoa. As is customary, we were conducting interviews with local priesthood leaders, asking each to suggest a few names of brethren of stature to be considered for a call.

One dignified branch president had walked from the other side of the island. He stood before us wearing a white shirt and a tie, with a lavalava, or skirt, tied about his waist. He wore no shoes; he had never owned shoes.

I asked for names. He gave but one. "Bishop Iono will be our stake president." He was right, for that had already been revealed to me. But I did not feel he should make the announcement.

So I asked for other names, for we had counselors to call as well. He replied, holding up his finger, "Just one man."

"But," I said, "suppose he could not serve, would you not like to name others?"

This humble priesthood president then asked me a question: "Brother Packer, are you asking me to go against the witness of the Spirit?"

How marvelous! This wonderful man had reminded me that each member of the Church, in prayer, can receive confirmation that the fifth article of faith has been honored. "We believe that a man [and this applies to sisters as well] must be called of God, by prophecy, and by the laying on of hands by those who are in authority, to preach the Gospel and administer in the ordinances thereof."

Follow Leaders and Be Saved

On one occasion Karl G. Maeser was leading a party of young missionaries across the Alps. As they reached the summit, he looked back and saw a row of sticks thrust into the snow to mark the one safe path across the otherwise treacherous glacier.

Halting the company of missionaries, he gestured toward the sticks and said: "Brethren, there stands the priesthood [of God]. They are just common sticks like the rest of us, . . . but the position they hold makes them what they are to us. If we step aside from the path they mark, we are lost." (In Alma P. Burton, *Karl G. Maeser, Mormon Educator* [Salt Lake City, Deseret Book Co., 1953], p. 22.)

Although no one of us is perfect, the Church moves forward, led by ordinary people.

The Lord promised:

If my people will hearken unto my voice, and unto the voice of my servants whom I have appointed to lead my people, behold, verily I say unto you, they shall not be moved out of their place.

But if they will not hearken to my voice, nor unto the voice of these men whom I have appointed, they shall not be blest. (D&C 124:45–46.)

I bear witness that the leaders of the Church were called of God by proper authority, and it is known to the Church that they have that authority and have been properly ordained by the regularly ordained heads of the Church. If we follow them we will be saved. If we stray from them we will surely be lost. That is true of the file leaders down through the ranks of the Church, of the heads of quorums and wards, of leaders of stakes and missions, of the prophet who stands at the head of the Church.

I sustain President Spencer W. Kimball as the prophet of God. I know that he is the prophet of God. I know that Jesus is the Christ, the Son of God; and that by His order, and in His order, is the Church moved forward in our generation. In the name of Jesus Christ, amen.

15

Youth's Obligation to Parents

I have appreciated, my brethren and sisters, the marvelous counsel given throughout this conference to parents with regard to their children. I wonder, would you object, would it be in order, if I ignored you for the next few minutes and spoke directly to children about their obligation to their parents.

No age is quite so carefree, so restless, so potential as high school years. Notwithstanding the outward turmoils and nonconformity, these are years of quiet inner growth. These are years of silent, restless maturing. It is to our youth of high school years that I speak.

A few days ago I visited a large automobile dealership, where I looked at many new automobiles. One in particular caught my eye —a convertible, sports model, with all of the fancy equipment you could imagine. It had push-button everything, and more horsepower than a division of cavalry. And it can be purchased for only $7,100. How I would have enjoyed a car like that when I was in

---

Address given at general conference April 1965.

high school! It occurred to me that you might be interested in owning such a car.

An Imagined Illustration

Do you have an imagination? Imagine with me that I am your benefactor; that I have decided to present to a typical teenager a car such as this, and you are the one who has been chosen. On the evening of the presentation I see that you are not quite financially able to run such a car, so I generously include free gas, oil, maintenance, tires, anything your car would use—all of this, and the bills would come to me.

How you will enjoy that car! Think of driving it to school tomorrow. Think of all the new friends you would suddenly acquire.

Now, your parents may be hesitant to let you use this car freely, so I will visit with them. I am sure they will be reluctant, but let us say that because of my position as one of the leaders of the Church they will consent.

Let us imagine, then, that you have your car, everything to run it, freedom to use it.

Suppose that one evening you are invited to attend a Church social. "There are just enough of you to ride in my station wagon," your teacher says. "You may leave your car home."

When they come to take you to the party, you suddenly remember your new convertible parked at the curb with the top down. You hastily go back into the house and give the keys to your father, asking that he put it in the garage, for it looks as though it might rain. Your father, of course, obediently agrees. (It is interesting how obedient parents have become these days.)

When you come home that evening you notice that your car is not at the curb. "Dear old Dad," you muse, "always willing to help out." But as the station wagon pulls into the driveway and the lights flash into the garage, you see it is empty.

You rush into the house, find your father, and ask that very urgent question.

"Oh, I loaned it to someone," he responds.

Then imagine, seriously imagine, a conversation such as this:
"Well, who was it?"
"Oh, that boy who comes by here regularly."

"What boy?"

"Oh, that boy . . . well, I have seen him pass here several times on his bicycle."

"What is his name?"

"I'm afraid I didn't find out."

"Well, where did he take the car?"

"That really wasn't made clear."

"Well, when will he bring it back?"

"There really wasn't an agreement on that."

Then suppose that your father should say to you, with some impatience, "Now, just calm down. He rushed in here. He needed a car. You weren't using it. He seemed to be in a frantic hurry over something, and he looked like an honest boy, so I gave him the keys. Now, relax, and go to bed. Calm down."

I suppose that under the circumstances you would look at your father with that puzzled expression and wonder if some important connection in his thinking mechanism had slipped loose.

It would take a foolish father to loan such an expensive piece of equipment on an arrangement such as that. Particularly one that belonged to you.

Use Wisdom in Dating

I am sure that you have anticipated the moral of this little illustration, you of high school age. It is in these years that dating begins; this custom of two sets of parents loaning their teenagers to one another for the necessary and the important purpose of their finding their way into maturity, and eventually into marriage. Perhaps for the first time you notice, and you begin to resent, the interest of your parents in and their supervision of your activities. Dating leads to marriage. Marriage is a sacred religious covenant, and in its most exalted expression it may be an eternal covenant. Whatever preparation relates to marriage, whether it be personal or social, concerns us as members of the Church.

Now, I speak very plainly to you, my young friends. If you are old enough to date, you are old enough to know that your parents have not only the right but the sacred obligation, and they are under counsel from leaders of the Church, to concern themselves with your dating habits.

If you are mature enough to date, you are mature enough to accept without childish, juvenile argument, their authority as parents to set rules of conduct for you.

No sensible father would loan your new convertible to anybody, to go anyplace, to do anything, to come back anytime. If you are old enough to date, you are old enough to see the very foolishness of parents who would loan their children on any such arrangement. Don't ask your parents to permit you—you, their most precious possession—to go out dating on such flimsy agreements.

Actually the loan of the car would not be as serious as you suppose, for should it be destroyed, completely, it could be replaced. But there are some problems and some hazards with dating for which there is no such fortunate solution.

When you are old enough you ought to start dating. It is good for young men and women to learn to know and to appreciate one another. It is good for you to go to games and dances and picnics, to do all of the young things. We encourage our young people to date. We encourage you to set high standards of dating.

When are you old enough? Maturity may vary from individual to individual, but we are rather of the conviction that dating should not even begin until you are well into your teens. And then, ideal dating is on a group basis. None of this steady dancing, steady dating routine. Steady dating is courtship, and surely the beginning of courtship ought to be delayed until you are almost out of your teens.

Dating should not be premature. You should appreciate your parents if they see to that. Dating should not be without supervision, and you should appreciate parents who see to that.

Some young people get the mistaken notion that the religious attitude and spirituality interfere with youthful growth. They assume that the requirements of the Church are interferences and aggravations which thwart the full expression of young manhood and young womanhood.

How foolish is the youth who feels that the Church is a fence around love to keep him out. Oh, youth, if you could know! The requirements of the Church are the highway to love and to happiness, with guardrails securely in place, with guideposts plainly marked, and with help along the way. How unfortunate to resent counsel and restraint! How fortunate are you who follow the standards of the Church, even if just from sheer obedience or habit! You will find a rapture and a joy fulfilled.

Now, be patient with your parents. They love you deeply. Because they are emotionally involved with you they may become too vigorous as they set their guidelines for you to follow. But be patient. Remember that they are involved in a big do-it-yourself child-raising project, and this is their first time through. They have never before raised a child just like you. Give them the right to misunderstand and to make a mistake or two. They have accorded you that right.

Recognize their authority. Be grateful for their discipline. Such discipline may set you on the path to greatness.

An example of what a little discipline can do is found in the comment President McKay made at Merthyr Tydfil, Wales, in 1963. "I was reminded," he said, "of a visit I made home when I was in college. Mother was sitting on my left at the dinner table, where she always sat. I said, 'Mother, I have found that I am the only one of your children whom you have switched.' She said, 'Yes, David O., I made such a failure of you, I didn't want to use the same method on the other children!' "

Be open with your parents. Communicate with them. Discuss your problems with them. Have prayer with them before a dating event.

Stay in group activities. Don't pair off. Avoid steady dating. The right time to begin a courtship is when you have emerged from your teens.

Heed the counsels from your bishop, from your priesthood and auxiliary teachers, from your seminary teacher.

Car Ownership for Youth

One further thought. When we talked about my giving you an automobile, that was make-believe. First, of course, at that price it had to be! But even if I could, while you are in high school I wouldn't, because I think too much of you.

Your parents would be very wise to know that car ownership in high school contributes to school dropout, to broken hearts, and to broken lives.

We have a son who is driving now. We also have another just ready to start. We have talked about a car for him. (That means he has talked and we have listened.) We have put this off by suggesting that if he is to have a car of his own he must earn the money for it. If it looks as though he may do this, I suppose we will have to pray that he has some kind of financial depression. In the meantime we will try as parents to be very generous with the use of the family car. We will try to see that he is not handicapped.

Young people, "honor thy father and thy mother," which is the first commandment with a promise, "that thy days may be long upon the land which the Lord thy God giveth thee" (Exodus 20:12).

I bear witness that God lives. You are old enough now to be told that we, your parents, are children also, seeking to follow His authority and to relate to His discipline. We love you, our youth; but more than this, we respect you. In the name of Jesus Christ, amen.

IV
Admonition

16

Keeper of the Faith

I wish I could express how good it is to be here and how much I have enjoyed and benefited from the classes I have been able to attend. I feel more equal—not quite equal, but *more* equal—to this assignment as a result of having had that experience.

I am amazed at the growth of the Seminary and Institute program. I kept in touch with it, of course, until three years ago when Sister Packer and I were called to go to New England. We were in touch with the program as it operates there, and many times we renewed and compounded our admiration for it and our certainty that it is an inspired program and actually does accomplish the things it was organized to accomplish. We have now seen case studies of this out there, so I know now better than I ever knew; and my prejudice for the program has not been diminished (in case there might have been any thought that that would happen). On the contrary, it has been sharpened and increased.

Now, you have spent the summer here at BYU, and I think today is your last day of classes. Tomorrow night is your banquet.

Address given to the Department of Seminaries and Institutes of Religion at Brigham Young University 17 July 1968.

You have been studying, working, associating, and, I suppose, commiserating with one another over problems teachers have. After today you go back to hundreds of classrooms, to tens of thousands of Latter-day Saint students.

In wondering what to say to you, my mind strangely enough took the theme from a rather unimportant incident that happened in Virginia some time ago. I was there on an assignment, and a friend of mine, a nonmember whom I hadn't seen for nearly twenty years, came to visit. He had been a navigator on a bomber in World War II, and we had roomed together for many months in Japan. He is now a district judge in Virginia. He had read in the newspaper of this meeting I was attending, and had seen there a picture of me, so he drove some distance to renew the acquaintance. We had a good visit.

He told me he had tried to keep track of me and in one way or another had learned a little about my activities. Then he said: "A few months ago I saw a couple of your missionaries on the street as I was going to court one morning. I stopped them, knowing who they were, and asked them if they might be acquainted with Boyd Packer. They said they had never heard of you." (When he pronounced my name in his deep Southern accent I could understand that the missionaries might have had trouble in interpreting it, but I laughed off his comment, "I tell you that because I think it will keep your ego in shape.") He added: "I told them that I thought you were a keeper of the faith or something and that they probably ought to know you. Both of them denied any knowledge, so it wasn't until I saw the notice in the newspaper that I was able to make contact with you."

Who Is a Keeper of the Faith?

Well, I got wondering about his thinking that I was a "keeper of the faith or something," and I wondered which it was. I began to wonder who is a keeper of the faith.

I learned the answer not too long thereafter when President Moyle was planning to go to Alaska. I was working very closely with him, and something had been said about my wife and me accompanying him on this tour. I didn't want to go. There were several reasons, one of them being that I knew Sister Moyle was going to go, and because of some financial pressures Donna wouldn't be able to go. (There were some other reasons, but I bring that in to kind of comfort you.)

I went to President Moyle's office one day, and he mentioned it again. I said, "Oh, President, why don't you just leave me here. I don't want to go. It just complicates things, so why don't you just leave me here and let me tend shop. I'll feel good about it!"

At this he became very serious, almost stern. "No," he said, "I want you to go. I've already talked to President McKay, and he wants you to come with me." Then he prophetically made a statement that had its fulfillment in scarcely a month. He said: "Boyd, I'm not going to be here very much longer. I know that. If what I know is worth anything, it ought to be preserved and kept. I don't know anywhere to keep it except in those of you who are younger. I want you to come along, and I want you to listen to me and stay close to me." Then I could see that he was a keeper of the faith and that the place he wanted to keep it was in those who were younger.

So I found out that that is where faith is kept. I think it is appropriate to address you, my brethren and sisters, probably as no other group in the Church, as keepers of the faith—keepers of the faith kept and preserved because it is embodied in those who are younger.

Now, faith relates to the unknown. It goes to the edge of the light and then a few steps into the darkness. I want to make that point. Faith is different from knowing something. I read from Alma 32:16:

> Blessed is he that believeth in the word of God, and is baptized without stubbornness of heart, yea, without being brought to know the word, or even compelled to know, before they will believe.
>
> Yea, there are many who do say: If thou wilt show unto us a sign from heaven, then we shall know of a surety; then we shall believe.
>
> Now I ask, is this faith? Behold, I say unto you, Nay; for if a man knoweth a thing he hath no cause to believe, for he knoweth it. . . . Faith is not to have a perfect knowledge of things; therefore if ye have faith ye hope for things which are not seen, which are true. (Alma 32:16–18, 21.)

In keeping faith I hope you are able to know that there are some things that must be taken on faith; and that, in our insatiable quest for knowledge, always preparatory to and preliminary to gaining spiritual knowledge there is the exercise of faith. As the prophet Moroni said, "Dispute not because ye see not, for ye receive no witness until after the trial of your faith" (Ether 12:6).

Now, as keepers of the faith and with the youth of the Church before you, how do you keep it? What do you teach them? I have two or three suggestions.

Teach Them About Preexistence

Teach them about preexistence. It's marvelous to me how in missionary work you mention the fact that we lived before we came here, and almost nobody resents that—virtually nobody even questions it. It's just that they have never thought of the preexistence. Teach our youth to know that they lived before they came here. It's marvelous to me that the world cannot see that if there is eternity before us in one direction there must of necessity have been an eternity behind us in the other. If there will not be an end, there must have not been a beginning, because beginnings and ends go together. Eternity is not like that.

Let me read a few lines from William W. Phelps:

If you could hie to Kolob in the twinkling of an eye,
And then continue onward with that same speed to fly,
Do you think that you could ever, through all eternity,
Find out the generations where Gods began to be?

Or see the grand beginning, where space does not extend?
Or view the last creation, where Gods and matter end?
Methinks the Spirit whispers, "No man has found 'pure space,'
Nor seen the outside curtains, where nothing has a place."

The works of God continue, and worlds and lives abound;
Improvement and progression have one eternal round.
There is no end to matter; there is no end to space;
There is no end to spirit; there is no end to race.

There is no end to virtue; there is no end to might;
There is no end to wisdom; there is no end to light.
There is no end to union; there is no end to youth;
There is no end to priesthood; there is no end to truth.

There is no end to glory; there is no end to love;
There is no end to being; there is no death above.
There is no end to glory; there is no end to love;
There is no end to being; there is no death above.

—*Hymns*, no. 284

Keep the faith to that end. Teach the youth that we lived before we came here; that there was a preexistence.

You Don't Have to Know All the Answers

The next suggestion as keepers of the faith is to you. Do you have to know all the answers? Well, if you do, as the scripture confirms, you don't need any faith. If you know it all, you don't need any faith. Read in the book of Ether that marvelous experience Mahonri Moriancumr had with the Lord, where it is said that "he had faith no longer, for he knew, nothing doubting" (Ether 3:19). So don't think you have to know all the answers.

I have come to know one thing that is increasingly important, particularly with our college-age students, who at the moment are under more stress from some of the directions that are apparent in society. I have come to know that more important than giving them all the answers is giving them something of a posture or a position in confronting the difficult and challenging questions that come to them. I believe this. Our youth will be content without knowing everything. They are content to take many things on faith. They don't want to know everything right now. They want to know what to do when they don't know everything—or even much of anything—on the questions they meet every day from their associates.

Help them to dismiss the idea that everybody around them is going to be comfortable. Our young people get the idea that they want to please everybody. They want everybody to feel good when they leave. They want everybody to agree. They want to be pleasing. But if they want this and yet are going to live the gospel, they want that which they will never have. Once they learn this lesson, it's marvelous what happens.

I had the privilege of teaching an institute class for the students at Harvard University. These students finally discovered that when they had a conversation on the gospel and came away having irritated or agitated or discomforted somebody, they probably had accomplished a good deal more than if everybody had agreed with them. And considering the frame of mind of many with whom they conversed, if the Latter-day Saint agreed with all they said that was some indication that he was wrong.

Well, it's a marvelous thing when youngsters can experience such a trial and stand on the position of testimony. The more excited or unnerved the other people become, the more calmed and reserved our young people are—and there's a security that comes from that. In other words, if they leave people a little uncomfortable when they talk about the Church position with reference to a particular issue, they can let it go at that.

We don't have to know everything or please everyone. The only way we could please everyone would be to yield, to stray from the truth. Teach our young people, then, that their lot in life is not easy. This isn't an easy gospel. It was never intended to be. It's upstream all the way, uphill all the way. It has been from the beginning and will continue to be so into the eternities. Teach them to know that, and their joy and their strength will increase.

Teach Them from the Scriptures

Teach them from the revealed word—the Bible, the Book of Mormon, the Doctrine and Covenants, and the Pearl of Great Price. Teach them! If you can induce in them a love for the scriptures, therein they can find the answers to the difficult questions. With this in mind, I think I'll read a verse or two from chapter 42 of Alma. (This is a teacher, a keeper of the faith, dealing with a student. It's a father dealing with his son.) Let me point out a couple of things in it. Alma is speaking to Corianton. (Notice that he could read his mind.)

"And now, my son, I perceive that there is somewhat more which doth worry your mind, which ye cannot understand—which is concerning the justice of God in the punishment of the sinner." Here was a boy wondering why sinners had to be punished. His father perceived that, and said, "for ye do try to suppose that it is injustice that the sinner should be consigned to a state of misery" (Alma 42:1).

As you read through chapter 42 of Alma, notice these verses:

Now behold, it was not expedient that man should be reclaimed from this temporal death, for that would destroy the great plan of happiness [for then death must be necessary, not a punishment].

Now, repentance could not come unto men except there was a punishment, which also was eternal as the life of the soul should be, affixed opposite to the plan of happiness, which was as eternal also as the life of the soul. [I would hate to live in a world where there was no repentance. I need it. I don't know whether you do—I suspect you do. If it takes punishment for repentance to be effective, I'm willing to take the one to have the other.]

Now, how could a man repent except he should sin? How could he sin if there was no law? How could there be a law save there was a punishment? (Alma 42:8, 16–17.)

Teach them the scriptures. Teach them that when their faith wanes and they need more knowledge, they should seek in the revealed word of the Lord.

I'm prompted to mention something I didn't have in my notes. Coming out to general conference this spring, Sister Packer and I got off the plane in Chicago, where a stopover was scheduled. We had the "occupied" cards in our seats, and, though the plane wasn't full, when we got back on the plane we noticed that a man was sitting in the seat next to me. I was irritated. I have a little trouble with cigarette smoke, and I thought he'd sit and blow smoke on me all the way. I glanced back and saw all the empty seats back of us and wondered why he didn't take one of those seats.

He was a fine-looking young man, and as missionaries will I was soon engaged in a conversation with him. It wasn't long before I could tell he didn't smoke. We had a visit. I asked him who he was, where he was going, and so forth—that always invites the inquiry and begins the conversation. As soon as I mentioned I was a member of the Church, he said, "Oh, my wife is a member of your church. She just became a member."

Then we had an interesting conversation in which he started talking about "our" bishop and "our" this and "our" that. I finally asked, "Why aren't you a member?"

Immediately his countenance changed. "I can't," he said. "I would give anything if I could, but I can't. It isn't anything personal with me, but it relates to other people. I just can't. There is something that has to be answered; I've just prayed that I could talk with somebody. I thought maybe of talking with one of the leaders or somebody about this question."

I asked, "Why do you suppose you're sitting in this seat?"

"What do you mean?" he responded.

I said, "Look back there." He glanced over, and I added, "See all those empty seats. Why do you suppose you're sitting here? Was that an accident?"

So we began to talk. We talked about the pioneer trail, and I talked to him about the scriptures, and for some reason I said, "Let me give you a sample of what's in the Book of Mormon." I read to him chapter 42 of Alma as we rode along in the plane. I just read it and he listened. Then we got off in Salt Lake City. He had some business there and was going on to the West Coast.

I asked him, "Has your wife ever been to a general conference of the Church?"

He replied, "No."

I said, "That would be a marvelous thing."

"Well," he responded, "we can't come."

I said, "Well, in case something should happen to change that, we'll be staying at Hotel Utah." Then we parted.

The next week, when general conference came, on Friday night near midnight I got a call from California. It was this same young man. "We're leaving right now," he said. "We're going to drive all night to come to conference."

So we met this couple and made arrangements so they could get into a session or two of conference, and then Sunday afternoon they came over to my office—a very lovely wife and a fine young man, a young professional engineer.

He told me, "I don't need to go into that problem anymore. It's solved, and the next time I see you. . . ."

I knew what he was going to say, but I interrupted him and said, "You'll hold the priesthood!"

He said, "That's right."

Then he told me something more about our flight together. "Do you know why I sat by you in Chicago? I was assigned that seat. Normally they only assign seats at the place of flight origin, and I was irritated that they gave me a seat assignment. I walked on the plane thinking, 'I won't sit there.' But then I thought, 'Well, there must be some reason for it.' That was the seat I was assigned to, and that's why I was sitting by you."

Well, I don't know what his problem was, but the answer was in the Book of Mormon. Teach them, if they are to keep the faith, to read the revealed word.

Teach Them to Testify

Teach them to testify. Let's talk just a minute about testimony. After hearing 206 missionaries stand up and make an expression, I finally came to the realization that we had heard 205 talks and only one testimony. The responses went something like this: "I'm grateful to be a missionary. I'm glad to be on a mission. I have a great companion. I love my companion. I've had good companions all the time. We had a great experience last week. We were tracting [and so on], and so you see how grateful I am to be on a mission. I have a testimony of this gospel. In the name of Jesus Christ, amen."

These missionaries had talked *about* testimony, but they had talked *around* and *through* it, *underneath* it and *over* it, but never *to* it. It was marvelous what happened when we were able to show them how one bears testimony.

There are two ways to spell *bear*. *Bear* means to carry. All of the missionaries were bearing testimonies—carrying them all over New England. Everywhere they went their testimony went with them. There's another spelling to that word (and I wonder if we don't use the wrong one). *Bare* means to expose or reveal or make known. So we may carry a testimony but not reveal it! Teach our young people to bear their testimonies instead of saying they have testimonies and then not saying what they are. Teach them to bear direct witness.

While a witness may come from hearing a testimony borne by another, I am convinced that *the* witness comes when the Spirit of the Lord falls upon a man or woman when he or she is bearing testimony personally. Teach them to bear testimony. If they don't have a testimony it may come when they start bearing it.

I have seen one or two brethren even in our program who are very hesitant about bearing testimony. They get so concerned about knowledge, and they say: "Well, I don't really *know* that! I don't know whether I can say it." Well, you never will know *until* you say it. It isn't that seeing is believing; it's that believing is seeing. Can't you see where it is hidden? The skeptic, the sophisticate, the experimenter, the insincere never take that step and bear a testimony, and the witness is therefore held from them. Teach our young people to bear testimony—to bear testimony that Jesus is the Christ, that Joseph Smith is a prophet of God, that the Book of Mormon is true, that we lived before we came here, that Christ died to redeem us, and that he is the Son of God. As they testify of those things the Holy Ghost will bear witness in their hearts, and it will be compounded a thousandfold more powerfully than if they just listen to a witness borne by others.

Teach our youth to bear testimony—direct, specific witness. I'm not offended at the testimony of little children who stand up and say, "I know." Some people criticize that, but it is the kindergarten of all spiritual learning. Teach our youth to bear witness and testimony, for therein they conform to a principle that opens the door so that great confirmation can come. As keepers of the faith, teach them to bear witness, to bear testimony.

Let me suggest that you read chapter 5 of Alma. As an example:

> And now, my brethren, I would that ye should hear me, for I speak in the energy of my soul; for behold, I have spoken unto you plainly that ye cannot err, or have spoken according to the commandments of God.
>
> For I am called to speak after this manner, according to the holy order of God, which is in Christ Jesus; yea, I am commanded to stand and testify unto this people the things which have been spoken by our fathers concerning the things which are to come.

Then notice these next two verses:

> And this is not all. Do ye not suppose that I know of these things myself? Behold, I testify unto you that I do know that these things whereof I have spoken are true. And how do ye suppose that I know of their surety?
>
> Behold, I say unto you that they are made known unto me by the Holy Spirit of God. Behold, I have fasted and prayed many days that I might know these things of myself. And now I do know of myself that they are true. (Alma 5:43-46.)

That kind of a testimony comes from the bearing of it.

Let me read from the book of Ether one other reference that I find very interesting in this regard, and I think it may help us as keepers of the faith. You remember that I mentioned earlier the incident in which the brother of Jared went up and had this interview with the Lord. "And the veil was taken from off the eyes of the brother of Jared, and he saw the finger of the Lord; and it was as the finger of a man, like unto flesh and blood; and the brother of Jared fell down before the Lord, for he was struck with fear."

The Lord told him to stand up, and asked him, "Why hast thou fallen?"

The brother of Jared replied, "I knew not that the Lord had [a body of] flesh and blood."

The Lord explained something about that and then asked, "Sawest thou more than this?" And this marvelously courageous man responded, "Nay; Lord, show thyself unto me."

But before this could be, there had to be a test. The Lord said unto him: "Believest thou the words which I shall speak?"

Notice that the brother of Jared had to answer whether he believed not what *was* said but what *would be* said. "Do you believe what I am *going* to say?" "And he answered: Yea, Lord, I know that thou speakest the truth, for thou art a God of truth, and canst not lie." (Ether 3:6–12.)

Teach them to bear witness. Teach them to bear witness a little ahead, maybe, of what they know, for in this they will get a confirmation.

Disease and Treatment

One more thing. I was on a plane once with a doctor, a member of the Church. While we were traveling, I noticed his interest in a man across the aisle. Finally he nudged me and said, "That man has got [something-or-other — he named a very dangerous disease]." I asked, "How do you know?" He said, "Well, the color of his skin."

I looked at his skin, and it looked kind of white and transparent. The doctor went on: "I saw his eyes and noticed what he ate. Did you notice what he ate?"

I said, "No. I noticed what I ate."

"He's got the disease all right," said the doctor. "I couldn't be sure without a lab test, but if he walked into my office I'd put him on medication immediately. The treatment wouldn't hurt him. I wouldn't wait even for the test, because this is serious."

I asked, "Do you think he knows he's got it?"

"Obviously not," was the reply, "or he wouldn't be on this airplane. I hope he gets to a doctor soon."

"Well, aren't you going to tell him?" I asked.

"Not me," he said, "not me."

"Well, why?"

Again, "Not me!"

"Well, aren't you going to do anything about it—just mention it?"

"Not me!"

Finally we stopped at a city. The man got off and I proceeded home.

A week or two later I was going out to Reno Stake Conference with another medical doctor who at that time was a member of the General Welfare Committee. I told him of this incident and chided him about his profession. "What kind of Christians are you anyway? If you had been there, you would have told him, wouldn't you?"

He said, "Not me! No sir!" Then he told me about once being on a plane when one of the stewardesses came back through the aisle asking, "Is there a doctor aboard? Is there a doctor aboard?" No one answered. Finally she became frantic: "Isn't there a doctor?" He leaned out into the aisle and could see that up in the front of the plane a man was stretched out in the aisle. Then he identified himself (he showed me a little kit he carried—a little of this and that for emergencies) and went forward. He told me, "I got the man conscious enough again to tell me what it was." The man knew what he had. The pilot came back and they held a little parley and decided that, since they were about halfway into their journey, instead of returning to their airport of origin they would radio ahead for an ambulance and a doctor to meet the plane. The doctor told me the interesting thing was that, when the flight resumed, three other men came over in the course of the next hour and identified themselves as doctors, wanting to know what was wrong with the man. They were interested in the case, but they wouldn't identify themselves.

Well, why? I think I know why. You do, too. Doctors' malpractice suits. They are scared to even stop and give first aid along the highway, for fear somebody may sue them for heavy damages. You know how a person would act if you tapped him on the shoulder and said, "Say, do you know you have such-and-such disease?" Well, you know how doctors get—you can hardly get a doctor to tell you what's wrong with you when you pay and go to his office.

Well, we see people dying of a spiritual disease—the disease of impenitence or immorality or selfishness or something else. We just want ever so much to tap them on the shoulder and say, "Brother, did you know that you're dying of a spiritual disease? You'd better get some treatment." If you do that a time or two, you get to be like a medical doctor who almost won't put a tourniquet on a bleeding accident victim.

Now, let me diagnose a disease among us. I think all of us come down with it now and again. Some of us have chronic cases of it, and if you're going to be a keeper of the faith you must positively "heal thyself, physician"—heal thyself. It's the disease of impenitence. Go before the Lord and become clean. Purify yourselves that your hearts and your hands and your feet will be clean before the Lord. As you go back to these hundreds of thousands of students, go in that spirit. Cease to be selfish; cease to complain; cease to be jealous; cease to be idle; live the gospel; heal thyself.

I bear to you, my brethren and sisters, the witness. Some people say He did not come, but He did. Some people say there was no plan, but there is. Some people say there is no Savior, but He lives—and I bear witness of Him. Some people say He has no servants here, but He has. I bear to you my witness that Jesus is the Christ, the Son of God, the Only Begotten of the Father; that in His gospel is salvation; and the faith, if kept, must be kept in those who are young—to their salvation and to the salvation of the generations to follow them. In the name of Jesus Christ, amen.

17

Moral and Spiritual Values in Character Education

I am very happy to be here this morning, and I want you to know I have not taken lightly this invitation to speak to you on the subject, "Moral and Spiritual Values in Character Education." I felt compelled to respond as a vote of confidence in your interest in considering moral and spiritual values in the teaching, in Utah, of 146,000 secondary school students.

Most of you preside over the largest institution in your community. You relate to a larger cross-section of the community, perhaps, than any other public figure, dealing with the students, their parents, with community leaders, and therefore your influence as an opinion maker in the community is pivotal. You have a tremendous opportunity and a great responsibility.

Morality in Decline

Morality is a very unstable element. Untended, it quickly combines with other things in the environment. What results may ap-

Address given to the Utah Association of Secondary School Principals 14 June 1977.

pear to have the same properties as highly refined morality but can be dangerous to society if left to spread unchecked.

Because morality is such an unstable element, it is very rare indeed to find it in its purified form. There are many counterfeits. Many an immorality now has currency disguised as morality. The same words are used to promote both of them. The same description is used for the counterfeit as we formerly used for the genuine product.

Some who merchandise freedom and relaxation are selling addiction. Others are selling slavery. Communists, for instance, talk incessantly about democracy and freedom.

Nowadays justice is so misrepresented that the victim of a crime often receives much less of it than the criminal. And legislation which is supposed to vouchsafe freedom of speech is cleverly twisted to protect the pornographer and penalize the victim.

And then there are the trends. We now hear the term "consenting adults" used to defend actions that were formerly known to be both immoral and illegal.

For a number of years I've been going to Europe on assignments. I have noticed, particularly in England (which might have a society comparable to ours), that they are just a year or two—I was going to say down the road, but on the skids, a little farther than we are. By looking at what they're doing now it isn't too difficult to see what we'll face here in two or three years.

We see this counterfeit morality moving across us like a cloud. Those who haven't carefully looked at it think mistakenly that it's beneficial.

Some say that morality should be left to be. They claim that the worst that would result from this "scientific neglect" would be an amoral society—neither moral nor immoral. Now, that's a silly notion!

Nature abhors a vacuum, and the idea of a so-called neutrality never has been maintained. If we do not plant moral and spiritual values firmly in place, something creeps in to replace them.

Some declare, "I'll let my children grow up uninfluenced; and when they are mature they'll choose for themselves, and then they'll not only be moral but they'll also be strong and free."

That's an interesting idea. Try it on your garden! Plant the seeds and leave the weeds, and see what you get.

If the nation's farmers did that, one season would see food shortages, another would produce a famine.

Morality, I repeat, is a very unstable element. Moral character does not develop by accident. It must be produced to exist, and it must be sustained to endure.

When we speak of teaching moral values and the development of moral character, we should understand this:

> If we oppose it, it can't happen.
> If we just permit it, it won't happen.
> If we stress it, it might happen.

And I suppose the purpose of this part of your conference is to somehow ensure that it will happen.

Need to Teach Values in Public Schools

Teaching moral and spiritual values and developing character is but a part of what *you* do. You have many other things that you are involved in. Fortunately others spend full time at it—every waking hour. And there have been developed some very highly refined processes for producing moral character.

The churches are (I think we should, in some cases, say *were*) concerned about these matters. But if we were to talk of what they do, the word *spiritual* would dominate the conversation, and then somehow we would be thought to be preaching instead of teaching.

As principals of our secondary schools, and as public servants, if there is no spiritual reason for you to be concerned about character and values and morality there are certainly some very practical reasons. There is more than sufficient evidence to document that.

I make just these passing comments about the school environment itself. You know these things better than I do, since you are involved totally in the school environment.

Student crime, violence, and vandalism have been escalating in one form or another to the extent that it is frightening. In *Education USA* the statement is made: "In-school assault and battery has increased 58 percent over 1970; school robberies, 117 percent; sex offenses, 62 percent; drug problems, 81 percent; serious crimes by girls under 18, 306 percent."

Los Angeles reports that on-campus incidents involving dangerous weapons have increased 159 percent, with 70 murders—teenage murders—so far this year.

Recently the *Religious News Service* pointed out that school vandalism is costing taxpayers $500 million a year. The Senate subcommittee on education sets that figure at $600 million. That's enough to purchase all of the textbooks that we use in this country for a year. Or it's enough to hire an additional fifty thousand teachers.

It has only been a year or two since here in Utah a school was burned—probably by an arsonist—and cost two million dollars to replace.

The School Law News quotes the Senate subcommittee as recommending such things as smaller classes, better police programs (interestingly, police in schools we now take matter-of-factly), better school and community liaison programs, better-trained security personnel, and more supplemental programs in art, music, and career education.

My question is: Why not address ourselves to the basic problem itself? Get at the root of it! That is precisely what I hope you have in mind here.

Isn't it interesting that a public that fidgets nervously when you talk about resolving problems for spiritual reasons is now concerned and forced to face those same problems for very temporal ones?

At last the pinch on the dollar compels us to look at such things, for instance, as one school district that spends $125,000 annually on a program for unwed mothers in secondary schools.

Churchill's Concern with Character and Morality

In order to get a perspective on this problem, I invite you to step back and look at a larger scene. I want to review a thread that runs through recent history.

One man had the best vantage point to see the formation of our society today. For ninety years he watched and recorded it. From the pages of the recent past I call Sir Winston Churchill to be our commentator.

While center stage for most of his life, he somehow managed to take careful notes. He added prodigious research, an uncanny ability to analyze, together with an almost prophetic sense of destiny. He then recorded it in such works as *A History of the English-Speaking Peoples, The Second World War,* and others.

Now, I don't think you need a history lesson, but I want to quote from here and there in his writings to illustrate the fact that concern for moral and spiritual values is not just academic.

During World War I Winston Churchill was Britain's First Lord of the Admiralty and was a keen observer of the world's circumstances. Following that war, in 1928 he wrote this:

> All the noblest virtues of individuals were gathered together to strengthen the destructive capacity of the mass. . . .
>
> Democratic institutions gave expression to the willpower of millions. Education not only brought the course of the conflict within the comprehension of everyone, but rendered each person serviceable in a high degree for the purpose in hand. . . .
>
> The war stopped as suddenly and as universally as it had begun. The world lifted its head, surveyed the scene of ruin, and victors and vanquished alike drew breath. In a hundred laboratories, in a thousand arsenals, factories, and bureaus, men pulled themselves up with a jerk, and turned from the task in which they had been absorbed. Their projects were put aside unfinished, unexecuted; but their knowledge was preserved; their data, calculations, and discoveries were hastily bundled together and docketed "for future reference" by the War Offices in every country. . . .
>
> It is in these circumstances that we entered upon that period of exhaustion which has been described as Peace. It gave us, at any rate, an opportunity to consider the general situation. Certain sombre facts emerge, solid, inexorable, like the shapes of mountains from drifting mist. It is established that henceforward whole populations will take part in war, all doing their utmost, all subjected to the fury of the enemy. It is established that nations who believe their life is at stake will not be restrained from using any means to secure their existence. It is probable—nay, certain—that among the means which will next time be at their disposal will be agencies and processes of destruction wholesale, unlimited, and perhaps, once launched, uncontrollable.
>
> Mankind has never been in this position before. Without having improved appreciably in virtue or enjoying wiser guidance, it has got into its hands for the first time the tools by which it can

unfailingly accomplish its own extermination. That is the point in human destinies to which all the glories and toils of men have at last led them. They would do well to pause and ponder upon their new responsibilities. Death stands at attention, obedient, expectant, ready to serve, ready to shear away the peoples *en masse;* ready, if called on, to pulverize, without hope of repair, what is left of civilization. He awaits only the word of command. He awaits it from a frail, bewildered being, long his victim, now—for one occasion only—his Master. (From *The Aftermath,* as quoted in Winston S. Churchill, *The Gathering Storm* [Boston: Houghton Mifflin, 1948], pp. 38–41.)

That was World War I, but it was to happen again because the lesson of World War I was missed. Morality was left untended. Spiritual values and character building were emphasized in a few places, but only here and there. Character was worse than ignored; it was tampered with. And it only takes a generation to bring about such a decline.

The next episode began in 1939 when Germany invaded Poland. Britain, they thought, would not resist. There was no honor left there. They had determined that with the dismemberment of Czechoslovakia.

But enough was enough, and on Sunday, 3 September 1939, after the "all clear," Sir Winston went to the House of Commons, knowing that he would participate in a declaration of war. He had received a note from the Prime Minister inviting him to come to the latter's room as soon as the debate died down. He wrote:

> As I sat in my place, listening to the speeches, a very strong sense of calm came over me, after the intense passions and excitements of the last few days. I felt a serenity of mind and was conscious of a kind of uplifted detachment from human and personal affairs. The glory of Old England, peace-loving and ill-prepared as she was, but instant and fearless at the call of honor, thrilled my being and seemed to lift our fate to those spheres far removed from earthly facts and physical sensation. I tried to convey some of this mood to the House when I spoke, not without acceptance. (*The Gathering Storm,* p. 409.)

I had to search for several months before I was able to find the proceedings of the House on that fateful Sunday and to read the text of Sir Winston's talk. It is very brief, and since it is but a paragraph and so meaningful with reference to what we are talking about, I want to read his speech in its entirety.

> In this solemn hour it is a consolation to recall and to dwell upon our repeated efforts for peace. All have been ill-starred, but all have been faithful and sincere. This is of the highest moral value—and not only moral value, but practical value—at the present time, because the wholehearted concurrence of scores of millions of men and women, whose cooperation is indispensable and whose comradeship and brotherhood are indispensable, is the only foundation upon which the trial and tribulation of modern war can be endured and surmounted. This moral conviction alone affords that ever-fresh resilience which renews the strength and energy of people in long, doubtful and dark days. Outside, the storms of war may blow and the lands may be lashed with the fury of its gales, but in our own hearts this Sunday morning there is peace. Our hands may be active, but our consciences are at rest. ("War"—The House of Commons, 3 September 1939.)

And so it happened again. Is it not interesting that this man, who was a politician and a statesman, in talking about those events centers on such words as *moral conviction, faithful, conscience, cooperation, sincere, comradeship, brotherhood, malice, wickedness, righteousness, virtue, scruples, honor, religion, prayer?* These are words having to do with morality and character and spirituality.

Sir Winston wrote this also:

> One day President Roosevelt told me that he was asking publicly for suggestions about what the war should be called. I said at once, "The Unnecessary War." There never was a war more easy to stop than that which has just wrecked what was left of the world from the previous struggle. The human tragedy reached its climax in the fact that after all the exertions and sacrifices of hundreds of millions of people and of the victories of the Righteous Cause, we have still not found peace or security, and that we lie in the grip of even worse perils than those we have surmounted.
>
> It is my earnest hope that pondering upon the past may give guidance in days to come, enable a new generation to repair some of the errors of former years and thus govern, in accordance with the needs and glory of man, the awful unfolding scene of the future. (*The Gathering Storm*, pp. v-vi.)

Well, his summation of the Second World War, like that of the first, ties our hopes to character and to moral and spiritual values, and I read just a few more lines.

> In the Second World War every bond between man and man was to perish. Crimes were committed by the Germans under the Hitlerite domination to which they allowed themselves to be subjected, which find no equal in scale and wickedness with any that have darkened the human record. The wholesale massacre by systemized processes of six or seven millions of men, women, and children in the German execution camps exceeds in horror the rough-and-ready butcheries of Genghis Khan, and in scale reduces them to pigmy proportions.

(They, of course, have been far exceeded in our generation in the last few years in Communist China and other areas where this horrible process of human annihilation has been practiced.)

> Deliberate extermination of whole populations was contemplated and pursued by both Germany and Russia in the Eastern war. The hideous process of bombarding open cities from the air, once started by the Germans, was repaid twentyfold by the ever-mounting power of the Allies, and found its culmination in the use of the atomic bombs which obliterated Hiroshima and Nagasaki.

And then this:

> We have at length emerged from a scene of material ruin and moral havoc the like of which had never darkened the imagination of former centuries. After all that we suffered and achieved, we find ourselves still confronted with problems and perils not less but far more formidable than those through which we have so narrowly made our way.
> It is my purpose, as one who lived and acted in these days, . . . to show how easily the tragedy of the Second World War could have been prevented; how the malice of the wicked was reinforced by the weakness of the virtuous. (*The Gathering Storm*, p. 17.)

Notice those words again: *wicked, virtuous, moral, malice.* Words having to do with character and morality. They are not essential, perhaps, in teaching chemistry or mathematics, or geography, or vocational arts. They have more substance in teaching political science, home and family living, social problems, or history, and perhaps a casual meaning in teaching languages. But they are words that must be taught! And they will not thrive on their own. These are words that must be cultivated and nurtured. The ideals they represent are absolutely essential to the survival of civilization.

Motivations Not Necessarily "Church Oriented"

I compliment you as the principals of the secondary schools for caring about these ideals. The state office for education has done some excellent work in character education and there are some districts that have ongoing programs that are very good. You have much, very much support in this intent to be concerned about moral and spiritual values.

If you proceed, however, your efforts can, and by some certainly will, be misconstrued. They'll say that you are out of your province.

Recently here at Brigham Young University we established an "Institute for the Studies in Values and Human Behavior." It took some doing to get the word *values* included in that, because the first proposals all centered only on the study of human behavior. But the word is there, and the Institute is off to a good start.

Dr. Allen E. Bergin, director of the Institute, recently gave an address to a symposium on values. In it he indicted the behavioral scientists for their efforts to analyze human behavior and to at once completely ignore the moral and spiritual dimensions of our lives.

The reaction to his address was most interesting. The fact that such a distinguished scholar would accuse his own profession of avoiding some essential ingredients in their field offended some of them and embarrassed others.

I think that response very strange, coming from a profession whose central effort over the last generation has been to get individuals to talk openly about their frailties as part of the healing process. Should they not be willing to do it as a profession?

The integrity of that profession may well now be judged on how they react and how thoughtfully they consider the declarations of Dr. Bergin. They cannot understand human behavior unless they include as an essential consideration the moral and spiritual dimensions of life. Otherwise they put themselves in the position which might be likened to a school for bakers where for some unknown reason they prohibit the discussion about, or the use of, leavening. Whatever else they do, or whatever else their students accomplish, the results of their efforts and that of their students ultimately must be described as flat and tasteless.

When you address yourselves to moral and spiritual values and character education, some will suppose that your motivation is "church oriented." But whatever your motivation is, it's an essential one. And the words we are talking about do not belong exclusively to the churches.

The Boy Scouts have demonstrated that. They operate under the sponsorship of a whole cross-section of agencies, churches, civic organizations, clubs, even governments. And they deal in a very straightforward manner with such words as *trustworthy, loyal, helpful, friendly, courteous, kind, obedient, thrifty, cheerful, brave, clean,* and *reverent.* They determine to make their participants physically strong, mentally alert, and *morally straight.*

You are not out of your province, or even near the borders of it, when you address yourselves to moral and character education. You are right in the center of what matters most, and you have a great deal of support.

How to Teach These Values

Now I want to say something about how teaching for character and how teaching of moral and spiritual values differ from most other disciplines.

Sometimes we think we're working at it and trying to accomplish it, yet we're failing and we don't quite know why. We're investing time and effort and the classroom space and the energy, but we're not getting it done. To do it well, we need to include it as a part of all the subjects. It is done best if, like leavening, it is a basic ingredient for all that's taught. But to do it at all you'll need a few specialized tools. Now, let me explain. This really should be another talk, but I just want to get far enough into the teaching of spiritual and moral values to make a point.

The best certification of man's intelligence is his ability to reproduce his environment in symbols. He can look at things around him, make symbols to represent them, put them on paper, and even record them in the database of a computer. The alphabet is perhaps the best and simplest example.

Three symbols from among the twenty-six, C-A-T, symbolize cat. Now, although there's no way to put those three letters, C-A-T, together in a line or upside down or leaning on one another to make them actually look like a cat, nevertheless it isn't too difficult to use them as a symbol and to teach youngsters what a cat is.

And then we can increase the information. B-I-G would make it a big cat. B-L-A-C-K would tell the color of it, and R-U-N-N-I-N-G would describe its motion.

We can convey, through the use of these little symbols that we put on charts and blackboards and so on, a great deal of information.

A cat has size and shape and color and texture. It can be described as big or little, soft or hard, black or white, this shape or that. We can get a picture of it. We can make films of it, and eventually we could even show a cat. And we can get the idea, cat, taught.

Most of the things we are obliged to teach, and most of the things you govern by way of instruction, can somehow be taught by using the tools we've just discussed. We can recreate the tangible, material world around us in symbols, utilizing some useful tools in making these symbols descriptive. We convey from one person to another the idea — cat, or most other ideas — by describing it in terms of size or shape or color or weight or texture, or a number of other features.

Now, the reason why ofttimes the teaching of moral and spiritual values is so difficult is that in that field it is our responsibility to teach such intangible principles as courage, faith, honesty, love, humility, reverence, modesty. In teaching morality we do not recreate the material world around us; we deal with the intangible world within us, and there is a very big difference. The ordinary teaching tools available to us just don't work very well. To convey to a youngster the idea of a cat is much simpler than to convey the idea of honesty.

Honesty is very difficult to describe. For instance, how big is honesty? We soon learn that size isn't helpful. Only vaguely can we talk to a youngster who knows nothing about honesty, by talking about the amount of honesty. Very honest, or not so honest — that's relative. We can't tell him what color it is. We can't tell him what shape it is. We can't tell him what texture it is. And that's the point.

When they are teaching moral and spiritual values, most teachers don't realize that the basic tools—the hammer, the saw, the ruler, the common basic tools for building material images in other people's minds—are not used in the same way as they are used in teaching anything else. They cannot be used directly. A whole new set of tools, designed in a different way, must be employed.

It is far, far easier to recreate the visible, tangible world around us in alphabetic symbols than to recreate the intangible, invisible world within us and have it understood.

What do we do, then, if we cannot use the regular basic tools of teaching to convey moral and spiritual values? What do we do with the intangibles? How do we teach them?

Well, of course there's a way. We can tell stories about people and their actions and demonstrate honesty, for instance, in that way. This is helpful and may put the idea of honesty into the mind of a student. But it is not the most effective way.

It is better to use symbols to represent them. A more effective way is to tie the invisible idea, honesty, to some tangible thing that a student already knows about and then build from that knowledge.

Your professors of education define this very useful process as apperception. Apperception is defined as "the process of understanding something perceived in terms of previous experience."

This means that if we have something difficult to teach, such as honesty, or reverence, or love, or courage, we should begin with the experience of the student and talk about things he already knows. Then when we make a transfer to or comparison with that which we want him to know, he will perceive the meaning.

If somehow we might associate honesty with something the student already knows about, something that is tangible and measurable in dimensions, then the teaching about it would become much easier. Then we could form words to describe it, create stories about it; we could measure it, draw pictures of it, make slides and films of it and show it, or present it as an object lesson. Then we would be on solid ground with the students, because students, generally speaking, are more interested in what they know about than those things they don't know about.

Now just one sentence as an example: The biblical symbol for faith is a seed—a mustard seed. But then, that's another talk!

The letters in the alphabet can be arranged in words which in turn become symbols for objects in the tangible world about us. We can open a book full of such symbols and read them, and in so doing we can see the things the symbols represent.

In a similar way the commonplace things that we already know about can be made to represent intangible, invisible ideals. We can learn to read those symbols and in so doing we can see the things that they represent, such as love, faith, charity, and obedience.

All of that, then, is for this one point: We, and you, and those whom you govern in our schools, could become very good indeed at teaching moral character, teaching values, if we put as much effort into developing specialized tools to do it as we do for the other subjects; for instance, mathematics. And it seems to me that if you could interest some of your teachers in the public schools—in a public way, not in a "church way"—to understand and develop the processes for teaching moral and spiritual values, we could accomplish what we need to accomplish as easily as we can teach any of the other disciplines.

Negative Religion Threatens Takeover

Our garden has gone untended and the weeds have almost choked out any concern for values from our system of public education. Beginning in the teachers colleges in the universities, prospective teachers, bombarded with humanism and secularism and pragmatism and atheism, have been graduated with a noticeable breach in their preparation. Concern for standards at colleges of education is reserved mostly for academic standards, and the students graduate to seek employment in schools that in some instances now have been described, and not without some truth, as jungles.

Again I make reference to the fact that I travel just a little, and given an interest in education it makes one shudder to think what they have there that we're going to have here, unless we wake up and do something about it.

The United States Supreme Court several years ago handed down a decision relating to prayer in the public schools. That decision was a partial decision. It was one-sided. Regardless of what the intent was—and I know what the intent was—the effect has been to offer great encouragement to those who would erase from our society every trace of reference to the Almighty. And an extension of that has been, as an effect, the abandonment of any concern for moral and spiritual values in the public schools.

The decision was partial because the plaintiff wanted to protect her son from any contact with religion in the public schools. Now her son is protected from my type of religion, and my son is exposed to hers.

There is a crying need for educators to understand and identify atheism for what it is—and that is, a religion. Though a negative one, nevertheless it is a religious expression.

We put sunshine and rain together under the heading of weather. It would be a little ridiculous to talk about clear skies and cloudy ones and claim that the two are not related and could not be considered under the single heading—weather. It is equally ridiculous to separate theism from atheism and claim that they are two separate matters. This is particularly so when we condone in the classroom, and in some instances encourage, the atheist's preaching of his doctrine and the standards of conduct and morality that accompany his beliefs, and then at once, with great vigor, eliminate any positive reference to theism and the standards that accompany that belief.

Administrators in our schools who intend to maintain academic freedom had better see to it that they administer impartially. Otherwise they offend the very principle that they claim to sustain.

We are very particular to forbid anyone from preaching sectarian religion in a public school in the classroom, and to define any decent standard of morality as sectarian; but for some reason we are very patient with those who teach negative religion and the degrading standards that accompany it.

In the separation of church and state we ought to demand more protection from the agnostic, from the atheist, from the Communist, from the skeptic, from the humanist, from the amoral and the immoral, than we have yet been given. The atheist has no more right to teach the fundamentals of his sect in public schools than does the theist. Any system of schools in our society that protects the destruction of faith and in turn forbids the defense of it must ultimately destroy the moral fiber of a people.

The Hour Is Late

Now, finally, is anything more abundantly clear in our present society? Is anything more evident in public schools in general? We're coming apart at the seams. Anyone can see that. It's time that you as administrators in the public schools in this state and across the nation recognize that, and I'm very grateful that you're doing something about it here.

A wise administrator would not allow a subject that has very significant moral implications to be taught without considering very seriously, as a part of that teaching, those very moral implications. The teaching of human maturation, so-called sex education, in our public schools is the best case in point. If you teach that and ignore the very significant moral implications surrounding it, it's only half taught.

A couple of years ago Neal A. Maxwell and I were sent to Europe, where we met with the minister of education in Denmark and spent some time reviewing their textbooks and their processes of education and seeing some of the things that are developing there. Since this is mixed company here, I'm not able to describe what is in those elementary school textbooks. But it's sufficient to say that it would be regarded as hard-core pornography in elementary and in secondary schools here. And the trend, as I said, is in the direction that we will one day face the same thing.

I repeat, a wise administrator would not allow a subject that has very significant moral implications to be taught without considering very seriously, as part of that teaching, those moral implications.

How encouraging, again I say, at last to see a group of administrators concerned, really concerned, about character education. I hope we're in time. We'd better be about it, because it's late; almost, but not quite, too late.

One final reference to Sir Winston Churchill. When Great Britain finally made the decision, they had passed up several moral commitments, and when they finally decided to act on it he responded:

> Here was decision at last, taken at the worst possible moment and on the least satisfactory ground, which must surely lead to the slaughter of tens of millions of people. Here was righteous cause deliberately . . . committed to mortal battle after its assets and advantages had been so improvidently squandered. Still, if you will not fight for the right when you can easily win without bloodshed; if you will not fight when your victory will be sure and not too costly; you may come to the moment when you will have to fight with all the odds against you and only a precarious chance of survival. There may even be a worse case. You may have to fight when there is no hope of victory, because it is better to perish than to live as slaves. (*The Gathering Storm*, pp. 347–48.)

Well, after that ominous comment I think I want to conclude on a note of optimism.

I used to worry a good deal more about some of these things than I do now. When Madeline Murray, or whatever her name is now, prospered in her effort that ended in that Supreme Court decision, that caused a chain reaction in a lot of things. And then I read somewhere this statement:

> Betwixt God and Mrs. Murray
> A battle royal rages,
> But it isn't fair, considering
> The difference in their ages!

I pondered over the question of how I should conclude this talk. You're all public school administrators, and we are, in a sense, in a public school environment. And then I had the happy thought that we're not on public school property right now!

So I have no hesitancy in exposing a very deep anxiety that comes from having visited in perhaps seventy countries, in public schools in those places, and seeing what's going on, and in praying that the Lord will bless you in your work and your efforts, that you can have inspiration beyond your training and beyond your experience as you consider the questions and the challenges of teaching moral and spiritual values. That particularly you can be supported in those times when you, as an administrator, must stand alone, that you will have a moral courage that will be exemplary.

What a great thing if you can go and reinforce yourself with your superintendent, with your board of education, and gain from them moral support for the teaching of character and values in your school, and for holding to a standard in which you have tremendous support that represents the cross-section of the public whose children you teach, and indeed whose servants we are, as educators!

So may the Lord bless you to remember those words that the politician and statesman thought so vital—morality, conviction, courage, honor, righteousness, wickedness, malice, prayer, religion, obedience, character, and values.

God bless you in your work, I pray in the name of Jesus Christ, amen.

18

Where Much Is Given, Much Is Required

Today it is my hope to inform those who are not yet members of the Church, and at once remind all of us who are members of the Church, of our responsibility to share the gospel.

Three weeks ago I was visiting in New York City awaiting a flight to Europe. An employee of the airlines left her place at the desk and came to where I was sitting. "Two of my nephews have joined your Church," she told me. "I can hardly believe the change that it's made in their lives."

In our brief conversation I asked how her sister felt about her sons joining the Church. "She couldn't be happier," she said, and she explained that the family had had real reason to be worried about the young men. They were two wanderers. "You wouldn't believe how they've changed," she said. "They've cut their hair and the whole bit," as she put it.

Later, as I left to board the plane, she thanked me again and said, "I don't know how you do it."

Address given at general conference October 1974.

Our Standards Are High

In answer to her question, let me explain that for one thing we hold to high standards of conduct. The principles of the gospel are anchored and secure. Some of the programs and methods change from time to time, but there is no altering of the standards. There is a great sense of security and of protection in this.

We continually strive to share the gospel with others, but we cannot dilute it to suit their taste. We did not set the standards; the Lord did. It is His church.

We ask those of you who are not yet members of the Church to be patient if we seem too anxious to share what we have. If we do not share it, we may lose it. That is one of the requirements if we are to keep it. Therefore, missionary work is not casual; it is very determined.

You should know that of the tens of thousands of missionaries serving full-time in the world right now, fewer than five percent of them have reached the age of twenty-one.

This accounts for both the vigor of the work and the great appeal that it has for young people. It takes a powerful conviction for a young person to give up two years of exciting, youthful activity and pay his own way to preach the gospel.

It should not be surprising that they succeed, for they teach the truth! It is the Church of Jesus Christ. By His own declaration, it is "the only true and living church upon the face of the whole earth" (D&C 1:30).

Notwithstanding our eager proselyting, this is not an easy church to join. For the average person it requires nearly a complete change in his way of life. This becomes a great challenge to some, even though every change required would be a sensible improvement in anyone's life, whether he joined the Church or not.

For instance, to join the Church you must forsake every kind of immorality. Husbands are placed under covenant to be faithful to their wives, and wives to their husbands. Young people are persuaded to reserve those sacred life-giving powers for marriage.

Responsible family membership is a great ideal in the Church.

Temperance is required. Members of the Church abstain from alcoholic beverages—all of them, all the time. The same is true with tobacco. And if that were not enough, habit-forming stimulants—tea and coffee—are not used. From this, of course, you could know our attitude on narcotics; that should be very clear.

And there are other improvements—in humility, in honesty, in reverence, keeping the Sabbath—all aimed at making each of us a decent person.

I repeat that in spite of our vigorous missionary activity it is not very easy to qualify for membership in the Church. Nor is it easy once you have joined. If it is an easy church you are looking for, if that is important to you, this is not it.

The Standards Attract

Several years ago I presided over one of our missions. Two of our missionaries were teaching a fine family, who had expressed a desire to be baptized; and then they suddenly cooled off. The father had learned about tithing, and he cancelled all further meetings with the missionaries.

Two sad elders reported to the branch president, who himself was a recent convert, that he would not have this fine family in his branch.

A few days later the branch president persuaded the elders to join him in another visit to the family. "I understand," he told the father, "that you have decided not to join the Church."

"That is correct," the father answered.

"The elders tell me that you are disturbed about tithing."

"Yes," said the father. "They had not told us about it; and when I learned of it, I said, 'Now, that's too much to ask. Our church has never asked anything like that.' We think that's just too much, and we will not join."

"Did they tell you about fast offering?" the president asked.

"No," said the man. "What is that?"

"In the Church we fast for two meals each month and give the value of the meals for the help of the poor."

"They did not tell us that," the man said.

"Did they mention the building fund?"

"No, what is that?"

"In the Church we all contribute toward building chapels. If you joined the Church, you would want to participate both in labor and with money. Incidentally, we are building a new chapel here," he told him.

"Strange," he said, "that they didn't mention it."

"Did they explain the welfare program to you?"

"No," said the father. "What is that?"

"Well, we believe in helping one another. If someone is in need or ill or out of work or in trouble, we are organized to assist, and you would be expected to help.

"Did they also tell you that we have no professional clergy? All of us contribute our time, our talents, our means, and travel—all to help the work. And we're not paid for it in money."

"They didn't tell us any of that," said the father.

"Well," said the branch president, "if you are turned away by a little thing like tithing, it is obvious you're not ready for this Church. Perhaps you have made the right decision and you should not join."

As they departed, almost as an afterthought he turned and said: "Have you ever wondered why people will do all of these things willingly? I have never received a bill for tithing. No one has ever called to collect it. But we pay it—and all of the rest—and count it as a great privilege.

"If you could discover *why*, you would be within reach of the pearl of great price, for which the Lord said the merchant man was willing to sell all that he had so that he might obtain it.

"But," the branch president added, "it is *your* decision. I only hope you will pray about it."

A few days later the man appeared at the branch president's home. No, he did not want to reschedule the missionaries. That would not be necessary. He wanted to schedule the baptism of his family. They had been praying, fervently praying.

This happens every day with individuals and entire families attracted by the high standards, not repelled by them.

We have in our custody the greatest thing on this earth. And, should the question be asked, yes, we intend to keep the commandments of the Lord, all of them. The only real inconvenience these high standards have caused us is in the rapid and continual growth of the Church. This has us constantly concerned with keeping the Church organized in small, efficient units for the benefit of each individual.

Even members who have difficulty in living the standards (and we have them) will generally defend those standards. Old members, as well as new members, need to be fellowshipped and trained so that when they come into the Church they at once come in out of the world.

"The kingdom of heaven is like unto a merchant man, seeking goodly pearls; who, when he had found one pearl of great price, went and sold all that he had," that he might obtain it (Matthew 13:45–46).

Now, lest some of you think all of this giving up of things and this rearranging of your habits is more painful than it really is, I should repeat a statement by Lady Astor. She had dreaded old age. When it finally came, she commented philosophically, "I always dreaded growing old, because then you can't do all of the things you want to. But it isn't so bad—you don't want to!"

To nonmembers I say that while you do not have to accept the gospel, we must offer it to you. There is something of great significance to you and to us in our having offered you a chance to accept it. The gospel stands as true for those who reject it as for those who accept it—both will be judged by it.

Bringing In the Lost

Now, as a reminder to Church members of our obligation to share the gospel I repeat an account from the history of the Church.

In the late 1850s many converts from Europe were struggling to reach the Great Salt Lake Valley. Many were too poor to afford the open and the covered wagons and had to walk, pushing their meager belongings in handcarts. Some of the most touching and tragic moments in the history of the Church accompanied these handcart pioneers.

One such company was commanded by a Brother McArthur. Archer Walters, an English convert who was with the company, recorded in his diary under 2 July 1856 this sentence: "Brother Parker's little boy, age six, was lost, and the father went back to hunt him."

The boy, Arthur, was next to the youngest of the four children of Robert and Ann Parker. Three days earlier the company had hurriedly made camp in the face of a sudden thunderstorm. It was then that the boy was missed. The parents had thought him to be playing along the way with the other children.

Someone remembered that earlier in the day, when they had

stopped, he had seen the little boy settle down to rest under the shade of some brush.

Now, most of you have little children and you know how quickly a tired little six-year-old could fall asleep on a sultry summer day and how soundly he could sleep, so that even the noise of the camp moving on might not waken him.

For two days the company remained, and all of the men searched for him. Then on July 2, with no alternative, the company was ordered west.

Robert Parker, as the diary records, went back alone to search once more for his little son. As he was leaving camp, his wife pinned a bright shawl about his shoulders with words such as these: "If you find him dead, wrap him in the shawl to bury him. If you find him alive, you could use this as a flag to signal us."

She, with the other little children, took the handcart and struggled along with the company.

Out on the trail each night Ann Parker kept watch. At sundown on July 5, as they were watching, they saw a figure approaching from the east! Then in the rays of the setting sun she saw the glimmer of the bright red shawl.

One of the diaries records: "Ann Parker fell in a pitiful heap upon the sand, and that night, for the first time in six nights she slept."

Under July 5, Brother Walters recorded: "Brother Parker brings into camp his little boy that had been lost. Great joy through the camp. The mother's joy I can not describe." (LeRoy R. Hafen and Ann W. Hafen, *Handcarts to Zion* [Glendale, California: The Arthur H. Clark Co., 1960], p. 61.)

We do not know all of the details. A nameless woodsman—I've often wondered how unlikely it was that a woodsman should be there—found the little boy and described him as being sick with illness and with terror, and he cared for him until his father found him.

So here a story, commonplace in its day, ends—except for a question. In Ann Parker's place, how would you feel toward the nameless woodsman who had saved your little son? Would there be any end to your gratitude?

To sense this is to feel something of the gratitude our Father must feel toward any of us who saves one of his children. Such gratitude is a prize dearly to be won, for the Lord has said, "If it so be that you should labor all your days in crying repentance unto this people, and bring, save it be one soul unto me, how great shall be your joy with him in the kingdom of my Father!'' (D&C 18:15.) Even so, I might add, if that soul should be our own.

Come As You Are

And so we appeal to all to come. We call you from the world, more for what you can give than for what you can get. You are needed here. Come by families if you can, or alone if you must.

Here all that the Father hath can be given unto you. But not without cost. ''For unto whomsoever much is given, of him shall be much required'' (Luke 12:48).

This is His church. In it you will not stand approved of all men. Many, perhaps most, will consider you strange. Some of the doctrines are not easy to understand or to accept. The commandments are not easy to live. The standards, I repeat, are high, but you can start where you are.

Many of you are burdened with unhappiness and worry and guilt. Many of you struggle under the bondage of degrading habits or wrestle with loneliness or disappointment and failure. Some of you suffer from broken homes, broken marriages, broken hearts.

We are not offended at all of these things. All of these things may be set aside—overcome. Whoever you are and whatever you are, we reach out to extend to you the hand of fellowship so that we can lift one another and lift others.

This is His church. I have that witness. Jesus is the Christ; He lives. It's commonly taught that He is but an influence in the world. I know Him to be Jesus Christ, the Son of God, the Only Begotten of the Father. I testify that He has a body of flesh and bones. This is His church. Of that I bear witness, in the name of Jesus Christ, amen.

19

The Saints Securely Dwell

In a temple meeting of the Brethren a short time ago there came to me the inspiration for the subject that I speak upon today. We sang the opening hymn in that meeting, "How Gentle God's Commands." Later in a prayer, President Harold B. Lee included the phrase from that hymn: "Beneath his watchful eye, His Saints securely dwell." He then reverently gave thanks to the Almighty for the security and protection of His Saints, and in that prayer he invited a continuation of that watch-care over them.

I was deeply touched with gratitude that in a world characterized by unrest, even by violence, there is a people who care for one another.

We Need Never Be Alone

Paul told the Saints at Ephesus: "Now therefore ye are no more strangers and foreigners, but fellowcitizens with the saints, and of the household of God" (Ephesians 2:19).

Address given at general conference October 1972.

To be a fellowcitizen with the Saints has great meaning. All can receive that citizenship through the ordinance of baptism, if they will repent and prepare themselves. Then, as members of The Church of Jesus Christ of Latter-day Saints, they never need be alone.

In this church the individual is regarded as a son or daughter of God. Family members are taught to sustain one another. In such families there is some fulfillment of the statement, "The Saints securely dwell." Then the family structure is marvelously fitted into the setting of Church organization.

When young men or women are living away from the parental circle they are not left alone, for the watch-care is kept over them. As they marry, the cycle begins again.

Some do not marry, but they are never left alone.

As children leave home and begin families of their own, the father and mother—now called "grandfather" and "grandmother" —face life together, as they did when they were newlyweds. This is the norm, the expected and the desirable pattern, for the course of the Lord is one eternal round. They are never left alone.

Children are taught to revere their parents, but sometimes they live at great distances away. In any case, the Church reaches out with a watch-care over them.

Then when one of them is gone, the aged widow is not left alone, for again the organization of the Church reaches out in watch-care over her to look after her needs—spiritually, and temporally also if that becomes necessary—that she might securely dwell.

The process is simple. Priesthood bearers are called in pairs by their quorum president and assigned by the bishop to visit the house of each member regularly, under the title of priesthood home teachers. They are guardians of the individual and of the family.

Watch-Care of Home Teachers

When I chose to talk of priesthood home teaching, I full well realized there are some activities in the Church that are more exciting and some more interesting. Perhaps even most have more appeal.

Some time ago I was in a home after a sacrament meeting. A mother asked her teenage son how the day had gone for him. The young man, bold in truth and unhesitant as youth usually is, said, "Fine, except for sacrament meeting."

The mother inquired about sacrament meeting and he said, "Well, if we could ever survive high councilors talking about priesthood home teaching and welfare, that would be the day!"

The humiliated mother said, "Why, David, Elder Packer here has charge of one of those programs for the whole Church."

"I know," he said. "Why doesn't he do something about it?"

My boy, I am, at this very moment, doing all that I know how to do about it. Let me explain something to you. Perhaps you'll find that these two programs—which are very closely related—can be most interesting. But interesting or not, they are vital to your security.

Incidentally, young man, you can list me with that high councilor who talks of basic priesthood programs. And list with us your coach, who talks about drill and exercise, and your music teacher, who insists on hours of practice for but a few minutes of performance. List with us your parents, who insist that you learn to work and to pay attention to fundamental things of life.

I repeat, some activities may have much more appeal, but there is none that is more important.

It is interesting that things so basic are so much taken for granted. For example, there is within us a coursing supply of blood delivering nourishment to sustain the body, carrying away waste materials, and armed with a protection against disease and infection. The blood supply is kept in motion by the incessant and dependable pumping of the heart. It is vital to life.

Ordinarily, however, a sliver in the finger gets more attention and is of more concern. No one pays much thought to the beating of the heart until there is the threat that it may be interrupted or stopped. It is then that we pay attention.

Home teaching, strangely enough, is taken so much for granted that most members pay little attention to it, participating routinely, sometimes almost with annoyance. Through it, nevertheless, there come to members of the Church a protection and a watch-care not known elsewhere.

Picture a man calling for his companion, generally a younger man in his teens, to spend an evening calling on the homes of five or six families. They come to bring them encouragement, to search out their spiritual needs, and to be concerned with their welfare so that everybody knows that there is somebody to call upon in time of need.

If illness strikes, help can be forthcoming. The children can be cared for, visits can be arranged. Here we join the priesthood home teachers with the visiting teachers from the Relief Society. Often the problem is not illness. It is a teenager with problems, or a little one not coming along in the way he or she should.

There can pour through this channel of priesthood home teaching a sustaining power to the limits of the resources of the Church on this earth. This is not all. There can flow through this channel a redeeming spiritual power — to the limits of heaven itself.

Through home teaching, tragedies have been averted. Sinking souls have been lifted. Material need has been provided. Grief has been assuaged. The infirm have been healed through administration. While the work goes on without being heralded, it is inspired of Almighty God and is basic to the spiritual nourishment of this people.

The Lord's Way

The leaders of the Church expend great effort to see that priesthood home teaching works. Though it is much taken for granted, it is always provided for and always will be. The principles of it have never changed. Not with changing society or the various additions to programming in the Church. Without it the Church could very quickly cease to be the Church. And I say again, though some activities may be more inviting, none is more important.

I am grateful for the many activity programs we have. They are a spice, a flavoring, or a dessert. They make life interesting, particularly for our young people. I am much in favor of them and would not see them neglected, nor could you persuade me to dispense with them.

I can see that a church with home teaching only might, to a young person, be quite as dull as a meal without flavoring or dessert. However, I have some concern when our local leaders concentrate entirely on activity programs and neglect home teaching.

I say to our bishops, you might as well try to raise up an athlete on a diet of chocolate bars and soda pop as to attempt to sustain your youth with activity programs only. They may be drawn to them, but they will not be much nourished by them. No effort to redeem our youth can be more productive than the time and attention given to priesthood home teaching. For the object of priesthood home teaching is to strengthen the home; and as the teenager would say—and he usually knows—"That is where it is all at." Can't you see that when you keep this lifeline to the home open not only do you strengthen the home but also you have much better, more flavorful activities?

There are many ways to lift our young people. We are very inventive and seem to be able to devise many exciting ways. Sooner or later we will be drawn to do it the Lord's way.

I am reminded of the story of a fur trapper who had earned a modest fortune trapping foxes. He decided to go south for the winter and left his trap lines in the care of a carefully trained young assistant. He taught him just how to set the traps and where to put the bait.

When he returned in the spring, to his disappointment there were very few fox furs.

"Did you do it just as I taught you?" asked the older man.

"Oh, no," was the reply. "I found a better way."

To you who are bishops and quorum leaders: I urge you to give adequate attention to priesthood home teaching. Do not release the home teachers by attempting to accomplish in other ways what they should do. You may invent a thousand ways in an effort to strengthen our youth, but sooner or later you must come back to doing it His way.

I am reminded of the scriptural declaration: "Who am I, saith the Lord, that have promised and have not fulfilled? I command and men obey not; I revoke and they receive not the blessing. Then say they in their hearts: This is not the work of the Lord, for his promises are not fulfilled. But wo unto such, for their reward lurketh beneath, and not from above." (D&C 58:31–33.)

To you who are home teachers—especially you who perform the "routine" visit, not infrequently considered a drudgery: Do not take the assignment lightly or pass it off as being routine. Every hour you spend in it and every step you take in it and every door you knock upon, every home you greet, every encouragement you give, is twice a blessing.

Home Teacher Is Taught

It is an interesting truth that the home teachers are often taught in the course of their visits to the family. In fact, it is often a question, even in a moment of sacrifice and service by a priesthood home teacher, who benefits the most—the family he serves or the home teacher.

In my experience I recall a very significant lesson I learned as a home teacher.

Shortly before I was married I was assigned with an older companion to serve as home teacher to an aged little lady who was a shut-in. She was a semi-invalid, and often when we knocked on the door she would call us to come in. We would find her unable to be about and would leave our message at her bedside.

We somehow learned that she was very partial to lemon ice cream. Frequently we would stop at the ice cream store before making our visit. Because we knew her favorite flavor, there were two reasons why we were welcome into that home.

On one occasion the senior companion was not able to go, for reasons that I do not remember, so I went alone. I followed the ritual of getting a half-pint of lemon ice cream before making the call.

I found the old lady in bed. She expressed a great worry over a grandchild who was to undergo a very serious operation the following day. She asked if I would kneel at the side of her bed and offer a prayer for the well-being of the youngster.

After the prayer—thinking, I suppose, of my coming marriage —she said, "Tonight I will teach you." She said she wanted to tell me something and that I was always to remember it. Then began the lesson I have never forgotten. She recounted something of her life.

A few years after her marriage to a fine young man in the temple, when they were concentrating on the activities of young married life and raising a young family, one day a letter came from "Box B." (In those days a letter from Box B in Salt Lake City was invariably a mission call.)

To their surprise they were called as a family to go to one of the far continents of the world to help open the land for missionary work. They served faithfully and well, and after several years they returned to their home to set about again the responsibilities of raising their family.

Then this little woman focused in on a Monday morning. It could perhaps be called a blue washday Monday. There had been some irritation and a disagreement; then some biting words between husband and wife. Interestingly enough, she couldn't remember how it all started or what it was over. "But," she said, "nothing would do but that I follow him to the gate, and as he walked up the street on his way to work I just had to call that last biting, spiteful remark after him."

Then, as the tears began to flow, she told me of an accident that took place that day, as a result of which he never returned. "For fifty years," she sobbed, "I've lived in hell knowing that the last words he heard from my lips was that biting, spiteful remark."

This was the message to her young home teacher. She pressed it upon me with the responsibility never to forget it. I have profited greatly from it. I have come to know since that time that a couple can live together without one cross word ever passing between them.

I have often wondered about those visits to that home, about the time I spent and the few cents we spent on ice cream. That little sister is long since gone beyond the veil. This is true also of my senior companion. But the powerful experience of that home teaching, the home teacher being taught, is with me yet, and I have found occasion to leave her message with young couples at the marriage altar and in counseling people across the world.

The Genius of Home Teaching

There is a spiritual genius in priesthood home teaching. Every priesthood holder who goes forth under this assignment can come away repaid a thousandfold.

I have heard men say in response to a question about their Church assignment, "I am only a home teacher."

Only a home teacher! Only the guardian of a flock! Only the one appointed where the ministry matters most! Only a servant of the Lord!

It is because of you, the priesthood home teacher, that a verse of the hymn stands true:

Beneath his watchful eye,
His Saints securely dwell;
That hand which bears all nature up
Shall guard his children well.
—*Hymns*, no. 125

I bear witness that Jesus is the Christ. This is His church and kingdom. We hold the priesthood and authority delegated of Him. There presides over us a prophet, who as a man cannot extend himself to the far reaches of the earth, to every branch, to every mission, or to every stake. Yet by delegation of the authority and the keys held by him, he can reach not just to the stakes and the wards and the branches but also into the homes, to the individuals, and bless and sustain them; that the Saints might securely dwell. In the name of Jesus Christ, amen.

20

The Relief Society

It will be my purpose to give an unqualified endorsement to an organization to which I have never belonged. It has greatly enriched my life and that of my family. I have never been eligible to hold membership; nevertheless, it continues to be an influence with me.

It is the Relief Society, one of the oldest women's organizations in the world. There are members in about seventy nations, numbering now well over a million. Each year the membership increases by thousands. Only women are eligible to join.

The Key Turned

When the Prophet Joseph Smith established it, he said to the women: "You will receive instructions through the order of the Priesthood which God has established, through the medium of those appointed to . . . direct the affairs of the Church in this last

Address given at general conference October 1978.

dispensation; and I now turn the key in your behalf in the name of the Lord, and this Society shall rejoice, and knowledge and intelligence shall flow down from this time henceforth" (*History of the Church* 4:607).

The Prophet told them that the organization would be "a charitable Society, and according to your natures," and then he added, "If you live up to your privileges, the angels cannot be restrained from being your associates" (*History of the Church* 4:605).

Thirty years ago, President George Albert Smith said:

> You are . . . more blessed than any other women in all the world. You were the first women to have the franchise; the first women to have a voice in the work of a church. It was God that gave it to you and it came as a result of revelation to a Prophet of the Lord. Since that time, think what benefits the women of this world have enjoyed. Not only you belonging to the Church have enjoyed the blessing of equality, but when the Prophet Joseph Smith turned the key for the emancipation of womankind, it was turned for all the world, and from generation to generation the number of women who can enjoy the blessings of religious liberty and civil liberty has been increasing. (*Relief Society Magazine*, December 1945, p. 717.)

Family Benefits from Relief Society

I would not press to join the Relief Society. I can get more from it if I leave it to be a women's organization. I then benefit more, much more, than I could by holding membership.

I hope the name, the Relief Society, will never be changed. It ties back to the very charter given to women by the Prophet. Its full, balanced program responds to every worthy need that is by nature a part of womanhood.

Each member is constantly exposed to literature, art, music, to current events, to *homemaking skills*, and, I emphasize, to *spiritual living*. She is encouraged to the full expression of every worthy feeling and impulse and talent.

When my wife returns from the grocery store, some things are set out for immediate use. Other things are set on the shelf until she, for instance, bakes again. Some are to be used only in time of an emergency.

Very frequently there are things that are not for us at all. They are to be given away to someone that she wants to *do for.*

She returns from Relief Society in much the same way, this time bearing spiritual commodities. Some are used right away; others are to be stored. But most of it she got for someone else.

Her store is replenished by attendance at Relief Society, and she still draws, now and again, on the very first Relief Society she ever attended.

I do not benefit, I repeat, from having membership in the Relief Society. We, as a family, benefit through association with women who do.

Many years ago there was published in the Church this statement: "The place of woman in the Church is to walk beside the man, not in front of him nor behind him" (John A. Widtsoe, *Evidences and Reconciliations,* G. Homer Durham, comp. [Salt Lake City: Bookcraft, 1960], p. 305).

In an organized way Relief Society symbolizes the relationship between man and woman in the Church.

All Women Needed There

Relief Society is for virtuous women, for steady women, for organized women. It is for reverent women, for spiritual women, for diligent women, for married women and for the unmarried, for women young and old.

Into its ranks are invited those women who are unsteady or disorganized, the lost, careworn women. The Relief Society is an unmeasured blessing to lonely women.

Shortly after the funeral held for the first wife of President Harold B. Lee, I was in a group which included his daughter Helen. Someone expressed sympathy to her for the passing of her mother and said: "She took such good care of your father. I'm sure he must be lonely and must miss all of the things she did for him."

Helen responded with an insight of remarkable wisdom. "You do not understand," she said. "It is not so much that he misses all of the things that Mother did for him. He misses her most because he needs *somebody to do for.*"

We all need *someone to do for.* When that is unfulfilled as a need, we become lonely. In the Lord's own way, Relief Society provides for that need.

Sister, you are needed there. We need women who will applaud decency and quality in everything from the fashion of clothing to crucial social issues.

We need women who are organized and women who can organize. We need women with executive ability who can plan and direct and administer; women who can teach, women who can speak out.

There is a great need for women who can receive inspiration to guide them personally in their teaching and in their leadership responsibilities.

We need women with the gift of discernment who can view the trends in the world and detect those that, however popular, are shallow or dangerous.

We need women who can discern those positions that may not be popular at all, but are right.

The Prophet Joseph Smith said, in organizing the Relief Society, that there is a need for "decision of character, aside from sympathy" (*History of the Church* 4:570).

The Relief Society is so vital a link in our welfare services that save it be strong we must surely fail.

I do not endorse the Relief Society for the sake of the organization, but for what accrues individually to the benefit of those who belong.

Now to the sisters in the Church I say that attendance at Relief Society, in an important way, is not really optional.

It is as obligatory upon a woman to draw into her life the virtues that are fostered by the Relief Society as it is an obligation for the men to build into their lives the patterns of character fostered by the priesthood.

What Do You Put Into It?

Recently I listened to several sisters discuss Relief Society. One young woman said: "We find it so difficult to interest both the older and the younger women. If we have a lesson or project the younger women are interested in, the older women do not come. It's so hard to get something to please everyone."

Sisters, to me there is something pathetic about those of our sisters who sit at home waiting to be enticed to Relief Society. That is not right!

When faithful sisters pray and work and make a worthy presentation, they deserve your support. Just to have you attend is a great help.

Some sisters, it appears, seem to pore over the offering of Relief Society like a fussy diner searching a menu for something to excite the taste.

Sisters, it is your duty to attend Relief Society, just as it is the duty of the brethren to attend their priesthood meetings.

I've heard some sisters say, "I don't attend Relief Society because I just don't get anything out of it."

Let me teach you a lesson.

In 1888 the Relief Society and the young women's organizations of the Church became charter members of the National Council of Women and of the International Council. These two organizations were established primarily to promote women's suffrage and to improve the lot of women and children everywhere.

During those years our delegates had their good days and their bad, depending upon circumstances, the leadership, and the leaders' attitude toward the Mormons.

In April of 1945 Belle Smith Spafford became the general president of the Relief Society. Only a week or two after she had been sustained a letter came from the National Council of Women announcing their annual meeting to be held in New York City.

Sister Spafford had attended those meetings before, and in view of her previous experience she and her counselors carefully considered the invitation for several weeks. They decided to recommend to the President of the Church that the Relief Society terminate its membership in those councils. They prepared a statement of recommendation, listing all of the reasons for so doing.

Trembling and uncertain, Sister Spafford placed the paper on the desk of President George Albert Smith, saying, "The Relief Society Presidency wishes to recommend that the general board terminate its membership in the National Council and in the International Council of Women, for the reasons listed on this paper."

President Smith carefully read the paper. Had they not held membership for well over half a century? he inquired.

Sister Spafford explained how costly it was to go to New York, the time it took, and described the humiliation they occasionally experienced. She recommended that they withdraw because "we don't get a thing from these councils."

This wise old prophet tipped back in his chair and looked at her with a disturbed expression. "You want to withdraw because you don't get anything out of it?" he questioned.

"That is our feeling," she replied.

"Tell me," he said, "what is it that you are putting into it?"

"Sister Spafford," he continued, "you surprise me. Do you always think in terms of what you get? Don't you think also in terms of what you have to give?"

He returned that paper to her and extended his hand. With considerable firmness he said, "You continue your membership in these councils and make your influence felt."

And so they did! Sister Spafford took the gentle correction from that wise prophet, and the day came that she was president of that organization.

Now, I pass that same message to each sister in the Church. If you are absenting yourself from Relief Society because "you don't get anything out of it," tell me, dear sister, what is it that you are putting into it?

Organized by Inspiration

I endorse the Relief Society without hesitation, for I know it to have been organized by inspiration from Almighty God. It has been blessed since its organization. I know that it is a rising and not a setting sun. I know that the light and the power that emanates from it will increase, not decrease.

I know that Relief Society today is led by wise and inspired and strong women. Through them the frustrations of the poorly trained, the lonely, the single will give way to security and happiness. The bewilderment of the uninspired and the misled will be replaced with assurance and direction.

After months of prayerful concern over this matter, having inquired of Him whose organization it is, without reservation, without hesitancy, I endorse and applaud the Relief Society of The Church of Jesus Christ of Latter-day Saints and pray God to bless these, our sisters, to strengthen them, for this is His church and we are led by a prophet. In the name of Jesus Christ, amen.

V
Understanding

21

Your Articles of Faith

The story is told around the Church Office Building that a student from Brigham Young University came up for a mission interview. The General Authority asked him a number of very searching questions. Finally he looked at him very intently and said, "Young man, do you smoke?" The young man answered, "No, thank you."

I respond to this invitation just as it was given: "Will you come down and talk to the students and the faculty at Brigham Young University?" That is what I am here to do. I am not going to give an address or an oration—I am not capable of either—or a research paper. I just want to talk to you. I wish somehow that we could create the illusion of an individual conversation, because I want to be intimate, personal, on a matter or two. So if you could, in your minds, disregard the persons sitting on either side of you and in front and around you. I will talk specifically and pointedly to *you*.

Here you are, students at Brigham Young University, attending classes in the various disciplines. You are in some classes because

Address given to the Brigham Young University student body 21 March 1962.

you want to be there. Others you were guided to by wise counselors. And some few you attend forced by unyielding graduation
requirements. You spend your time reading and studying, experimenting, editing, searching, listening, sometimes hearing (you
note that I separate the two), and there is little time for all that you
want to do. Then there may be a little postponing and avoiding
and ignoring—and maybe just a little dozing. In recognition of that
possibility some would-be philosopher or poet, I am not sure
which, wrote "The Poor Student's Soliloquy." I quote:

> I don't like the teacher;
> The subject is too deep.
> I'd quit this class
> But I need the sleep.

I would suppose that if each of us had an eternity to study at
Brigham Young University, or any other university, and we
pointed our efforts at *ourselves* only, we would fall far short of the
opportunity we have to educate ourselves.

Know Yourself

As the main point of what I would like to talk to you about, I
quote from the founder of Brigham Young University—President of
the Church, prophet, educated man—Brigham Young, who said:

> The greatest lesson you can learn is to know yourselves. When
> we know ourselves, we know our neighbors. When we know pre-
> cisely how to deal with ourselves, we know how to deal with our
> neighbors. You have come here to learn this. You cannot learn it
> immediately, neither can all the philosophy of the age teach it to
> you; you have to come here to get a practical experience and to
> know yourselves. You will then begin to learn more perfectly the
> things of God. No being can thoroughly know himself, without
> understanding more or less of the things of God; neither can any
> being learn and understand the things of God, without knowing
> himself: he must know himself, or he never can know God.
> (*Discourses of Brigham Young*, sel. John A. Widtsoe [Salt Lake City:
> Deseret Book Co., 1954], p. 269.)

Your challenge here, then, as I would appraise it, is to know
yourselves; and once you start getting acquainted with yourselves

—finding out who you are and where you belong and who your relatives are, spiritually speaking as well as in the earthly frame of reference—you come to the astounding, overwhelming realization that you *are* a child of God, that you belong to Him, that He is your Father. He is our Father.

I think it is not easy to discover this in a college frame of reference. Colleges in general, and maybe BYU to a degree, are so structured as almost to prevent one's really knowing oneself. It is a rare student, a rare and a gifted student, who in the course of his college education becomes acquainted with himself.

I recall being in a graduate class here a year or two ago taught by a visiting professor (I am grateful it was a visiting professor, or I could not tell this story), a capable, qualified teacher. Although the course title was something else, he was preoccupied with individual differences and spent the major share of the time emphasizing their significance to teachers. We were assigned a term paper. That is usual, isn't it? I thought, Since this teacher recognizes individual differences, here is my opportunity to write the kind of a term paper that would help me best. I can write the paper that will help me discover what I know or what I need to know about this subject.

We had to have an interview with the professor before we went ahead on our project. There I made the proposal that I would like to survey the literature of the field and then write, in my own words, without reference to any other authors, without including any quotations, the subject according to *me*. I indicated to the professor that I did not care how carefully he edited it or how severe he was in his judgment. His appraisal would be the more helpful. Then I expressed myself as being willing to read references and cite any number of references in the bibliography, but *not* to list quotations.

I mention here that I resent the necessity most often imposed upon students of racing to the library and looking through books, trying to find a place where somebody said something approximately in the direction the student would take, extracting the quotations, tying them together with a few meaningless connecting sentences, and then handing it in as a term paper. Hence my proposal to the professor.

I remember that he considered the proposal very carefully, and then he said, "You mean, *no* quotations?"

"Exactly."

"You mean, spin it out of whole cloth?"

"I do."

He pondered rather deliberately, then he said: "Oh, no. I don't think we could let you do that."

Before I left the office I had been assigned one book and several articles from which I could quote.

Well, I am not critical of the use of expert opinion, but I think it is often misused. I think that in the course of always searching for someone else, in the course of always looking for what others have done, and what others have thought, and what others have felt, often we overlook what is in here, in our hearts, and thus we never make the most important of all discoveries.

Speaking of expert opinion, I was in another graduate class where a student was reporting on the prominent pioneer educator, Horace Mann. Another student in the class challenged some of the information he was presenting. He stopped and said: "I want to tell you that these are not my own words. I am quoting directly from the author—these words came straight from Horace's mouth."

In your search for yourself I would like to make a suggestion or two, which is the burden of what I want to talk to you about this morning.

Let me recommend that you as a Latter-day Saint student have a chat with yourself. (Now, if you are going to do this, you might do it privately so as not to excite some suppositions about yourself.) When you do, realize that this talk is for your own benefit—nobody else included, not anyone. Then there can be no misrepresenting, no counterfeiting, no avoiding, no covering up, no inventing. Just look at yourself.

How Does Your Gospel Compare?

Once you are ready, I pose two questions for you to answer. I suggest that these be answered to yourself alone. It is recognized, isn't it, that the whole purpose of this university is to promote and disseminate the gospel of Jesus Christ? That is what we are here for. That is why there is a Brigham Young University—to disseminate the gospel of Jesus Christ. If you are about to graduate and have not answered these questions to yourself, let me suggest that you do it right away.

One: Just what is the gospel according to *you* like? How does it compare with the gospel as revealed to us in the scriptures? Is it a full gospel or have you left out some essentials? Are you satisfied that the plan of the gospel according to you, if you live by it, will ensure your salvation?

I know what the gospel according to President David O. McKay is like, for I have heard and read his sermons and sensed his spirit. I know what the gospel according to President Joseph Fielding Smith is like, and that of others of the Brethren, for I have heard them declare it. I know what the gospel according to Brigham Young is like, for I have read much about him. And I find that they are full and whole and coordinate with the revealed word. But the most amazing discovery, one that was most helpful and one that was a humbling experience, was to determine one day what the gospel was like according to *me*. I found that I had left some things out; I found I was guilty of the game of pick and choose. Some things that I needed most but liked the least I had deleted. I didn't make this discovery until I asked myself the question, "What is the gospel like according to you?" I suggest that you do the same.

After you have answered this question and know a little about what you feel about it, the second question I pose, for you to decide for you alone, is "What are your articles of faith?"

If my memory serves me correctly, it was in *Measure for Measure* that Shakespeare wrote, "Go to your bosom; knock there, and ask your heart what it doth know."

Somewhere along the long journey that you face in your college career there ought to be a time when you commune with yourself—a time when you find out, besides what all the experts are thinking and what is in the library, a little about *you* and your gospel. Somewhere we may learn that the gospel can and should be *our* gospel.

Let me urge you to be mature and honest in your judgment of yourself. You might, of necessity, be making comparisons. Our little brown-eyed boy came home one day from kindergarten a year or two ago and he was chuckling, all amused. I asked him what was so amusing.

He said, "Nuphin'."

I said, "What is so funny?"

"Nuphin'."

And then he chuckled the more, so I pressed him a little bit and said again, "Well, what is so funny?"

He said, "Oh, deys a tid over in tindadarten what tan't tok pwain."

I suggest that sometimes our grown-up judgments of one another, and maybe our judgments of ourselves, are about that mature.

If it is so that you are not outlining your articles of faith and that you are not discovering your relationship with Christ in the process of obtaining your education here at Brigham Young University, one of two things is apparent. Either you are not learning to the fulness of your opportunity, or the members of the faculty are not teaching to the fulness of their obligation. If I were a student, which I am, I would more quickly suppose the first. My testimony to you would be that the gift is here for us if we will but seek; but it cannot be imposed upon us, however fervent the faculty members can be and are, and however determined they are to help make the gospel according to you coordinate with the gospel according to the Lord Jesus Christ. It cannot be done unless somehow we look at ourselves.

Deal with Your Strengths and Weaknesses

Now several words of counsel and advice. When you look at yourself, why don't you make a list of your strengths and weaknesses. Do not try to hide them. You know them. You can look right through yourself. The Lord knows them and looks at you. I have learned from personal experience that His servants can do the same—look into you and *see you.*

After you have appraised your weaknesses, start acting like a Latter-day Saint. As you do this, avoid the circumstances that bring out your weaknesses. Stay away from them. When you look at yourself, if you find something unpleasant there (I have, a time or two—I guess all of you have or will), get rid of it.

If it is of severe intensity and ugly too and you do not quite know what to do, go see your bishop. He is a judge in Israel—an agent of the Lord. He has the formula. And there is no use your carrying this about. I interview many young men going into missions and see them weep with relief after they have had a burden lifted from them that they have carried needlessly for so long. Why don't you talk with yourself, and if there *is* something there, be *done* with it.

I notice this, that there is a heavy incidence of "I" trouble among our youth. It does not show up on the physical examinations because it is spelled the other way. It is not E-Y-E. It is *I*. When we look at ourselves and find our relationship to God, we change perspective a bit, and the individual himself loses some of his importance in his own eyes. Once you have drawn a circle around you, look yourself over, and then maybe if you would step out of that circle and put Christ in, it would have significant effect in the way you live.

I have another question to ask you. What difference does the Lord Jesus Christ make to you? Any at all? I know He makes a difference in the sociology here, the University, the companions you keep. These have an effect. But do you have any personal relationship with Him? Do your articles of faith include Him? I recall reading in the Book of Mormon a scripture that was as important to me as any ever has been. It reads: "But charity is the pure love of Christ, and it endureth forever; and whoso is found possessed of it at the last day, it shall be well with him" (Moroni 7:47).

As I read that, I thought how valuable a gift it would be if I could have charity, if Christ could love *me*, if I could win the love of Christ. Then the day of discovery came and I found that I was reading it backwards; that charity was something I was *to give*, not to get. (That is, I was to be charitable to others while praying to receive the full spiritual gift of charity, as Mormon recommended in the verse that followed.) It was something that I was indebted to give, something that I owed, not something that someone was indebted to give to me. Suddenly my relationship with my Father in Heaven took on an entirely new and more important perspective.

The First Four Principles

Now, here are four points for you to remember. Does the gospel according to *you* include these? Are these your articles of faith?

1. *Faith in the Lord Jesus Christ.* I recognize two kinds of faith. The first is the kind which is apparent in the world. It is the common denominator of most everything that goes on. It is the thing that lets us exist. It is the thing that gives us some hope of getting anything done. Everyone has it, some in a larger measure than others. The second kind of faith, remarkably rare, unusual to find, is the kind of faith that causes things to happen. Faith is a power as real as electricity but a thousand times more powerful. Now, did you ever exercise faith—exercise it, practice it, you see, not just take it for granted? When you look at yourself, ask yourself how faithful you are. Faith in the Lord Jesus Christ is a first principle of the gospel according to the Lord. Is it a first principle in the gospel according to you?

2. *Repentance.* This should be obvious—repentance—to turn from paths that are not correct and to do whatever is necessary to make the adjustments and get back on the path that is correct. I ask you students and faculty, are you so enamored with one of the disciplines, the one that interests you so much here, that you are willing to judge the gospel principles against it?

Is it true that whenever a principle of the gospel happens to coordinate with a principle or theory of your favorite discipline you will accept it, but that otherwise you will reject it? Are your articles of faith based particularly on some field of intellectual learning, or are they articles of *faith?* Is the gospel according to you a shoddy, makeshift conglomeration? If it is, let me suggest that some of the greatest minds in human history have attempted to produce a gospel of their own. In some cases they have organized a church to implement it. I suggest that it may be just a little difficult for any one of us as an individual to formulate a gospel according to us that is superior to the gospel according to Christ. As you discover, as you look at yourself, that you have been unconsciously making this attempt, you may do well to include in your articles of faith the principle of repentance.

3. *Baptism.* Does the gospel according to you include renewing your covenants? We have all had baptism, and that makes us agents of Christ. We have taken upon ourselves His name. We should develop a relationship with Him. We should have constant communication with Him.

4. *The laying on of hands for the gift of the Holy Ghost.* Is this included in your articles of faith? If so, do you live by it?

The Brethren were in a meeting the other day when a very important matter was being discussed at great length. Finally a course of action was decided upon. As the meeting concluded, Elder Harold B. Lee was called on to offer the closing prayer. He stood, and it was an inspiring thing to be present and hear him pray. He said words to this effect: "We thank thee, Father, that the light which is due this, thy chosen servant [referring to the member of the First Presidency who had led the deliberations and had proposed the course of action] has been apparent here today, and that we are witnesses of thy love and thy revelation to thy servants."

Center Your Life in Christ

Now, if you are not taking advantage of the full blessing of Church membership when you look yourself over carefully and formulate your articles of faith, it may be time to start. When you look at you and you want to center everything in you and to use the word *I*, use just a little caution. Be humble and prayerful, lest the gospel according to you and your articles of faith differ materially from those of the Lord. Sometimes the term *I* can mislead us. Remember William Ernest Henley's poem "Invictus."

> Out of the night that covers me,
> Black as the Pit from pole to pole,
> . . . .

It ends with these four lines:

> It matters not how strait the gate,
> How charged with punishments the scroll,
> I am the master of my fate,
> I am the captain of my soul.

Some years ago Elder Orson F. Whitney of the Council of the Twelve, seeing this poem held up as a great example of courage, sensed maybe a thread of egotism in it, and he penned an answer that he entitled "The Soul's Captain." In answer to the declaration, "*I* am the master of my fate, *I* am the captain of my soul," he wrote:

Art thou in truth? Then what of him
    Who bought thee with his blood?
Who plunged into devouring seas
    And snatched thee from the flood?

Who bore for all our fallen race
    What none but him could bear?
The God who died that man might live,
    And endless glory share.

Of what avail thy vaunted strength,
    Apart from his vast might?
Pray that his Light may pierce the gloom,
    That thou mayest see aright.

Men are as bubbles on the wave,
    As leaves upon the tree.
Thou, captain of thy soul, forsooth!
    Who gave that place to thee?

Free will is thine—free agency,
    To wield for right or wrong;
But thou must answer unto him
    To whom all souls belong.

Bend to the dust that head "unbowed,"
    Small part of Life's great whole!
And see in him, and him alone,
    The Captain of thy soul.

    —*Improvement Era*, April 1926, p. 611

I submit to you students that if you follow the injunction of President Brigham Young and learn of yourself, and that if you are honest with yourselves and evidence enough faith to accept the gospel according to revealed word where the gospel according to you may be lacking, somewhere at the end of that road you will find a companionship, an intimate, priceless, eternal companionship, with the Lord Jesus Christ.

As you know, I belonged here at the University, and I still do. About six months ago—maybe prematurely, certainly without notice—I was catapulted into association with the General Authorities of the Church. There comes with that a great conviction, and I could say nothing more important to you, as you seek on your own behalf, than to bear witness to you that God lives. This I know. I bear witness of Christ, that He lives, an actual being; that this is His Church; that the destiny of it is in His hands; and that as we discover ourselves we discover our relationship with Him. May our companionship with Him be perfect, I pray in the name of Jesus Christ, amen.

22

Revelation in a Changing World

Following baptism, one is confirmed a member of The Church of Jesus Christ of Latter-day Saints in a brief ordinance, during which there is conferred the gift of the Holy Ghost. Thereafter, all through life, men, women, even little children have received the right to inspired direction to guide them in their lives—personal revelation! (See Alma 32:23.)

The Holy Ghost communicates with the spirit through the mind more than through the physical senses. This guidance comes as thoughts, as feelings, through impressions and promptings. It is not always easy to describe inspiration. The scriptures teach us that we may "feel" the words of spiritual communication more than hear them, and see with spiritual rather than with mortal eyes.

The patterns of revelation are not dramatic. The voice of inspiration is a still voice, a small voice. There need be no trance, no sanctimonious declaration. It is quieter and simpler than that.

Address given at general conference October 1989.

The Book of Mormon teaches that "angels speak by the power of the Holy Ghost" (2 Nephi 32:3) and records that even though an angel spoke to some, they "were past feeling, that [they] could not feel his words" (1 Nephi 17:45). If you have experienced inspiration, you understand.

Bodily Impurities Can
Impair Spiritual Communication

Our physical body is the instrument of our spirit. In that marvelous revelation the Word of Wisdom we are told how to keep our bodies free from impurities which might dull, even destroy, those delicate physical senses which have to do with spiritual communication.

The Word of Wisdom is a key to individual revelation. It was given as "a principle with promise, adapted to the capacity of the weak and the weakest of all saints" (D&C 89:3).

The promise is that those who obey will receive "great treasures of knowledge, even hidden treasures" (v. 19). If we abuse our body with habit-forming substances, or misuse prescription drugs, we draw curtains which close off the light of spiritual communication.

Narcotic addiction serves the design of the prince of darkness, for it disrupts the channel to the holy spirit of truth. At present, the adversary has an unfair advantage. Addiction has the capacity to disconnect the human will and nullify moral agency. It can rob one of the power to decide. Agency is too fundamental a doctrine to be left in such jeopardy.

It is my conviction, and my constant prayer, that there will come through research, through inspiration to scientists if need be, the power to conquer narcotic addiction through the same means which cause it. I plead with all of you to earnestly pray that somewhere, somehow, the way will be discovered to erase addiction in the human body.

It is not just human suffering, even human life, which is at risk; it is all of the personal and social and political and spiritual freedoms for which humanity has struggled for ages. At risk is all that was purchased by the blood of martyrs. Moral agency itself is in jeopardy! If we all pray fervently, the Lord will surely help us. And with those prayers, teach your children to obey the Word of Wisdom. It is their armor and will protect them from habits which obstruct the channels of personal revelation.

Revelation Is Intended for All

Things of the Spirit need not—indeed should not—require our uninterrupted time and attention. Ordinary workaday things occupy most of our attention. And that is as it should be. We are mortal beings living in this physical world.

Spiritual things are like leavening. By measure they may be very small, but by influence they affect all that we do. Continuing revelation is fundamental to the gospel of Jesus Christ.

And I assure you that revelation attends our prophet President and those ordained as Apostles, as prophets, seers, and revelators. But revelation is not limited to them. The Lord desires that "every man might speak in the name of God the Lord, even the Savior of the world" (D&C 1:20).

Not all inspiration comes from God (see D&C 46:7). The evil one has the power to tap into those channels of revelation and send conflicting signals which can mislead and confuse us. There are promptings from evil sources which are so carefully counterfeited as to deceive even the very elect (see Matthew 24:24).

Nevertheless, we can learn to discern these spirits. Even with every member having the right to revelation, the Church can be maintained as a house of order. Revelation comes in an orderly way in the Church. We are entitled to personal revelation. However, unless we are set apart to some presiding office, we will not receive revelations concerning what others should do.

Revelation in the Church

Revelation in the Church comes to those who have been properly called, sustained, ordained, or set apart. A bishop, for instance, will not receive any revelation concerning a neighboring ward, because that is out of his jurisdiction.

Occasionally someone will claim to have received authority to teach and bless without having been called and set apart. Less than a year after the Church was organized (February 1831), a revelation was received which the Prophet specified "embrac[ed] the law of the church." It contains this verse: "It shall not be given to any one to go forth to preach my gospel, or to build up my church, except he be ordained by some one who has authority, and *it is known to the church that he has authority* and has been regularly ordained by the heads of the church" (D&C 42:11, italics added).

That is why the process of sustaining those called to office is so carefully protected in the Church—that all might know who has authority to teach and to bless.

An unusual spiritual experience should not be regarded as a personal call to direct others. It is my conviction that experiences of a special, sacred nature are individual and should be kept to oneself.

Few things disturb the channels of revelation quite so effectively as those who are misled and think themselves to be chosen to instruct others when they are not chosen.

Others, fearing they also might go astray, then hold back and do not seek the source of divine revelation. Obedience to constituted priesthood authority will protect us from going astray.

There are those within the Church who are disturbed when changes are made with which they disagree or when changes they propose are not made. They point to these as evidence that the leaders are not inspired. They write and speak to convince others that the doctrines and decisions of the Brethren are not given through inspiration.

Two things characterize them: they are always irritated by the word *obedience,* and always they question revelation. It has always been so. Helaman described those who "began to disbelieve in the spirit of prophecy and in the spirit of revelation; and the judgments of God did stare them in the face." They "were left in their own strength," and "the Spirit of the Lord did no more preserve them; yea, it had withdrawn from them." (Helaman 4:23, 13, 24.)

Changes Indicate Ongoing Revelation

Changes in organization or procedures are a testimony that revelation is ongoing. While doctrines remain fixed, the methods or procedures do not.

For instance: When the current editions of the scriptures were published, many corrections were made in the Book of Mormon on the basis of original or printer's manuscripts, some of which had not previously been available. In Alma chapter 16, verse 5, for example, the word *whether* had appeared. The original manuscript for that verse does not exist. However, when we found the printer's copy we saw that the Prophet Joseph Smith had changed the word to *whither*. *Whether* means "if"; *whither* means "where." The next verse verifies *whither* to be correct.

Another example: In Alma chapter 32, verse 30, the words "sprouteth and beginneth to grow" occurred three times. An obvious typesetting error left one of them out. In the 1981 edition, thirty-five words were restored. It now conforms to the original text.

There were many such changes. None altered the doctrine. Each change, however small in detail, was carefully and prayerfully considered and approved by the Council of the First Presidency and the Quorum of the Twelve Apostles in a meeting in the temple. All such matters are determined in that way. The Lord established that process when He gave revelations relating to temple ordinances.

In 1841 the Saints were commanded to build a temple in Nauvoo in which to perform baptisms for the dead, and they were given time to do it. They would be rejected if they failed. He said: "I command you, all ye my saints, to build a house unto me; . . . and if you do not these things at the end of the appointment ye shall be rejected as a church, with your dead, saith the Lord your God." (D&C 124:31–32.)

The Saints did not fail. However impossible it may have seemed to them, given the terrible opposition they faced, the Lord promised to guide them through His appointed servants: "If my people will hearken unto my voice, and unto the voice of my servants whom I have appointed to lead my people, behold, verily I say unto you, they shall not be moved out of their place. But if they will not hearken to my voice, nor unto the voice of these men whom I have appointed, they shall not be blest." (D&C 124:45–46.)

Later, speaking on the same subject of temple ordinances, the Lord affirmed again that He would reveal His will to His authorized servants: "For him to whom these keys are given there is no difficulty in obtaining a knowledge of facts in relation to the salvation of the children of men" (D&C 128:11).

That principle of revelation has been with the Church ever since. Those who hold the keys have obtained knowledge on what to do. When changes have come, they have come through that process. The Lord does as He said He would do: "I, the Lord, command and revoke, as it seemeth me good" (D&C 56:4). "I command and men obey not; I revoke and they receive not the blessing" (D&C 58:32).

He told the Saints that when enemies prevented them from keeping a commandment, He would no longer require them to do so. And He said: "The iniquity and transgression of my holy laws and commandments I will visit upon the heads of those who hindered my work, unto the third and fourth generation, so long as they repent not" (D&C 124:50).

Doctrines Fixed, Methods
Subject to Revealed Change

The gospel plan was revealed line upon line, precept upon precept, here a little, and there a little. And it goes on: "We believe that He will yet reveal many great and important things pertaining to the Kingdom of God" (Articles of Faith 1:9).

There will be changes made in the future as in the past. Whether the Brethren make changes or resist them depends entirely upon the instructions they receive through the channels of revelation which were established in the beginning.

The doctrines will remain fixed, eternal; the organization, programs, and procedures will be altered as directed by Him whose church this is.

We who have been called to lead the Church are ordinary men and women with ordinary capacities struggling to administer a church which grows at such a pace as to astound even those who watch it closely. Some are disposed to find fault with us; surely that is easy for them to do. But they do not examine us more searchingly than we examine ourselves. A call to lead is not an exemption from the challenges of life. We seek inspiration in the same way that you do, and we must obey the same laws which apply to every member of the Church.

We are sorry for our inadequacies, sorry we are not better than we are. We can feel, as you can see, the effect of the aging process as it imposes limitations upon His leaders before your very eyes.

But this we know. There are councils and counselors and quorums to counterbalance the foibles and frailties of man. The Lord organized His church to provide for mortal men to work as mortal men, and yet He assured that the spirit of revelation would guide in all that we do in His name.

And in the end, what is given comes because the Lord has spoken it, "whether by [His] own voice or by the voice of [His] servants, it is the same" (D&C 1:38). We know His voice when He speaks.

Revelation continues with us today. The promptings of the Spirit, the dreams, and the visions and the visitations, and the ministering of angels all are with us now. And the still, small voice of the Holy Ghost "is a lamp unto [our] feet, and a light unto [our] path" (Psalm 119:105). Of that I bear witness, in the name of Jesus Christ, amen.

23

Can I
Really Know?

Some time ago a representative of the Church on a plane bound for a large West Coast city was drawn into conversation with a young attorney. Their conversation centered on the front page of a newspaper, a large city tabloid with the sordid, the ugly, the tragic openly displayed.

The attorney said the newspaper was typical of humanity and typical of life—miserable, meaningless, and in all ways useless and futile. The elder protested, holding that life was purposeful, and that there lives a God who loves His children, and that life is good indeed.

The Skeptic's Challenge

When the attorney learned that he was speaking to a minister of the gospel, he said with some emphasis: "All right! We have one hour and twenty-eight minutes left on this flight and I want you to

Address given at general conference October 1964.

tell me what business you or anyone else has traipsing about the earth saying that there is a God or that life has any substantial meaning."

He then confessed himself to be an atheist and pressed his disbelief so urgently that finally he was told: "You are wrong, my friend. There is a God. He lives. I *know* He lives." And he heard the elder proclaim with fervor his witness that Jesus is the Christ.

But the testimony fell on doubtful ears. "You don't *know*," he said. "Nobody *knows* that! You can't *know* it."

The elder would not yield, and the attorney finally said condescendingly: "All right. You say you know. Then [implying 'If you are so smart'] tell me how you know."

The elder had been faced with questions before, in written and oral examinations attendant to receiving advanced degrees, but never had a question come which seemed to be so monumentally significant.

I mention this incident because it illustrates the challenge that members of the Church face—all of them. This challenge particularly becomes a stumbling block to our youth. They face a dilemma when the cynic and the skeptic treat them with academic contempt because they hold to a simple childlike faith. Before such a challenge many of them turn away—embarrassed and ashamed that they cannot answer the question.

As our friend attempted to answer this question, he found himself helpless to communicate with the attorney, for when he said, "The Holy Ghost has borne witness to my soul," the attorney said, "I don't know what you are talking about."

The words *prayer* and *discernment* and *faith* were meaningless to the attorney, for they were outside the realm of his experience.

"You see," said the attorney, "you don't really know. If you did, you would be able to tell me how you know." The implication being that anything we know, we readily can explain in words alone.

But Paul said:

> Now we have received, not the spirit of the world, but the spirit which is of God; that we might know the things that are freely given to us of God.
>
> Which things also we speak, not in the words which man's wisdom teacheth, but which the Holy Ghost teacheth; comparing spiritual things with spiritual.

> But the natural man receiveth not the things of the Spirit of God: for they are foolishness unto him: neither can he know them, because they are spiritually discerned. (1 Corinthians 2:12-14.)

The elder felt that he may have borne his testimony unwisely and prayed in his heart that, even if the young attorney could not understand the words, he could at least feel the sincerity of the declaration.

"Not all knowledge can be conveyed in words alone," he said. And then he asked the attorney, "Do you know what salt tastes like?"

"Of course I do," was the reply.

"When did you taste salt last?"

"Why, just as we had dinner on the plane."

"You just think you know what salt tastes like," said the elder.

"I know what salt tastes like as well as I know anything," said the attorney.

"If I gave you a cup of salt and a cup of sugar and let you taste them both, could you tell the salt from the sugar?"

"Now you're getting juvenile," was his reply. "Of course I could tell the difference. I know what salt tastes like. It is an everyday experience—I know it as well as I know anything."

"Then," said the elder, "may I ask you one further question? Just assume that I have never tasted salt. Can you explain to me, in words, just what it tastes like?"

After some thought the attorney ventured, "Well—I—it's not sweet and it's not sour."

"You have told me what it isn't," was the answer, "not what it is."

After several attempts he admitted failure in the little exercise of conveying in words knowledge so commonplace as what salt tastes like. He found himself quite as helpless as the elder had been to answer his question about God.

The Believer's Knowledge

As they parted in the terminal the elder bore testimony once again. "I claim to know there is a God. You ridiculed that testimony and said that if I did know I would be able to tell you exactly how I know.

"My friend, spiritually speaking, I have tasted salt. I am no more able to convey to you in words how this knowledge has come than you are able to perform the simple exercise of telling me what salt tastes like. But I say to you again, there is a God. He does live. And just because you don't know, don't try to tell me that I don't know, for I do."

Young people, do not apologize or be ashamed because you cannot frame into words that which you know in your heart to be true. Do not repudiate your testimony merely because you have no marvelous manifestations to discuss.

Lehi saw in his dream those who "tasted the fruit," and "were ashamed, because of those that were scoffing at them; and they fell away into forbidden paths and were lost" (1 Nephi 8:28).

We sympathize with you and know how difficult it is to hold to the truth, particularly when professors of worldly knowledge—some of them counterfeit Christians—debunk and scoff. We know from personal experience that you may have some doubts. You may wonder at times, "Can I ever really know for sure?' You may even wonder, "Does anyone really know for sure?"

President David O. McKay told of his search for a testimony as a youth. "I realized in youth," he said, "that the most precious thing that a man could obtain in this life was a testimony of the divinity of this work. I hungered for it." He continued:

> I remember riding over the hills one afternoon thinking of these things and concluded that there in the silence of the hills was the best place to get that testimony. I stopped my horse, threw the reins over his head. . . . I knelt down and with all of the fervor of my heart poured out my soul to God and asked him for a testimony of this Gospel. I had in mind that there would be some manifestation, that I should receive some transformation that would leave me without doubt.
>
> I got up, mounted my horse, and as he started over the trail I remember rather introspectively searching myself, and involuntarily shaking my head, saying to myself, "No, sir, there is no change; I am just the same boy I was before I knelt down."
>
> The anticipated manifestation had not come. Nor was that the only occasion. However, it did come, but not in the way that I had anticipated. Even the manifestation of God's power and the presence of His angels came, but when it did come it was simply a confirmation; it was not the testimony. (*True to the Faith*, Llewelyn R. McKay, comp. [Salt Lake City: Bookcraft, 1966], p. 262.)

In answer to your question, "Can I ever really know for sure?" we answer, "Just as certainly as you fill the requirements, that testimony will come." The Lord has never said, nor was it ever pretended, that this testimony yields itself to scientific investigation, to mere curiosity, or to academic inquiry.

In answer to your question, "Does anybody really know?" yes, tens of thousands know. The Brethren know. Your parents know.

I have respect for the truth. It is wrong to fabricate, to invent, to mislead.

There is another dimension also. When one has received that witness, and is called to testify, for him to dilute, to minimize, to withhold would be grossly wrong. It is in the face of this that I feel the urgency to bear witness. And I bear my solemn witness that Jesus is the Christ. I say that I know Jesus is the Christ, that the gospel of Jesus Christ was restored to Joseph Smith, a prophet of God, that David O. McKay who presides over this Church is a prophet of God. In the name of Jesus Christ, amen.

The Mystery
of Life

I want to tell you of an incident that happened many years ago. Two of my sons, then little boys, were wrestling on the rug, and they had reached that line which separates laughter from tears. So I worked my foot carefully between them and lifted the older one back to a sitting position on the rug. As I did so, I said, "Hey there, you little monkeys. You'd better settle down."

To my surprise he folded his little arms, his eyes swimming with deep hurt, and protested, "I *not* a monkey, Daddy, I a *person!*"

The years have not erased the overwhelming feeling of love I felt for my little sons. I was taught a profound lesson by my little boy. Many times over the years his words have slipped back into my mind: "I *not* a monkey, Daddy, I a *person!*"

The Cycle of Life

Now the cycle of life has moved swiftly on, and both of those sons have little boys of their own, who teach their fathers lessons.

Address given at general conference October 1983.

They now watch their children grow as my wife and I watched them. They are coming to know something as fathers that they could not be taught as sons. Perhaps now they know how much their father loves them. Hopefully, they know as well why prayers begin, "Our *Father* who art in heaven."

All too soon their children will be grown and will have little "persons" of their own, repeating the endless cycle of life.

There is on the West Coast a statue by Ernesto Gazzeri which depicts in marble that cycle of life. There are toddlers and children, teenagers, young lovers, the mature and the aged, gazing at a newborn baby. Two figures to the back, however, face away from the group. An aged couple, supporting one another, haltingly moves away from the family circle.

Persons enter life through mortal birth and, in due time, disappear through the veil of death. Most of them never sense why we are here.

Nothing is more obvious than what the statue represents, but the sculptor entitled it *The Mystery of Life*.

Why the Inequities

Occasionally, as at the time of birth, we pause in awe of what nature has to say. We see patterns of creation so ordered and so beautiful as to sponsor deep feelings of reverence and humility. Then, just when we might discover the meaning of life, we are jerked back by the wild, uncontrolled things that humanity is doing to itself.

There are so many unanswered questions. Why the inequities in life?

Some are so rich, some so wretchedly poor.

Some are so beautifully formed, and others have pitiful handicaps.

Some are gifted and others retarded.

Why the injustice, the untimely death? Why the neglect, the sorrow, the pain?

Why divorce, incest, perversion, abuse, and cruelty?

If there be order and meaning to life, they are hardly visible in what mortals do to one another and to themselves.

In counterpoint, we see love and devotion, sacrifice, faith, and humility; we see humanity in exalted expressions of courage and heroism.

When at last the mystery of life is unraveled, what will be revealed?

I know a man who studied for the ministry. Then just before his ordination he dropped out because there were so many unanswered questions. He still regarded himself as a devout, if somewhat disillusioned, Christian. He found another profession, married, and was raising a family when our missionaries found him.

He made a very superficial study of the doctrines of the Church and found them tolerable enough. The fundamentals of Christianity were visible. But he was most interested in programs and activities that would benefit his family.

It was *after* he was baptized that he made the discovery of his life. To his surprise he found, underlying the programs of the Church, a solid foundation of doctrine. He had no idea of the depth and breadth and height of our theology. When once he moved from interest in the programs to a study of the gospel of Jesus Christ, he found answers which explained to his full satisfaction the deep questions that had left him unable to accept ordination as a clergyman.

Doctrine of Premortal Life

One doctrine was completely new to him. Although he was a student of the Bible, he had not found it there until he read the other revelations. Then the Bible was clear to him and he understood.

The doctrine is so logical, so reasonable, and explains so many things that it is a wonder that the Christian world rejected it. It is so essential a part of the equation of life that, if it is left out, life just cannot add up; it remains a mystery.

The doctrine is simply this: Life did not begin with mortal birth. We lived in spirit form before we entered mortality. We are spiritually the children of God.

This doctrine of premortal life was known to ancient Christians. For nearly five hundred years the doctrine was taught, but it was then rejected as a heresy by a clergy that had slipped into the Dark Ages of apostasy.

Once they rejected this doctrine, the doctrine of premortal life, and the doctrine of redemption for the dead, they could never unravel the mystery of life. It was as if they were trying to assemble a strand of pearls on a string that was too short. There was no way they could put them all together.

Why is it so strange a thought that we lived as spirits before entering mortality? Christian doctrine proclaims the resurrection, meaning that we will live after mortal death. If we live beyond death, why should it be strange that we lived before birth?

The Christian world in general accepts the idea that our condition in the resurrection will be determined by our actions in this life. Why can they not believe that some circumstances in this life were determined by our actions before coming into mortality?

The scriptures teach this doctrine, the doctrine of premortal life. For His own reasons, the Lord provides answers to some questions with pieces placed here and there throughout the scriptures. We are to find them; we are to *earn* them. In that way sacred things are hidden from the insincere.

Of the many verses revealing this doctrine, I will quote two short phrases from the testimony of John in the ninety-third section of the Doctrine and Covenants. The first, speaking of Christ, says plainly, "He was in the beginning, before the world was" (D&C 93:7). And the other, referring to us, says with equal clarity, "Ye were also in the beginning with the Father" (D&C 93:23).

Essential facts about our premortal life have been revealed. Although they are sketchy, they unravel the mystery of life.

When we comprehend the doctrine of premortal life, we know that we are the children of God, that we lived with Him in spirit form before entering mortality. We know that this life is a test, that life did not begin with birth, nor will it end with death. Then life begins to make sense, with meaning and purpose even in all of the chaotic mischief that mankind creates for itself.

Tests Meet Individual Needs

Imagine that you are attending a football game. The teams seem evenly matched. One team has been trained to follow the rules. The other, to do just the opposite; they are committed to cheat and disobey every rule of sportsmanlike conduct.

While the game ends in a tie, it is determined that it must continue until one side wins decisively.

Soon the field is a quagmire. Players on both sides are being ground into the mud. The cheating of the opposing team turns to brutality. Players are carried off the field. Some have been injured critically; others, it is whispered, fatally. It ceases to be a game and becomes a battle.

You become very frustrated and upset. "Why let this go on? Neither team can win. It must be stopped."

Imagine that you confront the sponsor of the game and demand that he stop this useless, futile battle. You say it is senseless and without purpose. Has he no regard at all for the players?

He calmly replies that he will not call the game. You are mistaken. There is a great purpose in it. You have not understood.

He tells you that this is not a spectator sport—it is for the participants. It is for their sake that he permits the game to continue. Great benefit may come to them because of the challenges they face.

He points to players sitting on the bench, suited up, eager to enter the game. "When each one of them has been in, when each has met the day for which he has prepared so long and trained so hard, then, and only then, will I call the game."

Until then it may not matter which team seems to be ahead. The present score is really not crucial. There are games within games, you know. Whatever is happening to the team, each player will have his day.

Those players on the team that keeps the rules will not be eternally disadvantaged by the appearance that their team somehow always seems to be losing.

In the field of destiny, no team or player will be eternally disadvantaged because they keep the rules. They may be cornered or misused, even defeated for a time. But individual players on that team, regardless of what appears on the scoreboard, may already be victorious.

Each player will have a test sufficient to his needs; how each responds is the test.

When the game is finally over, you and they will see purpose in it all, may even express gratitude for having been on the field during the darkest part of the contest.

I do not think the Lord is quite so hopeless about what's going on in the world as we are. He could put a stop to all of it at any moment. But He will not! Not until every player has a chance to meet the test for which we were preparing before the world was, before we came into mortality.

The same testing in troubled times can have quite opposite effects on individuals. Three verses from the Book of Mormon, which is another testament of Christ, teach us that

> they had had wars, and bloodsheds, and famine, and affliction, for the space of many years.
>
> And there had been murders, and contentions, and dissensions, and all manner of iniquity among the people of Nephi; nevertheless for the righteous' sake, yea, because of the prayers of the righteous, they were spared.
>
> But behold, because of the exceedingly great length of the war between the Nephites and the Lamanites many had become *hardened*, because of the exceedingly great length of the war; and many were softened because of their afflictions, insomuch that they did humble themselves before God, even in the depth of humility." (Alma 62:39–41, italics added.)

Surely you know some whose lives have been filled with adversity who have been mellowed and strengthened and refined by it, while others have come away from the same test bitter and blistered and unhappy.

Premortality Doctrine
Makes Sense of Mortality

There is no way to make sense out of life without a knowledge of the doctrine of premortal life. The idea that mortal birth is the beginning is preposterous. There is no way to explain life if you believe that. The notion that life ends with mortal death is ridiculous. There is no way to face life if you believe that.

When we understand the doctrine of premortal life, then things fit together and make sense. We then know that little boys and little girls are not monkeys, nor are their parents, nor were theirs, to the very beginning generation.

We are the children of God, created in His image.

Our child-parent relationship to God is clear.

The purpose for the creation of this earth is clear.

The testing that comes in mortality is clear.

The need for a redeemer is clear.

When we do understand that principle of the gospel, we see a Heavenly Father and a Son; we see an atonement and a redemption. We understand why ordinances and covenants are necessary. We understand the necessity for baptism by immersion for the remission of sins. We understand why we renew that covenant by partaking of the sacrament.

I have but touched upon the doctrine of premortal life. We cannot, in these brief conference talks, do more than that. Oh, if we but had a day, or even an hour, to speak of it!

I assure you there is, underlying the programs and activities of this church, a depth and breadth and height of doctrine that answers the questions of life.

When one knows the gospel of Jesus Christ, there is cause to rejoice. The words *joy* and *rejoice* appear through the scriptures repetitively. Latter-day Saints are happy people. When one knows the doctrine, parenthood becomes a sacred obligation, the begetting of life a sacred privilege. If everyone understood these things, abortion would be unthinkable; no one would think of suicide; and all the frailties and problems of men would fade away.

We have cause to rejoice and we do rejoice, even celebrate.

"The glory of God is intelligence, or, in other words, light and truth" (D&C 93:36).

God bless us that we and all who will hear His message can celebrate the Light! Of Him I bear witness, in the name of Jesus Christ, amen.

25

Live by
the Spirit

Dear brethren and sisters, I feel very grateful this morning to be able to attend this general conference for Scandinavia.

Although the name Packer is an English name, I am in fact Scandinavian by ancestry. My grandfather on my mother's side emigrated from Denmark, bringing with him his two-year-old son. He worked in the smelter's to earn money to bring his Swedish wife to America. My father's mother also was Danish.

They came as converts to the Church. When my mother was six, Grandmother died. Mother then went to live with Grandma Jensen, who spoke no English. My mother, therefore, grew up speaking Danish.

In those days, when the converts arrived from overseas they were sent to the outlying settlements surrounding the Church headquarters. Brigham City, where I was raised, was settled almost entirely by converts from Scandinavia. The names in our town were Danish names and Swedish names and Norwegian

Address given at the Scandinavia general conference 17 August 1974.

names—Olsen, Johnson, Jensen, Jeppsen, Andersen, Christensen, Isaacson, and many others.

My wife also traces her ancestry to Denmark. Her grandfather immigrated to America in 1853. He was devoted to the gospel of Jesus Christ. When the Logan Temple was built he hiked over the mountains each Monday morning, a distance of twenty-five miles, to work on the temple. On Saturday evening he would hike the steep trails back over the mountains to spend the weekend with his family.

A Great Lesson

Today I wish to share with you a great lesson I learned from my little Danish mother. Many times she told us children of this incident in her life. She was teaching us a lesson every Latter-day Saint must learn. It is that message I would leave with you today.

In the early days of their marriage my father and mother lived on a little farm at Corinne. It was very difficult to raise crops, so they were very poor.

One morning, my father had to go into town. He had broken a piece of farm equipment and it had to be welded before he could continue planting. He came to the house and told Mother he must go to the blacksmith in Brigham City, a distance of seven miles. Although Mother was in the middle of doing the weekly washing, she quickly made arrangements to go with him, for it was not often that she could go to town.

On the cook stove in the kitchen she had been heating water for the washing. She also had a kettle of water heating on top of a little stove in the bedroom. While she set her washing things aside, banked the fires, and quickly got the little children ready for the trip to town, she thought of all the things she could do while Father was at the blacksmith's.

In the meantime Father harnessed the horse and brought the buggy to the front gate. Mother hurried out with the children and lifted them into the buggy. As she began to climb into the buggy herself, she hesitated a moment and then said, "I think I won't go with you today."

"What's the matter?" Father asked.

"I don't know," she answered. "I just have the *feeling* that I shouldn't go."

When she said *feeling*, that meant something to my father. He was wise enough not to tease her or try to talk her out of it. He simply said, "Well, if you have that feeling, perhaps you had better stay home."

As she lifted the children out of the buggy, you can imagine what they did!

She watched Father as the buggy went down the road then clattered across the bridge over the Bear River, up the bank on the opposite side, and out of sight. She stood at the gate with the children, who were crying in disappointment, and said to herself, "Now, wasn't that silly of me!"

She returned to the little house with the thought of finishing the washing.

I should tell you that that was a very humble home. The ceiling was not wood or plaster, but was made of cloth stretched and sized with glue and then wallpapered. They did that in homes in those days—not in the expensive homes but in the very humble homes.

The chimney pipe of the little stove in the bedroom was insulated with a brass ring at the point where it went through the fabric ceiling. No one knew that above the ceiling the pipe had rusted through. Now, sparks had escaped into the attic and settled into the dust. Mother had been back in the home only a few minutes when she smelled smoke and found the ceiling afire.

The little youngsters formed a bucket brigade from the pump. Mother stood on a chair and threw the water to the ceiling, and soon the fire was out.

And so the incident closes, except to ask the very important question: Why didn't she go to town that day?

Father and Mother had prayed earnestly that the Lord would bless them to be able to raise their family—feed them, clothe them, and provide shelter for them. They had been saving money to pay for their farm, and their savings were hidden away in that little house. All they owned was somehow centered in that humble home. To lose it would have been a great tragedy.

This little Danish mother of mine had prayed many times that they might be blessed. On that day her prayers were dramatically answered.

Again the question: Why did she not go to town that day?

She did not hear an audible voice saying, "Emma, you'd better not go to town today, I'm going to answer your prayers." Nor did a written message descend from which she could read, "Emma, you'd better stay home today." She stayed home because of a feeling; a still, small voice had spoken to her. She told my father, "I just have the *feeling* that I shouldn't go."

It was a great lesson my little Danish mother taught us.

Learn to Live by the Spirit

This is my counsel to you, my brethren and sisters in Scandinavia, and particularly to the young people among you: Learn to live by the Spirit.

Following baptism, each of us was confirmed a member of The Church of Jesus Christ of Latter-day Saints. We were blessed to receive the Holy Ghost, which was to be a gift and a blessing to us in our lives.

Through the Holy Ghost we may always have a very clear signal to follow. If we are living worthily that signal will be a constant guide to us.

It is a quiet gift. It is unknown in the world. To Latter-day Saints it is a great blessing. It can guide us in all we do in life. All of us, particularly our young people, must learn to trust in that Spirit. We must learn to be spiritually minded. The prophet said, "To be carnally-minded is death, and to be spiritually-minded is life eternal" (2 Nephi 9:39).

That voice of inspiration is so quiet and still that it can be explained away. It is easy to be disobedient to that voice. It often takes great courage to follow it. But to Latter-day Saints it is a clear signal.

There is a very important message on this subject in the Book of Mormon. On one occasion Nephi scolded his brothers Laman and Lemuel for their unbelief, telling them: "Ye are swift to do iniquity but slow to remember the Lord your God. Ye have seen an angel, and he spake unto you; yea, ye have heard his voice from time to time; and he hath spoken unto you in a still small voice, but ye were past *feeling*, that ye could not *feel* his words." (1 Nephi 17:45, italics added.)

Someone once criticized the Book of Mormon by saying that it did not use correct language, and pointed to the above verse as the example: "You were past *feeling*, that ye could not *feel* his words."

You don't *feel* words, the person insisted, you *hear* them. If the book were true, the passage would read, "You were past *hearing*, that you did not *hear* his words."

That correction would only be made by someone who did not know about the Spirit. There are literally millions of members of the Church across the world who know what that word *feel* means in this context. Many, perhaps most of you, could bear testimony of being prompted by the Spirit in this way.

Members of the Church should learn to trust in that guidance; to be prayerful, and live so that the Spirit of the Lord can operate through us.

Honor Your Baptismal Covenants

In order to have that Spirit guide us we must prepare ourselves for it. To do that, to be worthy of constant inspiration, we must keep the covenants we made at the time of baptism.

The Lord set forth in the scriptures the qualifications for being accepted by baptism:

> And again, by way of commandment to the church concerning the manner of baptism—All those who humble themselves before God, and desire to be baptized, and come forth with broken hearts and contrite spirits, and witness before the church that they have truly repented of all their sins, and are willing to take upon them the name of Jesus Christ, having a determination to serve him to the end, and truly manifest by their works that they have received of the Spirit of Christ unto the remission of their sins, shall be received by baptism into his church (D&C 20:37).

When we have complied with those requirements the ordinance of baptism carries with it a remission of our sins. Think how marvelous that is—to be able to stand clean and worthy before our Heavenly Father.

It is not an easy thing in this world to stay worthy, to stay clean and pure. Each day may bring little irritations and temptations and mistakes. Our Heavenly Father has provided a way that we can renew the covenants we made with him at the time of our baptism. Each week we can gather together to partake of the sacrament for that purpose.

It is not very likely that during the course of a week, between sacrament meetings, we will get so far off the path of righteousness that we will lose our way. There is always that still, small voice to guide us.

I reverently quote from the sacramental prayer.

> O God, the Eternal Father, we ask thee in the name of thy Son, Jesus Christ, to bless and sanctify this bread to the souls of all those who partake of it; that they may eat in remembrance of the body of thy Son, and witness unto thee, O God, the Eternal Father, that they are willing to take upon them the name of thy Son, and always remember him, and keep his commandments which he hath given them, that they may always have his Spirit to be with them. Amen. (Moroni 4:3.)

Note the last clause, "that they may always have his Spirit to be with them."

The prayer on the water concludes:

> that they may witness unto thee, O God, the Eternal Father, that they do always remember him, that they may have his Spirit to be with them. Amen. (Moroni 5:2.)

Discerning Right in a Wicked World

We live in a day when evil is everywhere. At times it almost seems that right is wrong and wrong is right. We would hardly know which way to go if we did not have somewhere to turn in making many of the decisions we must make in life.

As members of the Church we are not just cut loose and left to shift for ourselves in this world. That would be a terrible thing. We are not left adrift. That constant spiritual guidance that we have in the Church is a clear signal, if we live for it and if we follow it.

There is no more wonderful time than now to be alive. And there is no finer place to live than in Denmark, or Finland, or Norway, or Sweden. The inspiration of the Lord can come to members of the Church in Scandinavia as readily as in any other place on this earth.

The remission of our sins, which we received at the time of baptism, can remain with us.

Humble yourselves even in the depths of humility, calling on the name of the Lord daily, and standing steadfastly in the faith of that which is to come, which was spoken by the mouth of the angel.

And behold, I say unto you that if ye do this ye shall always rejoice, and be filled with the love of God, and always *retain a remission of your sins;* and ye shall grow in the knowledge of the glory of him that created you, or in the knowledge of that which is just and true. (Mosiah 4:11-12, italics added.)

Inspiration can come, of course, from sources other than through the Holy Ghost. How, then, can we tell the difference?

The prophet Mormon left this counsel for us:

Wherefore, take heed, my beloved brethren, that ye do not judge that which is evil to be of God, or that which is good and of God to be of the devil.

For behold, my brethren, it is given unto you to judge, that ye may know good from evil; and the way to judge is as plain, that ye may know with a perfect knowledge, as the daylight is from the dark night.

For behold, the Spirit of Christ is given to every man, that he may know good from evil; wherefore, I show unto you the way to judge; for every thing which inviteth to do good, and to persuade to believe in Christ, is sent forth by the power and gift of Christ; wherefore ye may know with a perfect knowledge it is of God.

But whatsoever thing persuadeth men to do evil, and believe not in Christ, and deny him, and serve not God, then ye may know with a perfect knowledge it is of the devil; for after this manner doth the devil work, for he persuadeth no man to do good, no, not one; neither do his angels; neither do they who subject themselves unto him. (Moroni 7:14-17.)

Leaders Can Assist with Counsel

It is to the leaders of the Church that members tend to turn when they have not yet learned to discern inspiration. The gift of the Holy Ghost is a great and priceless gift. It is essential that leaders of the Church keep themselves worthy in order that they can be constantly guided by that Spirit.

To be called to a position in the Church is no small thing. We have an obligation to live, then, as perfectly as we know how to live.

Very often when a member of the Church has a decision to make, he or she may pray about it and yet still feel unsettled, not quite knowing whether one path of action represents an opportunity or a temptation. What does he do then? He can seek counsel. He can seek the counsel of wise and inspired leaders.

First, he can go to the father and head of the family. Then, following the order of the Church, he may go to his branch president or bishop. There he will find counsel from one who has the right to receive inspiration, to be guided by that Spirit.

Quite often people will come to Church headquarters wanting to see the President of the Church. They have a personal problem of one kind or another and they want his counsel. They say: "I want him to tell me what to do. I have prayed about this matter, and I still do not know quite what to do."

Fortunately, it is not necessary for members of the Church to have an interview with the President of the Church in order to solve these problems. And as a practical matter, if he should open his door to every member of the Church who came with problems, he would not have time for the ministry that he is ordained to perform.

The Lord taught this lesson in the Old Testament. Moses opened his tent to all of Israel. They came in such numbers that they were lined up from morning until evening waiting to have a chance to talk over their problems with Moses.

One of them perhaps had a wayward son or daughter whom he wanted to talk about. Another had difficulty with his neighbor. Moses listened to them and judged these matters.

One day Jethro, Moses' father-in-law, saw what was going on. He said to Moses:

What is this thing that thou doest to the people? why sittest thou thyself alone, and all the people stand by thee from morning unto even?

And Moses said unto his father-in-law, Because the people come unto me to inquire of God.

When they have a matter, they come unto me; and I judge be-

tween one and another, and I do make them know the statutes of
God, and his laws.

And Moses' father-in-law said unto him, The thing that thou
doest is not good.

Thou wilt surely wear away, both thou, and this people that is
with thee: for this thing is too heavy for thee; thou art not able to
perform it thyself alone.

Jethro then told Moses:

[Choose] out of all the people able men, such as fear God, men of
truth, hating covetousness; and place such over them, to be rulers
of thousands, and rulers of hundreds, rulers of fifties, and rulers of
tens:

And let them judge the people at all seasons: and it shall be,
that every great matter they shall bring unto thee, but every small
matter they shall judge: so shall it be easier for thyself, and they
shall bear the burden with thee. (Exodus 18:14–18, 21–22.)

And so it is today in the Church. When we are confused and at
a loss to know which way to go, we can turn first to the local leader
of the Church—to our branch president or bishop. As appropriate,
he in turn can counsel with the stake president, or the mission
president, who if necessary can counsel with the General Authorities, who themselves are in constant counsel with the prophet
himself.

As with the Israelites in the wilderness, it is not necessary to
have the President of the Church or the other General Authorities
hear all of the problems of the people. It is not necessary for the
stake president or the mission president to personally judge all of
these matters.

Even the bishops or branch presidents do not need to hear all
of these matters, although it is true that they will hear more of them
than the leaders above them will. The point is that each of us
should live in such a way as to be able to follow the inspiration of
that still, small voice. We must have the courage to follow these
feelings. Such inspiration will always lead us to do right, to be active in the Church. This inspiration will always teach Latter-day
Saints to be Latter-day Saints indeed.

Influence Others
with the Spirit You Carry

I close with another experience.

At one point when I was president of a mission I was interviewing a young missionary assigned to St. Johns, Newfoundland, located nearly two thousand miles from mission headquarters. He seemed reluctant to let the interview end, and finally he said, "I feel strong now and I'm not discouraged, but you are going to go away."

"But you have my assistants who come and visit you," I said.

"Yes," he said, "they come for a brief visit, but they go away."

"What about the zone leaders?" I asked.

"It is the same with them. They will come every few weeks and pay us a brief visit, and then they will go away." He added, "I feel strong and inspired when you are here, but it seems that all of you go away and then I am discouraged and don't know which way to go."

I then could see that we had failed to teach this elder a very important lesson. So I said to him: "Elder, do you not know that when we are gone and you are here, you are to the people here as we are to you? That is, you must be a strength and an inspiration to them. We should only need to visit you infrequently. You should *carry* the Spirit with *you*, and give of the Spirit to all among whom you labor."

He had never thought of that!

Right at this moment there are a number of General Authorities here with you. But in a day or two we will be moving to assignments elsewhere in the world. When we are gone and you are here, just remember that you have the responsibility to convey inspiration to those with whom you associate—your families, the other members of the Church, and nonmembers.

How can you do that? You can simply carry the spirit of this conference with you, and you can carry the spirit of the gospel with you at all times. You can be guided and prompted and inspired. In this Church we are not left comfortless. The Lord said:

If ye love me, keep my commandments.

And I will pray the Father, and he shall give you another Comforter, that he may abide with you for ever;

Even the Spirit of truth; whom the world cannot receive, because it seeth him not, neither knoweth him: but ye know him; for he dwelleth with you, and shall be in you.

I will not leave you comfortless: I will come to you. (John 14:15-18.)

This is the great lesson that I learned from my little Danish mother—that we have the right to be prompted and inspired, and that if we are living righteously and if we are prayerful the Lord will guide us.

I have come to know that it is not always easy to follow these promptings. I have come to know also that we need to stay faithful and active in the Church. And I have come to know that if we do this and constantly improve in righteousness and spiritual living the Lord will bless us with the guidance we need and seek. For this is the one true Church, and hence its faithful members are entitled to that guidance; Jesus Christ is at its head, directing its course; Joseph Smith was the great prophet called to lead this final gospel dispensation; and we have a living prophet leading us today. These things I have come to know. Of them I bear witness in the name of Jesus Christ, amen.

VI
Assurance

26

"*Let Not Your Heart Be Troubled*"

I begin with a testimony that the gospel of Jesus Christ is true, that in its exalted principles rest the keys to the nature of man, his relationship to God, and the ideal pattern of his regard for himself and his fellowmen. Any position which ignores revealed truth concerning the nature of man and his relationship to God must ultimately prove to be inadequate, if not downright erroneous and destructive.

The challenge that you will face in this generation is best summed up by a little girl I know who imagined that she was cornered by all the frustrations and confusions of a fast-moving technologically oriented society. She assessed our plight in eloquent simplicity when she said, "Life gets complicateder and complicateder."

One could hardly ignore the unnecessarily high incidence of problems, even among our people, relating to emotional stress and emotional breakdown. This incidence is unnecessarily high because there are ways to prevent it—ways to relieve it.

Address given to the Brigham Young University student body 4 October 1966.

In the New England Mission during the last year we have had a substantial drop in medical expenses for missionaries, most of which expenses were for the relief of psychosomatic illnesses. In this school environment you are not immune from pressures which relate to schoolwork; from tensions and problems and the long list of attendant, emotionally oriented difficulties and disorders—insecurity, worry, stress, confusion, dependency, suspicion, withdrawal, fear, and, ultimately, failure. Life does, indeed, get complicateder and complicateder.

Areas of Challenge

I think it is fair to say that the pressures of Grandfather's day, with all the challenge of wresting a place from the hostile frontier, had a certain tranquility about it that we will never know again. Inasmuch as you face these challenges in your college environment, I thought it might be helpful to you to list a few of the difficulties a college-aged person might face and make some rather practical observations which may be of assistance to you.

I list, then, these areas of challenge:

1. Dissatisfaction over the shape and proportion of your body. Young men, because you are not the tall, firmly muscled, athletically proportioned male with the "collar ad" features, and, young women, because you do not fit the image of "Miss Something-or-Other," worshipped so generously by society, you have the tendency to become dissatisfied, miserable over something that you cannot change.

2. Frustration because of physical impediments or handicaps, sometimes real and formidable, often imagined and without real physiological basis.

3. The restless feeling of inferiority because of little success experienced socially. You never were president or chairman, you never were captain of the team or preferred man or woman. You never were "Miss-Somebody-or-Other." You have a feeling of restless inadequacy because you feel you never have arrived.

4. Worry at your age over some real or imagined inadequacy to fulfill the physical and emotional and occupa-

tional responsibilities attendant in a happy marriage relationship.

5. Strangely enough, humiliation over being "poorly born." It is not unusual to find young people of your age who are aspiring for a place in the world to be needlessly ashamed of family relationships. Embarrassment because your family is "ordinary."

6. Concern over academic competency—feeling you are not scholastically competent or competitive.

7. The most serious of all, the corrosion of guilt because of unsettled transgression.

These are the pitfalls—quiet, inner, and personal. Before them one may feel frail and helpless. These are the silent, the lonely battles.

As I list these rather practical suggestions, I hope you will ponder them carefully—measure yourself against them and, perhaps, try them out.

The Weather

First: Declare your independence from the weather! Now, I readily recognize that changes in the barometric pressure and in weather have certain physiological effects. It is interesting to note, however, the large percentage of people who seem to be completely subjugated in their moods to the flimsy, variable, uncontrollable exigencies of weather. Their attitudes are wafted to and fro not just by every "wind of doctrine" but literally by every wind.

It was interesting to see the effect on missionaries when they were invited to declare their independence from weather. (There are two hundred of you here who know that in New England we have a marvelous variety of good weather.) Even inclement weather can be tolerable, perhaps enjoyable, if we have asserted our agency and decided that we are going to be pleasant regardless of what the barometer says.

> Isn't it true that man's a fool?
> When it's hot he wants it cool.
> When it's cool, he wants it hot.
> Always wanting what it's not.

It is time that we begin to achieve that degree of maturation which is necessary so that we can be emancipated from the influences of meteorological phenomena—that is college language for, "Why not grow up!"

What a marvelous thing it is to see young men and women who have learned not to care greatly what the weather is! They dress against it if it is inclement and for it if it is not. They go about their purposes of life undisturbed by weather or its variations. When it starts to rain, they simply say: "Let it rain. We got here first." Surely you of college age can find some more important index for your disposition than the viscissitudes of the weather.

Your Body

The next suggestion I make has been the subject of thousands of volumes. Simply this: Take care of your body. It is the instrument of your mind and the foundation of your character. Within it are kindled the life-giving capacities suited to prepare mortal bodies for the coming generations.

> Know ye not that ye are the temple of God, and that the Spirit of God dwelleth in you? If any man defile the temple of God, him shall God destroy: for the temple of God is holy, which temple ye are. (1 Corinthians 3:16–17.)

When will we learn to do the following simple things:

1. Eat nourishing, balanced meals, particularly a well-balanced, sustaining breakfast.
2. Make sure that your body has plenty of rest. "Cease to sleep longer than is needful; retire to thy bed early, that ye may not be weary; arise early, that your bodies and your minds may be invigorated" (D&C 88:124).
3. Get proper exercise through both labor and recreation. Keep your bodies clean. It is marvelous at the university to have the vigor of youth developed through competitive athletic activities. But I urge you to pay attention to those instructions concerning the well-being of your bodies, not only in the vigor of youth but also in the childbearing, the middle, and the later years. The inseparable relationship between mind and body demands this.

A Healthy Depression

Did you know that it is normal and healthy to be depressed occasionally? As General Authorities, we face a long line of people who call upon us because they are unhappy—they are depressed. They are worried about this and that and really not certain what they are worried about. They are a little like the man who insisted: "You can't tell me that worry doesn't help. The things I worry about never happen!"

When we search the revealed word for some evidence of the nature of man, we find statements such as this:

> For it must needs be, that there is an opposition in all things. If not so, . . . righteousness could not be brought to pass, neither wickedness, neither holiness nor misery, neither good nor bad. (2 Nephi 2:11.)

If you happen to hit a good sorry mood once in a while, relax and enjoy it—it is a good sign that you are normal. It is all right to worry about things now and again, I suppose, but when you get worried about being worried, that is when you are getting off the track.

I really was hesitant to put this "literature" in here, but it has a thought:

> If you can smile when things go wrong,
> And say it doesn't matter,
> If you can laugh off cares and woe,
> And trouble makes you fatter,
> If you can keep a cheerful face
> When all around are blue,
> Then have your head examined, bud,
> There's something wrong with you.
> For one thing I've arrived at:
> There are no ands and buts,
> A guy that's grinning all the time
> Must be completely nuts.

February

Watch out for February! We learned in supervising teaching that after the interesting beginnings of school—you have the football season, the holidays, the beginning of the basketball season—then, after the first of the year, come the cold, dreary days of winter. We noted that at that time the teacher would fail and the students would have problems. Depressions are then accentuated. It has been interesting to notice this and to point it out when people come in during those dreary days of winter, depressed and unsettled. Then they find out that there was not anything wrong—it was just February. It is worthwhile to know that.

Unsettled Transgression

I have mentioned the corrosive guilt of unsettled transgression. Be wise enough to learn *not* to talk about your problems with the wrong people. Unfortunately, many young people who have made mistakes, particularly if these are in the category of moral transgression, end up telling a roommate about it. If there is something weighing heavily on your mind, talk it over first with the Lord in prayer, and then with your parents. Learn what a bishop is for, and confide in him when faced with such problems. There may be one here who has been immorally involved; if so, you should *get it settled*—get that page torn out of your life so that you can go on.

With reference to all of the other little things that seem to loom so big, forget them—just get them out of your mind. Go ahead. Face the sunlight of truth in order that the shadows of sin, doubt, and error will be cast behind you.

Innocence Brings Power

Innocence brings great power. I have managed to read a biography or two—one of them of Theodore Roosevelt, the rugged, individualistic, forceful president of the United States. There is a very interesting statement by the author, Noel F. Busch:

> He never suffered from the "repressed guilt feelings" which provide the sand in the gears of most less happily adjusted humans. T.R.'s total clarity of conscience can be deduced not only from his own by no means infrequent affirmations, but also from circumstantial evidence in the form of other character traits and

tendencies. One of the latter might be the capacity for intense and uninterrupted enjoyment, which he possessed to a degree unthinkable for anyone with a psyche clouded by any trace of self-doubt or accusation. Corollary evidence might be supplied by the excellence of his memory. Like a sundial which records only the shining hours, memory, most psychologists agree, tends to erase unpleasant experiences while taking full note of pleasant ones. Roosevelt's astounding ability to recall events, ideas and people may well have been derived at least in part from the obvious fact that for him all experiences tended to be happy ones. (*T. R., The Story of Theodore Roosevelt and His Influence on Our Times* [New York: Reynal and Company, Inc., 1963], pp. 9–10.)

There was great power in his innocence, and when you see great men with that quality you find that they are unclouded by things that are unsettled. Sweeter words were never spoken than these spoken by the Lord: "I will remember your sins no more" (see D&C 58:42).

Troubles and Dependency

We have reached a state when evidently we cannot get any considerable number of people together in school, business, society, the military, or anywhere else without having them attended by a sufficient number of counselors, psychologists, and psychiatrists. I look with concern on the increased dependency upon psychologists and psychiatrists. Now, explicitly, I did *not* say I look with concern upon the use of them. I said I look with concern upon our growing *dependency* upon them. I have misgivings about the growing tendency to diagnose every aberration of behavior as the beginnings of "psycho-something-or-other."

Let me caution you to be careful. Do not tell your troubles to the wrong people. We do not call a neurosurgeon every time we have a slight headache, and you had better be careful before going to an analyst.

May I say that I recognize the need for professional help from psychiatrists. I have at times referred individuals to them, but I say again that I look with concern upon our growing *dependency* upon them. I would suppose that when there is that measure of difficulty or disorder which requires professional attention, that attention ought to be given on the referral from the bishop and from the medical doctor. But we are at the point now where at the slightest aberration in behavior we are sent for professional clinical inspection.

I am not always sure that the measures that are taken are wise. For instance, I am not sure it is always wise to try to erase grief with sedatives. Perhaps when we know the true nature of man, we may be more discriminating in the administering of sedatives in an attempt to erase grief or bring peace to broken hearts, and we may be more careful in the buffering of individuals from life through the use of tranquilizers.

Act—Not React

Take courage! Do not continually be reacting. Be independent in your moods. Search yourself. Start to act. Be selective in your emotional diet. How unfortunate it is to see someone with a well-structured physical body who lives on intellectual and emotional garbage. Just because Jean-Paul Sartre points out the miserable all of the time does not mean that you have to join him.

Sydney Harris wrote, in the *Chicago Daily News:*

> I walked with my friend, a Quaker, to the newsstand the other night, and he bought a paper, thanking the newsie politely. The newsie didn't even acknowledge it.
>
> "A sullen fellow, isn't he?" I commented.
>
> "Oh, he's that way every night," shrugged my friend.
>
> "Then why do you continue to be so polite to him?" I asked.
>
> "Why not?" inquired my friend. "Why should I let him decide how I'm going to act?"

Disorders with Moral Implications

Now we are in a touchy area! There are some emotional disorders and psychological beginnings that have their fulfillment in the ugliness of perversion. There are disorders that, while psychological in beginning, have moral implications and may ultimately be acted out physically. It is a critically serious thing when we get that mixed up in our feelings and thinking about our relationships to other people. Some yield to these neurotic feelings and find themselves immorally involved, guilty of perverted acts. It is heartbreaking to have someone come pitifully seeking help yet tangled in a mesh of tragic experiences.

I have a simple and practical suggestion with regard to this matter. This may seem like strange counsel for a member of the Board of Trustees to give at a university; nonetheless, I say this is well-considered counsel. The counsel is simply this: If at sometime in your life you go through one of these phases—and there are some elements of normalcy about them—do *not* be attracted to read all of the books on the subject.

Some years ago Dr. Dale Tingey and I were at the Washington State University at Pullman. We had called upon a friend who was the director of the medical services. In his outer office was a long table stacked with several dozen pamphlets on physical illnesses: tuberculosis, cancer, encephalitis, and so forth. Dale motioned to the table and said: "Well, there they are. Pick one out. If you read enough about it and think about it long enough, you will be sure you have it." And to his expression I might add parenthetically that, if it is emotionally oriented, you may cause yourself to get it. Sometimes study can magnify rather than reduce these problems, particularly when they are psychologically oriented. Again, I repeat: Any position which ignores the revelations of the Lord pertaining to the nature of man must ultimately prove to be inadequate, if not downright false and destructive. Virtually none of the writers on these subjects are sensitive to such revelations.

I have almost come to believe that the chances of rescuing people from these addictions are inversely proportional to the number of books they have read on the subject. If they have been to the library seeking out all of the long treatises on perverted activities, they become almost, if not entirely, convinced that there is no hope for them. Their faith is extinguished and their chances for rescue are diminished. They ought to understand that their problem is not a basic presetting of their nature so much as an addiction. Habit patterns strengthen addiction, but a cure can be effected. A cure *must* be effected.

The greatest source for stability is a strong home life. If somehow this was denied you, or if somehow you have denied it, know that the deficiency is not likely to be supplied by the professional counselor, by the psychologist, or by the psychiatrist. For unless those who try to fill in that void—to fill in those yearning vacancies—are conversant with the nature of man, they cannot prescribe accurately. And unless they can regard man in his true status as a son or daughter of a divine being possessed of divine capacity, unless they have reverence for life which comes from truth, they likewise cannot prescribe accurately. Thank the Lord that here at this university we have men as counselors, psychiatrists, and psychologists who are amply trained and competent in their field and yet humbly and reverently conversant with the operations of the Spirit of the Lord. Again, any position which ignores revealed truth concerning the nature of man and his relationship to divinity must ultimately prove to be inadequate.

Purpose in the Challenge

Well, those are the simple suggestions. I commend them to you with the hope that you will recognize that there is purpose in the challenges of life. Disappointment, sorrow, pain—these are all flames for the Refiner's fire, but they are meant to temper us only, not to consume us:

> In the furnace God may prove thee,
> Thence to bring thee forth more bright,
> But can never cease to love thee;
> Thou art precious in his sight.
> God is with thee, God is with thee;
> Thou shalt triumph in his might.

> —*Hymns*, no. 43

It was never intended that we float in an effortless environment at 72 degrees and bathe constantly in the sensation of physical, sensational, and spiritual pleasures. We are here to grow.

Now pull yourselves together. If you are having some of these strains and stresses, *pull yourself together.*

I am reminded of a story of two men who were crossing the country on a bicycle built for two. On a hot July day they had negotiated a very steep hill, and the man on the back, panting from exhaustion, said, "I didn't think we were going to make it!" The man in front, wiping his brow, said, "I didn't either. If I hadn't had the brakes on all the way up, we would have gone backwards for sure!''

Now pull yourself together.

Your body, with all its limitations, is priceless. I remember from some years ago a few lines from the Thornton Wilder play *Our Town*. Emily had noticed that George noticed that she noticed him, and this little touching conversation took place as Emily and her mother sat shelling peas:

"Mama, am I good-looking?"

There was a little discussion, then Mama said, "Emily, now stop it! You are pretty enough for all normal purposes."

"Keep My Commandments"

I conclude with these few verses from the book of John:

If ye love me, keep my commandments.

And I will pray the Father, and he shall give you another Comforter, that he may abide with you for ever;

Even the Spirit of truth; whom the world cannot receive, because it seeth him not, neither knoweth him: but ye know him, for he dwelleth with you, and shall be in you.

I will not leave you comfortless: I will come to you. . . .

These things have I spoken unto you, being yet present with you.

But the Comforter, which is the Holy Ghost, whom the Father will send in my name, he shall teach you all things, and bring all things to your remembrance, whatsoever I have said unto you.

Peace I leave with you, my peace I give unto you: not as the world giveth, give I unto you. Let not your heart be troubled, neither let it be afraid. (John 14:15-18, 25-27.)

I bear my witness that Jesus is the Christ, that there is a sustaining power that will overrule the troubles that come to us in our youth, in the name of Jesus Christ, amen.

27

Keeping Covenants

My dear brothers and sisters, especially the young people. For many years I was a seminary teacher for the Church, and I have a great deal of love for the young people in the Church. I pray that the Spirit of God may be with me during my address. Please pray for me. I desire to speak about covenants.

This is a sacred occasion, the dedication of a temple. It is a joyful time, a time to rejoice and a time to consider very soberly our obligation. President Joseph Fielding Smith was ninety-five when he died. I shall never forget his prayers. He would pray without fail that he would be faithful, that he would endure to the end, and that he would keep his covenants and obligations.

Doctrine and Covenants section 132 speaks of being sealed by the Holy Spirit of Promise. *Promise* is an interesting word. It is found often in the scriptures. The Lord said to us, "I, the Lord, am bound when ye do what I say; but when ye do not what I say, ye have no promise" (D&C 82:10).

Address given at the dedication of the Buenos Aires Argentina Temple 19 January 1986.

"He Did Not Keep His Covenants"

I would like to tell the young people of an experience I had when I was a very young man and was talking with a very old man. This is the story he told me.

When he was a little boy—that would be nearly one hundred years ago—he lived in a very small community a long way from Salt Lake City. One of the men in the ward, a close relation to the President of the Church, had passed away. When the funeral was held, everyone in the ward went to the funeral, as was the custom. So this little boy went with his father and mother to the funeral. Just as the service was about to begin, to their great surprise in walked the prophet, the President of the Church. He had come a long way by train and then by buggy to attend the funeral service of his relative.

The service was similar to those of other funerals. Some kind things were said about the deceased man. He was described as a good man. Someone said that he had given flour to the widows, and he had helped those in the ward. We like to say kind things at funerals, of course.

The concluding speaker was the President of the Church. What he said was not comforting. He gave a talk that perhaps only the President of the Church could give; and he perhaps could speak in that way only because he was speaking about a relative. He confirmed that this man had been a good man and said that the good things he had done would earn him a reward; but then he said: "The fact is, he did not keep his covenants."

This man, when he was young, had gone to the temple to be married, to be sealed. Some sweet young girl had persuaded him to change his habits and become worthy, so he stopped doing some wrong things, began to pay his tithing and attend church, eventually received a temple recommend; and then the couple went to the temple and were sealed. But after a while, because the temple was a long way away and they did not return, he forgot. He began to slip back into some of his old habits. He forgot to pay his tithing. He ceased being the man he had become.

His relative, the President of the Church, knew all this, so he acknowledged that all the good he had done would earn him rewards, but he said, "The fact is, he did not keep his covenants." There were things he did that he should not have done, for he had covenanted not to do them. Similarly there were things he had covenanted to do that he had not done. So he had covenanted not to do some things and covenanted to do some things, and he had become loose and lazy on those things. He was basically a good man, maybe a good Christian as far as the world would judge it. But he had not kept his covenants, his agreements.

When you young people go to the temple to be married, you will hear about the importance of your marriage being sealed by the Holy Spirit of Promise. "I, the Lord, am bound when ye do what I say." And if you do what He says, He cannot break those promises; you will receive what is promised. But if you do not keep your part of the covenant the promises will not be fulfilled. There cannot be justice in your receiving the reward if you have not earned it.

Covenants in Ancient Israel

The ancient Israelites used to make contracts and covenants. Sometimes these were in connection with their business, and they would write them on a piece of wood. If I made a covenant with my brother here, we would write the agreement on the wood. We would each sign it, and perhaps he would agree to pay me some money. Then we would split the board down the middle. He would take one half and I would take the other. In order for this contract to be consummated, both halves would have to be brought together and I would have to fulfill my part of the bargain and he would have to fulfill his part. That is where the illustration in the Old Testament comes from, wherein Ezekiel mentions the stick of Judah and the stick of Joseph—referring to the Bible and the Book of Mormon—which when brought together fulfill a covenant, a contract. The purpose of that coming together is to testify that Jesus is the Christ, the Book of Mormon being another testament of Jesus Christ.

The Lord Is Bound
When We Keep Covenants

Now, the Lord is very generous. He tells us to strive to be perfect, so that he may bless us even more richly as we travel that path. It is very difficult to be perfect. I am not sure I know anyone who is perfect. Someone asked Brigham Young, "Are you perfect?" He said, "No, I am not. If I were perfect, I would be taken to heaven so fast it would scare this whole congregation." But he was striving for perfection. He was trying to do everything he could to be perfect. He was keeping his covenants. If we will keep our covenants and do as we promise to do, then the Lord is bound and we will receive the blessing.

When we prepare for the temple, we will be asked questions. One question will be about the Word of Wisdom. "Do you keep the Word of Wisdom?" Well, do you or don't you? Quite often when I am interviewing leaders, I will say, "Are you worthy of a temple recommend?" Often they will say, "Well, I feel I am." And I will say, "But are you worthy?" It does not matter how you feel. It matters whether you are worthy. Then the brother will smile and he will say, "I am worthy." "Do you keep your covenants?" "I keep my covenants." That is a commendable thing.

I remember an occasion many years ago when I went for a temple recommend. I had a very good bishop, and we were friends. He said to me: "I think I can just sign your recommend. I know you well enough. You are the supervisor of the seminaries. I will just sign this recommend." But I said: "Bishop, I cannot accept it. It is your responsibility to ask those questions and it is my privilege to answer them."

Now, we must keep our covenants. "Are you morally clean?" "Do you pay your tithing?" "Do you sustain the authorities of the Church?" "Well, yes, everybody but Brother Somebody." No, that is not the way it works. Brother Somebody probably needs your sustaining influence more than anyone. Keep your covenants. Keep your covenants.

When you come to the temple and receive your endowment, and kneel at the altar and be sealed, you can live an ordinary life and be an ordinary soul—struggling against temptation, failing and repenting, and failing again and repenting, but always determined to keep your covenants—and that marriage ordinance will be sealed by the Holy Spirit of Promise. Then the day will come when you will receive the benediction: "Well done, thou good and faithful servant: thou hast been faithful over a few things, I will make thee ruler over many things; enter thou into the joy of thy lord" (Matthew 25:21).

God grant that we will be a covenant-keeping people, that we will not take our covenants lightly. I bear witness that Jesus is the Christ, that He lives, that the marvelous gospel and the ordinances and the covenants were revealed of Him to us for our exaltation, in the name of Jesus Christ, amen.

28

Bruce R. McConkie,
Apostle

A few days ago I had my last visit with our beloved Brother Mc-Conkie. He was resting on the bed, dressed, alert, patient. We expressed our deep love for one another and said our good-byes.

President Lee told me on one occasion how the passing of one certain member of the Twelve had affected him more deeply than had any other. Now I understand. I cannot express the loneliness and the deep, personal loss I feel.

Brother McConkie and I shared a witness that, I have come to believe, few men share. I could, and I did, speak more openly to him of sacred things than to any other man. We had talked in recent months of his coming graduation from mortality. On those occasions, despite his great regret at leaving his family and his brethren, he spoke in terms of anticipation. He was absolutely devoid of any fear.

As we said our good-byes I inquired whether I could do anything else for him. He asked for a blessing.

Address given at the funeral service of Elder Bruce R. McConkie 23 April 1985.

The faithful will understand President Romney's statement, "I know when I speak with the power of the Holy Ghost because then I always learn something from what I have said." We learned something from that blessing a few days ago. I will share part of it with you at the conclusion of my tribute to my beloved Brother Bruce.

Miracles in His Life

We were told more than a year ago that he would live only a few weeks. Miraculously he returned to full service, in full vigor. Later he and I traveled together to South America. In the Quorum we teasingly called Bruce the archbishop of South America. He organized more stakes there than any two of us.

He pressed for a different pattern for stakes in those developing countries. As they were approved, the work flourished. Brother Oaks and Brother Maxwell are in South America today. Perhaps they would have hurried back from any other place to be at this service, but not from there. They asked to stay to press the work that was so dear to him, the ministry that was his, as something of a tribute to him.

It was a miracle that he could deliver his final inspired testimony at general conference a couple of weeks ago. That was the exclamation point to his ministry.

These recent miracles were not the first. His life began as a miracle. When he was born, it was a very difficult birth. He was thought to be stillborn and was set aside. Then as they worked frantically to save his mother, someone heard a tiny cry and turned to him.

Later, when his own firstborn son died in infancy, he surely wondered why his son could not have been spared, as *he* was. But he and Amelia suffered through it; kept their faith. Bruce lived to be a disciple and a special witness of another firstborn son who, when His time came, was not spared.

I will recall in Bruce's own words another experience, another miracle:

"One of my earliest childhood recollections is of riding a horse through an apple orchard. The horse was tame and well broken, and I felt at home in the saddle.

"But one day something frightened my mount, and he bolted through the orchard. I was swept from the saddle by the overhanging limbs, and one leg slipped down through the stirrup. I desperately hung to an almost broken leather strap that a cowboy uses to tie a lariat to his saddle.

"Suddenly the horse stopped, and I became aware that someone was holding the bridle tightly and attempting to calm the quivering animal. Almost immediately I was snatched up into the arms of my Father.

"My father had been sitting in the house reading the newspaper when the Spirit whispered to him: 'Run out into the orchard.'

"Without a moment's hesitation, not waiting to learn why or for what reason, my father ran. Finding himself in the orchard without knowing why he was there, he saw the galloping horse and thought, 'I must stop this horse.' He did so and found me.

[His father did not know Bruce was there until after he had stopped the horse.]

"I was saved from death or serious accident because my father hearkened to the voice of the Spirit. If he had not responded instantly to the whisperings of the still small voice, my life might have ended then or had its course totally changed."

But there was a work for him to do.

Raised Up to a Purpose

To me there was one great crowning contribution and achievement in Brother McConkie's ministry. Some may not agree, because he accomplished and contributed so many things. But I am sure, quite sure of this: If ever there was a man who was raised up unto a very purpose, if ever a man was prepared against a certain need, it was Bruce R. McConkie. That purpose and need had to do with the scriptures.

All members of the First Presidency and the Quorum of the Twelve had important work to do in the publication of the new editions of the scriptures with all of the aids, the footnotes, the corrections, the Topical Guide, the dictionaries, the indexes, the reversification, the new chapter headings, additional revelations, and more.

This work, while hardly appreciated yet, will one day emerge as a signal, inspired event of our generation. Because of it we shall raise up generations of Latter-day Saints who will know the gospel and know the Lord.

Brother Monson and I served for years with Brother McConkie on the Scriptures Publication Committee. I know full well that the work could have been accomplished without me. I venture to suggest, as well, that Brother Monson was not crucial to that work.

But it could not have been done without Elder Bruce R. McConkie. Few will ever know the extent of the service he rendered. Few can appraise the lifetime of preparation for this quiet, crowning contribution to the onrolling of the restored gospel in the dispensation of the fulness of times.

I should not have felt right about participating in the recent satellite broadcast on the scriptures had Bruce been unable to participate. Only Amelia knows the pain he endured during the many hours it took to record that program. But it is recorded and his testimony is preserved.

His preparation for the work began in the home, where his father and his mother invited scriptural discussions around the family table. Before his mission he had read the Book of Mormon three times. He was on a single scriptural track that would lead to the apostleship and to his crowning achievement in mortality.

His main interest centered in the scriptures. He was in the mission field when the Cumorah Pageant started. All missionaries participated in the pageant, as he joked, "according to our talents." His talent was scriptural. "I parked cars."

Knew the Law and the Prophets

S. Dilworth Young wrote:

> It was while walking to and from law school that Elder McConkie developed a habit of study. . . . He would think of a subject in the gospel, such as repentance, and would then, in his mind, make up an outline for a sermon on the subject.
>
> He would, from memory, add the appropriate scripture and material supporting the outline. He had memorized a verse of scripture a day while in the mission field, and so he had a large amount to draw upon.

> Doing this daily, as he walked, gave him practice in analysis and logic of doctrinal subjects. . . . He continued this until this method of thinking became second nature to him.

Elder McConkie came to know two things as few mortals have known them: The law and the prophets.

He came to know the *law* and he came to know the *prophets.* When he was called as a General Authority, I am sure there were snide remarks about nepotism, for he had married the daughter of Joseph Fielding Smith of the Council of the Twelve Apostles. People making such remarks did not know that the President of the Church had kept his call from her father until it had to be announced. If they could not see then, can they see now that in that union this chosen man was brought under the constant tutelage of Joseph Fielding Smith, scripturalist, son of a prophet, grandson of Hyrum the patriarch, and a prophet himself?

And Amelia, the very image of her father, was perfect, just perfect, as his help meet for this ministry.

If you know ecclesiastical history at all, if you know the dealings of the Lord with men and of men with men, you should not be surprised that the one characteristic which the Lord pressed upon him was the very thing that many, even some close to him, misunderstood. As is often true, the great ones are not fully understood or appreciated while they live.

A Great Man Walked Among Us

Perhaps one day we will see how great a man has walked among us. He was not less than Elder Talmage or the others we revere from the past. His sermons and writings will live on. In these, he will live longer than any of us. The scriptures have something to say about testimonies being in fuller force after the death of the testator.

His manner of delivery was unique, with something of an Old Testament scriptural quality about thm.

It was not granted to Brother McConkie to judge beforehand how his discourses would be received and then to alter them accordingly. He could not measure what ought to be said and how it ought to be said by, "What will people think?" Would his sermons leave any uncomfortable? Would his bold declarations irritate some in the Church? Would they inspire the critics to rush to their anvils and hammer out more "fiery darts," as the scriptures call them?

Would his manner of delivery offend? Would his forthright declarations, in content or in manner of presentation, drive some learned investigators away? Would he be described as insensitive or overbearing?

Would his warnings and condemnations of evil undo the careful work of others whose main intent was to have the world "think well of the Church?" Perhaps it was given to other men to measure their words in that way, but it was not given to him.

He and I have talked of this. And when he was tempted to change, the Spirit would withdraw a distance and there would come that deep loneliness known only to those who have enjoyed close association with the Spirit, only to find on occasion that it moves away. He could stand what the critics might say and what enemies might do, but he could not stand that.

He would be driven to his knees to beg forgiveness and plead for the renewal of that companionship with the Spirit which the scriptures promise can be constant. Then he would learn once again that what was true of holy men of God who spake in ancient times applied to him as well. He was to speak as he was moved upon by the Holy Spirit. What matter if it sounded like Bruce R. McConkie, so long as the Lord approved! I knew him well enough to know all of that.

Brother McConkie was as sensitive a man as ever I have known. I have had my arms around him as he wept openly over what some had said or done. I have delighted in his sparkling sense of humor that few men could equal. I have sensed that he was quite as much an Apostle as was Peter, James, John, or Paul.

President Kimball spoke in public of his gratitude to Elder McConkie for some special support he received in the days leading up to the revelation on the priesthood.

We did learn much from that final blessing we gave Brother McConkie. In it I quoted from verses in section 138 of the Doctrine and Covenants. That section is one of the revelations added to the scripture as part of recent editions. It is a revelation given to Amelia's grandfather, President Joseph F. Smith, on 3 October 1918 and is referred to as "The Vision of the Redemption of the Dead."

The heading of that section (which, incidentally, Bruce wrote) says this:

In his opening address at the eighty-ninth Semi-annual General Conference of the Church, on October 4, 1918, President Smith declared that he had received several divine communications during the previous months. One of these, concerning the Savior's visit to the spirits of the dead while his body was in the tomb, he had received the previous day.

President Smith had been reading and pondering certain verses from First Peter in the New Testament, including this one:

> For for this cause was the gospel preached also to them that are dead, that they might be judged according to men in the flesh, but live according to God in the Spirit (1 Peter 4:6).

The following verses were the ones from which I quoted in that blessing:

> And as I wondered, my eyes were opened, and my understanding quickened, and I perceived that the Lord went not in person among the wicked and the disobedient who had rejected the truth, to teach them;
>
> But behold, from among the righteous, he organized his forces and appointed messengers, clothed with power and authority, and commissioned them to go forth and carry the light of the gospel to them that were in darkness, even to all the spirits of men; and thus was the gospel preached to the dead (D&C 138:29–30).

One more verse:

> I beheld that the faithful elders of this dispensation when they depart from mortal life, continue their labors in the preaching of the gospel of repentance and redemption, through the sacrifice of the Only Begotten Son of God, among those who are in darkness and under the bondage of sin in the great world of the spirits of the dead (D&C 138:57).

Following the blessing, Brother McConkie wept and said, "It is now all in the hands of the Lord." He affirmed his willingness to do as the Lord should wish.

After we left his home that day, for the first time he took off his clothes and went to bed.

Last Thursday as the Brethren met in the temple, the message came from him and from his Amelia that he was ready now to go.

Would we ask the Lord? At the altar that was done. The following day at Amelia's invitation his family knelt around the bed for a final family prayer. His son Joseph was voice. At last they were willing to let him go, and at the very moment they asked the Lord, his passing came. It was a tender and sweet experience for the family.

He Is with His Lord

Where is Bruce McConkie now? He is with his Lord. When the refining process is complete, I know something of how he will appear. He will be glorious! What will he do? Whatever the Lord wills him to do. I believe he shall be, as the revelation describes them, "a chosen messenger, clothed with power and authority to go forth and carry the light of the gospel to them that were in darkness" (see D&C 138:30–31).

President Priday of the Provo Temple called to tell me of an experience. When Bruce died, his ninety-five-year-old mother was in the temple doing ordinance work for the dead. This was her daily work. Bruce's sister Margaret rushed to the temple and found her, and there, in that sacred sanctuary, she learned that her noble son was now beyond the veil.

Now he may preach the plan of redemption to complement the sacred ordinance work that this lovely little lady has performed so faithfully for so many years. For the temple workers, that was a sweet experience. President Priday, who knew nothing of my speaking today, said he was just prompted to call to tell me of it.

Now Bruce is gone. What will we do without him? Others, of course, will receive the fiery darts fashioned on the anvils of the adversary. And, in his own words, "the wagon train will move on." His brethren will share the extra burden and "the wagon train will move on!"

If you heard at the last conference the sermons of Elder Nelson and Elder Oaks, who had been duly called to the Quorum of the Twelve, you will know that the Lord is preparing others as he prepared Bruce R. McConkie for the holy apostleship. "The wagon train will move on."

And now, in testimony, let him speak for himself, and let him speak for me, as well:

Let it now be written once again—and it is the testimony of all the prophets of all the ages—that he is the son of God, the Only Begotten of the Father, the Promised Messiah, the Lord God of Israel, our Redeemer and Savior: That he came into the world to manifest the Father, to reveal anew the gospel, to be the great exemplar, to work out the infinite and eternal atonement: and that not many days hence he shall come again to reign personally upon the earth and to save and redeem those who love and serve him.

And now let it also be written both on earth and in heaven, that this disciple, . . . does himself also know of the truth of those things of which the prophets have testified. For the things have been revealed unto him by the Holy Spirit of God. And he therefore testifies that Jesus is Lord of all, the Son of God, through whose name salvation cometh.

President Wilford Woodruff included this sentence in his last will and testament: "If the laws of the spirit world permit, and I shall be governed by them, I should like to attend my own funeral."

And I have known other occasions when that was permitted. Should Bruce be here, I would say:

God bless you, our beloved Brother Bruce R. McConkie. We love you deeply, we know that you now are with Him. God grant that all of us may finish the race as you have done, and that one day where He is, and where you are, we may be also, in the name of Jesus Christ, amen.

29

The Book of Mormon

It will be our objective to examine the structure of the Book of Mormon, Another Testament of Jesus Christ, and to show from the record itself, in the words of the ancient prophets, what purpose the Lord had for the preservation of the record.

To present the Book of Mormon properly, a missionary or member should know how it is put together and why it is structured in the way it is; for there is something of an obstacle which prevents most beginners from reading the entire book. Following this examination I shall recommend a way for the Book of Mormon to be presented to investigators so as to overcome that obstacle.

I have chosen as a title for this presentation:

"The Things of My Soul"

The source for this will emerge as we proceed.

From the title page we read:

From the Church video presentation *The Things of My Soul*.

The Book of Mormon
An account written by the hand of Mormon
upon plates
taken from the plates of Nephi

and that it was "written by way of commandment, and also by the spirit of prophecy and of revelation. . . ."

Notice the words *commandment, prophecy,* and *revelation.* Then comes this threefold statement of purpose:

1. "To show unto the remnant of the House of Israel what great things the Lord hath done for their fathers."
2. "That they may know the *covenants* of the Lord."
3. "To the convincing of the Jew and Gentile that *Jesus is the Christ,* the Eternal God, manifesting himself unto all nations."

Book of Mormon Sources: The Plates

Many records and plates are mentioned in the Book of Mormon (see 1 Nephi 1:17; Mosiah 8:9; 25:5; Helaman 3:15; 3 Nephi 5:19). Of these we will consider five (see "A Brief Explanation about the Book of Mormon," in the front of the book):

1. *The brass plates of Laban,* which Lehi brought from Jerusalem.
2. *The large plates,* named the plates of Nephi, also referred to as the "other" plates (see 1 Nephi 9:2–5; 2 Nephi 5:33).
3. *The small plates of Nephi,* which will be the center of our attention.
4. *The twenty-four gold plates of the Jaredites.*
5. *The plates of Mormon,* from which Joseph Smith translated the Book of Mormon.

The Brass Plates of Laban

First, the brass plates of Laban. When Nephi obtained these plates, he said:

It is wisdom in God that we should obtain these records, that we may preserve unto our children the language of our fathers;

And also that we may preserve unto them the words . . . of all the holy prophets, which have been delivered unto them by the Spirit and power of God (1 Nephi 3:19–20; see also 5:13).

Nephi found

that they did contain the five books of Moses, which gave an account of the creation of the world, and also of Adam and Eve, . . .

And also a record of the Jews from the beginning, even down to the commencement of the reign of Zedekiah, king of Judah;

and a genealogy of his fathers (1 Nephi 5:11, 12, 14).

Nephi wrote that the plates of brass were "of great worth unto us, insomuch that we could preserve the commandments of the Lord unto our children" (1 Nephi 5:21).

Lehi prophesied "that these plates of brass should go forth unto all nations, kindreds, tongues, and people who were of his seed," and that they "should never perish; neither should they be dimmed any more by time." (1 Nephi 5:18–19.)

Eight generations later (see Omni 1:14) Lehi's descendants discovered the Mulekites, whose ancestors also had come out of Jerusalem. The Mulekite situation taught a profound lesson. "Their language had become corrupted [because] they had brought no records with them; and they *denied the being of their Creator*" (Omni 1:17, italics added).

That corruption of language was particularly sad, for there were records of metal and of stone which they could not read.

The Mulekite leader, Zarahemla, was overjoyed to find that the Nephites had the brass plates. Mosiah caused that the Mulekites should be taught his language, so that they could receive the scriptures and their genealogies. Benjamin, prophet-king, taught the value of the sacred records, saying:

I would that ye should remember that were it not for these [brass] plates, which contain these records and these commandments, we must have suffered in ignorance, . . . not knowing the mysteries of God (Mosiah 1:3).

Were it not for these things, which have been kept and preserved by the hand of God, that we might read and understand of his mysteries, and have his commandments . . . even our fathers would have dwindled in unbelief (Mosiah 1:5).

Then Benjamin bore testimony of the record:

These sayings are true, and also . . . these records [the brass plates] are true. And behold, also the [small] plates of Nephi, which contain the records and the sayings of our fathers . . . are true; and we can know of their surety. (Mosiah 1:6.)

The Large Plates of Nephi

The second record, the large plates of Nephi, which he also called "mine other plates," were largely a secular history handed down through the lineage of the kings (see Jarom 1:14; Words of Mormon 1:10). They are, for the most part, written in the third person. Nephi wrote: "Upon [these] other plates should be engraven an account of the reign of the kings, and the wars and contentions of my people" (1 Nephi 9:4).

The large plates were many in number. In fact, many plates and records which we do not now have are mentioned in the book.

And now there are many records kept of the proceedings of this people, by many of this people, which are particular and very large, concerning them.

Behold, there are many books and many records of every kind, and they have been kept chiefly by the Nephites.

And they have been handed down from one generation to another by the Nephites. (Helaman 3:13, 15–16.)

At least four times in his abridgment of these plates Mormon repeats that he cannot write "a hundredth part" of what is in the records (see Words of Mormon 1:5; Helaman 3:13–16; 3 Nephi 5:8; 26:6).

We know also that these plates contained genealogies (see 1 Nephi 6:1; 19:2; Omni 1:18).

Nephi faithfully kept the secular history on the large plates. After his death these plates were kept by the kings. No doubt they contained a great resource of historical information. They were by no means the most valuable record, however, for Nephi was commanded to keep another account; not a secular history this time, but a record of the ministry. This record was written on the small plates of Nephi.

The Small Plates of Nephi

The purpose of the small plates was best explained when Nephi gave the records to his brother Jacob, for they were to remain with Jacob's seed. Notice that they are written in the first person.

> And he gave me, Jacob, a commandment that I should write upon these [small] plates a few of the things which I considered to be most precious; that I should not touch, save it were lightly, concerning the history of this people. . . .
>
> For he said that the history of his people should be engraven upon his other [large] plates, and that I should preserve these [small] plates and hand them down unto my seed, from generation to generation.
>
> And if there were preaching which was sacred, or revelation which was great, or prophesying, that I should engraven . . . them upon these [small] plates, and touch upon them as much as it were possible, for Christ's sake, and for the sake of our people. (Jacob 1:2-4.)

Did you notice that he was "*not* to touch (save it were lightly) on the *history* of the people" but he *was* to touch upon the *sacred things* "as much as possible"? To know that is to know how the prophets and Apostles of today must regard the records of our people and whether or not we are obliged to please the world in what we do with them.

Nephi made this clear statement on the relative value of the two histories:

> It mattereth not to me that I am particular to give a full account of all the things of my father, for they cannot be written upon these [small] plates, for I desire the room that I may write of the things of God.
>
> For the fulness of mine intent is *that I may persuade men to come unto the God of Abraham, and the God of Isaac, and the God of Jacob, and be saved.*

Wherefore, the things which are pleasing unto the world I do not write, but the things which are pleasing unto God and unto those who are not of the world.

Wherefore, I shall give commandment unto my seed, that they shall not occupy these plates with things which are not of worth unto the children of men. (1 Nephi 6:3–6, italics added.)

This I do that the more sacred things may be kept for the knowledge of my people.

. . . I do not write anything upon plates save it be that I think it be sacred. (1 Nephi 19:5–6.)

Again notice why he did as he did:

I have received a commandment of the Lord that I should make these plates, for the special purpose that there should be an account engraven of the ministry of my people (1 Nephi 9:3).

Wherefore, the Lord hath commanded me to make these plates for a wise purpose in him, which purpose I know not.

But the Lord knoweth all things from the beginning; wherefore, he prepareth a way to accomplish all his works among the children of men. (1 Nephi 9:5–6.)

Then this verse from which we take our title:

And upon these [small plates] I write *the things of my soul*, and many of the scriptures which are engraven upon the plates of brass. For my soul delighteth in the scriptures, and my heart pondereth them, and writeth them for the learning and the profit of my children.

Behold, my soul delighteth in the things of the Lord. (2 Nephi 4:15–16, italics added.)

For that very reason, Nephi copied the prophecies of Isaiah from the brass plates onto his small plates. He wrote:

Wherefore I, Nephi, to be obedient to the commandments of the Lord, went and made these plates upon which I have engraven these things.

And I engraved that which is pleasing unto God. And if my people are pleased with the things of God they will be pleased with mine engravings which are upon these plates. (2 Nephi 5:31–32.)

After Nephi died, eight others wrote upon the small plates.

Nephi passed them to his brother Jacob, admonishing him, as already noted, "not [to] touch, save it were lightly, concerning the history of this people," but "if there were preaching which was sacred, or revelation which was great, or prophesying," he should "touch upon them as much as it were possible." (Jacob 1:2, 4.)

The seven chapters Jacob wrote are most precious and include the provoking allegory of the olive vineyard from the writings of the prophet Zenos.

Jacob gave the record to his son Enos, a worthy man who told how he "wrestled before the Lord" and received forgiveness for his sins. His words are worthy of a prophet.

Enos passed the record to his son Jarom, who wrote that the prophets persuaded the people to "look forward unto the Messiah and believe in him to come as though he already was" (Jarom 1:11). Among his concluding words he wrote: "And I, Jarom, do not write more, for the plates are small. But behold, my brethren, ye can go to the other [large] plates of Nephi; for behold, upon them the records of our wars are engraven, according to the writings of the kings." (Jarom 1:14.)

Jarom gave the record to his son Omni, who confessed: "I of myself am a wicked man, and I have not kept the statutes and the commandments of the Lord as I ought to have done" (Omni 1:2). It may seem strange that a book is named after him, but even this self-confessed wicked man knew the sacred nature of the record and delivered it to his son Amaron for safekeeping (see Omni 1:3).

Amaron passed the record on to his brother Chemish, who recorded: "Now I, Chemish, write what few things I write, in the same book with my brother; for behold, I saw the last which he wrote, that he wrote it with his own hand; and he wrote it in the day that he delivered them unto me" (Omni 1:9).

Chemish in due course gave the records to his son Abinadom, who wrote: "I know of no revelation save that which has been written, neither prophecy; wherefore, that which is sufficient is written" (Omni 1:11).

Abinadom's son Amaleki was the last to write on the small plates. A better man than his father, he told how Mosiah discovered the Mulekite people. Amaleki wrote: "Having no seed, and knowing King Benjamin to be a just man before the Lord, wherefore, I shall deliver up these plates unto him." Finally he added, "These plates are full." (Omni 1:25, 30.)

Benjamin, who was both prophet and king, "took [the small plates] and put them with the other [large] plates, which contained records which had been handed down by the kings" (Words of Mormon 1:10).

It was at this point that the small plates of Nephi, the sacred history handed down from father to son, and the large plates of Nephi, the secular history kept by the kings, came together. And they were still together when Mormon found them more than four hundred years later.

When Mormon was a boy of ten, Ammaron (who had received the records from his brother Amos II) told him where they were hidden. He instructed the boy: "When ye are about twenty and four years old . . . ye shall take the [large] plates of Nephi . . . and the remainder shall ye leave in the place where they are." (Mormon 1:3–4.)

Mormon began to abridge the large plates. When he came to the reign of King Benjamin, surely he read his testimony that the small plates of Nephi "are true; and we can know of their surety" (Mosiah 1:6).

Can we doubt that Benjamin's testimony inspired Mormon to return to Jashon and look for that precious record? (See Mormon 2:17.)

Mormon wrote:

After I had made an abridgment from the [large] plates of Nephi down to the reign of this king Benjamin, of whom Amaleki spake, I searched among the records which had been delivered into my hands [those words "searched among" assure us that there were many records—see Helaman 3:13–16], and I found these plates, which contained this small account of the prophets, from Jacob down to the reign of this king Benjamin, and also many of the words of Nephi.

And the things which are upon these plates pleasing me, because of the prophecies of the coming of Christ; . . .

Wherefore, I chose these things, to finish my record upon them, which remainder of my record I shall take from the [large] plates of Nephi; and I cannot write the hundredth part of the things of my people.

But behold, I shall take these [small] plates, which contain these prophesyings and revelations, and put them [as they were written, without abridgment] with the remainder of my record, for they are choice unto me; and I know they will be choice unto my brethren.

And I do this for a wise purpose; for thus it whispereth me, according to the workings of the Spirit of the Lord which is in me. And now, I do not know all things; but the Lord knoweth all things which are to come; wherefore, he worketh in me to do according to his will.

And my prayer to God is concerning my brethren, that they may once again come to the knowledge of God, yea, the redemption of Christ. (Words of Mormon 1:3–8.)

I have the conviction that Mormon's reading of the small plates of Nephi greatly influenced what he chose from the large plates to include in the rest of his abridgment; for while we have some history of the people, we have much "preaching which [is] sacred, [and] revelation which [is] great, [and] prophesying" (Jacob 1:4).

Being able to choose but a hundredth part, Mormon chose the better part. He was, however, not able to resist putting in a generous amount of military science and tactics—for he was a general. This unusual human insight is also a testimony!

Mormon was drawn to the prophecies concerning the coming of Christ. The inspiration that came to him as he abridged the records resulted in his work being, indeed, another testament of Jesus Christ.

Mormon finished the abridgment and wrote of his last days (see Mormon chapters 1–7). He then suffered death at the hands of the Lamanites (see Mormon 8:3). His son Moroni finished his record (see Mormon 8:3–5). Moroni then abridged the plates of the Jaredites as something of an appendix to the record. Later he wrote the obvious "I have not as yet perished" (Moroni 1:1), and added his own book of Moroni.

The Plates of Mormon

The plates of Mormon, as delivered to Joseph Smith, consisted of the following:
  — Mormon's abridgment of the large plates of Nephi
  — The record of Lehi

— The small plates of Nephi, unabridged
— The Words of Mormon explaining why he included the small plates
— Mormon's abridgment of the remainder of the large plates of Nephi
— Mormon's account of the history of his day, completed by Moroni
— Moroni's own book
— Moroni's abridgment of the twenty-four gold plates, the book of Ether
— The title page added by Moroni
— The sealed portion

Surely the purposes of the Lord were being worked out when Nephi concentrated on the things of his soul: the preachings which were sacred, and the revelations which were great, and the prophesying; and when Mormon placed the small plates of Nephi, intact, without abridgment, into his record.

Centuries later the Prophet Joseph Smith translated the record of Lehi from the plates of Mormon down to the reign of King Benjamin. Then the manuscript of that translation, consisting of 116 pages, was lost or stolen.

The sacred history on the small plates of Nephi became the providential replacement (see D&C 10:37–46). At that time the Lord consoled Joseph Smith and confirmed the purpose as stated on the title page of the Book of Mormon:

> Remember, remember that it is not the work of God that is frustrated, but the work of men (D&C 3:3).

> And for this very purpose are these plates preserved, which contain these records—that the promises of the Lord might be fulfilled, which he made to his people;
> . . . That they may believe the gospel and rely upon the merits of Jesus Christ, and be glorified through faith in his name, and that through their repentance they might be saved. (D&C 3: 19–20.)

The Christ: The Message of the Book

To present the Book of Mormon properly to others, members and missionaries must know that the message of the book is a testimony to the world that Jesus is the Christ. That message recurs through the pages like a golden thread. Indeed, the Book of Mormon is another testament of Jesus Christ.

Long before Christ was born in the flesh, Nephi recorded visions of His ministry which have no equal in the Old Testament.

Lehi had a vision in which he saw the tree of life (see 1 Nephi chapter 8). Nephi was deeply moved by the things his father had told him. He later wrote: "Believing that the Lord was able to make [these things] known unto me, as I sat pondering in mine heart I was caught away in the Spirit of the Lord" (1 Nephi 11:1). Of the spirit personage who attended him he wrote: "I beheld that he was in the form of a man; yet nevertheless, I knew that it was the Spirit of the Lord" (1 Nephi 11:11).

Nephi desired "to behold the things which [his] father saw." Before that was granted, there was a test, a question. The Spirit said to him: "Believest thou that thy father saw the tree of which he hath spoken?" The answer shows Nephi's great faith: "Yea, thou knowest that I believe all the words of my father" (1 Nephi 11:1-5).

After he was shown the vision of the tree of life, the Spirit asked, "What desirest thou?" (1 Nephi 11:10.) When Nephi replied that he wanted to know the interpretation of that vision, there was then opened to him a supernal vision in which he saw
— A virgin, beautiful and fair.
— The virgin bearing a child in her arms.
— The ministry of the Son of God.
— John the Baptist, the prophet who should prepare the way.
— Twelve others following Jesus.
— The heavens opened and angels ministering unto the Twelve.
— The multitudes blessed and healed.
— Christ lifted upon the cross and slain for the sins of the world.
— The wisdom and the pride of the world and the fate of those who fight against the Twelve Apostles of the Lamb. (See 1 Nephi 11:1-36.)

That testimony of Christ is repeated through the pages of Book of Mormon history up to the crowning event: the appearance of the Lord to the Nephites in fulfillment of prophecy.

The account of His appearance to the Nephites is consistent with the New Testament account of His ministry in Jerusalem.

He called and gave authority to twelve.

He announced that the law of Moses was fulfilled.

He taught as He taught in Jerusalem.

He blessed and healed the people.

He blessed their little children.

He instituted the sacrament as He had in Jerusalem, with that one crucial difference—when they brought the bread, "He brake and blessed it" (3 Nephi 18:3) instead of blessing it first, as He had in Jerusalem.

He did many other things—two of which, of great significance, are often overlooked.

First, He dictated to the Nephites what we have in our Bible as the third and fourth chapters of Malachi and caused them to be written. Then He expounded them. These chapters contain prophecies of the coming of Elijah and the turning of the hearts of the fathers to the children and of the children to their fathers. That return of Elijah and the bestowal of the sealing power is the foundation of the sacred work for the dead. It is of consummate importance to all mankind in this dispensation of the fulness of times. (See 3 Nephi chapters 24 and 25.)

Second, He gave a commandment to them concerning the writings of the prophet Isaiah:

> And now, behold, I say unto you, that ye ought to search [the words of Isaiah]. Yea, a commandment I give unto you that ye search these things diligently; for great are the words of Isaiah.
>
> For surely he spake as touching all things concerning my people which are of the house of Israel; therefore it must needs be that he must speak also to the Gentiles.
>
> And all things that he spake have been and shall be, even according to the words which he spake. (3 Nephi 23:1–3.)

Twenty-one chapters of Isaiah are duplicated in part or in whole in the Book of Mormon. They are in Old Testament prophecy language. Much of it is symbolism and allegory. They are not easily read nor understood. They form a barrier to the casual reader.

Most people who open the cover of the Book of Mormon do not feel able to go beyond the Isaiah chapters. They lay the book aside, thinking perhaps they will try another day. If they complete reading the book at all, it is after several attempts to surmount this unusual barrier.

Few people indeed ever complete the reading of the Book of Mormon on the first try.

Let me illustrate.

The Book of Mormon begins, "I, Nephi, having been born of goodly parents," and so forth. At chapter 20 of 1 Nephi stands a barrier—two chapters of Isaiah. If the reader goes beyond that, to chapter 8 of 2 Nephi, another similar barrier looms like a mountain.

The reader becomes discouraged and lays the book aside. Then, in the future, he tries once more—"I, Nephi, having been born of goodly parents," and so on—and it happens again. And yet a third time, perhaps a fourth. Finally, the persistent reader surmounts that barrier. Then he does not stop reading in Alma or Helaman or 3 Nephi; he finishes the Book of Mormon.

The twenty-one chapters are not the only quotations from Isaiah in the Book of Mormon. Single verses and paraphrases appear throughout the book.

Isaiah is the most quoted prophet in the New Testament. The Lord Himself quoted Isaiah seven times, the Apostles forty times more. In addition there are ninety partial quotes or paraphrases of Isaiah's words.

Isaiah is the most quoted prophet in the Doctrine and Covenants. Sixty-six quotations from thirty-one chapters of Isaiah attest to the singular importance of this great prophet.

All of this confirms that the Lord had a purpose in preserving Isaiah's words, notwithstanding they have a winnowing effect upon the harvest gathered in from all nations, and thus some precious souls may be lost.

The Book of Mormon has great converting power only if it is read. It is not too difficult to place copies of the book. It is another thing to have it read.

It is our conviction that an answer to that challenge rests in the way the Book of Mormon is first introduced to the investigator or reintroduced to the members of the Church.

The Book of Mormon is often introduced as "a history of the ancient inhabitants of the American continent, the ancestors of the American Indians." We have all seen missionaries about the world with street boards displaying pictures of American Indians or pyramids and other ruins in Latin America.

That introduction does not reveal the contents of this sacred book any better than an introduction of the Bible as "a history of the ancient inhabitants of the Near East, the ancestors of the modern Israelites" would reveal its contents.

The presentation of the Book of Mormon as a history of the ancestors of the American Indians is not a very compelling nor a very accurate introduction. When we introduce the Book of Mormon as such a history—and that is the way we generally introduce it—surely the investigator must be puzzled, even disappointed, when he begins to read it. Most do not find what they expect. Nor do they, in turn, expect what they find.

We have a study which shows that most investigators read very few pages in the Book of Mormon. And, sadder still, most converts do little more. Very few of them finish reading the book.

We can do much better than we have hitherto done in introducing the Book of Mormon. In doing so we can foster in the heart of the missionary and the member a reverence for the sacred testament.

A Suggestion on Placing Copies of the Book of Mormon

We present now this suggestion.

In substance, the following message should accompany the placement of each Book of Mormon by every missionary and by every member. Every missionary should be familiar enough with the Book of Mormon to present such an introduction in his own words. We recommend that this introduction not be memorized nor read.

Each one receiving a copy of the book by purchase or by gift should be told:

"Except for the Bible, the Book of Mormon is different from any book you have read. It is not a novel. It is not fiction. For the most part it is not difficult to read. However, like all books of profound value, it is not casual reading. But if you persist, I assure you it will prove to be the most rewarding book you have ever set your mind to read.

"The Book of Mormon is not biographical, for not one character is fully drawn. Nor, in a strict sense, is it a history.

"While it chronicles a people for a thousand and twenty-one years and contains the record of an earlier people, it is in fact not a history of a people. It is the saga of a message, a testament. As the influence of that message is traced from generation to generation, more than twenty writers record the fate of the individuals and civilizations that accepted or rejected that testament.

"The history in the Book of Mormon is incidental. There are prophets and dissenters, and genealogies to move them from one generation to another, but the central purpose is not historical.

"As the saga of the message is traced, one writer requires 160 pages to cover 38 years (Alma), while seven other writers together use only six pages to cover over three hundred years (Enos, Jarom, Omni, Amaron, Chemish, Abinadom, Amaleki). In either case, the testament survives.

"The Book of Mormon is a book of scripture. It is another testament of Jesus Christ. It is written in biblical language; the language of the prophets.

"For the most part it is in easy-flowing 'New Testament' language, with such words as *spake* for *spoke*, *unto* for *to*, with 'and it came to pass,' with *thus* and *thou* and *thine*.

"You will not read many pages until you catch the cadence of the language and the narrative will be easy to understand. As a matter of fact, most teenagers readily understand the narrative of the Book of Mormon.

"Then, just as you settle in to move comfortably along, you will meet a barrier. The style of the language changes to 'Old Testament' style; for interspersed in the narrative are chapters reciting the prophecies of the Old Testament prophet Isaiah. They loom as a barrier, like a roadblock or a check point beyond which the casual reader, prompted by idle curiosity, generally will not go.

"You, too, may be tempted to stop there, but do not do it! Do not stop reading! Move forward through those difficult-to-understand chapters of Old Testament prophecy, even though you understand very little of it. Move on, if all you do is skim and merely glean an impression here and there. Move on, if all you do is look at the words. Soon you will emerge beyond those difficult chapters to the easier 'New Testament' style which is characteristic of the rest of the Book of Mormon.

"Being forewarned about that barrier, you will be able to surmount it and finish reading the book.

"You will follow the prophecies of the coming of the Messiah through generations of the Nephite people to that day when those prophecies are fulfilled and the Lord appears to them. You will be present, through eyewitness accounts, at the ministry of the Lord among the 'other sheep' of whom He spoke in the New Testament (see John 10:16).

"Thereafter you will understand the Bible as never before. You will come to understand the Old Testament and know why we, as a people, hold it in such esteem. You will come to revere the New Testament, to know it is true. The account of the birth and life and death of the man Jesus as recorded in the New Testament is true. He is the Christ, the Only Begotten Son of God, the Messiah, the Redeemer of mankind.

"This testament, the Book of Mormon, will verify the Old and the New Testaments.

"Perhaps only after reading the Book of Mormon and then returning to the Bible will you sense that the Lord had purpose in preserving the words of Isaiah in the Book of Mormon, notwithstanding they become a barrier to the casual reader.

"Christ quotes Isaiah seven times in the New Testament—the Apostles forty more times. One day you may revere these prophetic words in both books.

"Those who never move beyond the Isaiah chapters miss the personal treasures to be gathered along the way. For instance, a knowledge of

— The purpose of mortal death.
— The certainty of life after death.
— What happens when the Spirit leaves the body.
— The description of the resurrection.
— How to receive and retain a remission of your sins.
— What hold justice may have on you, or mercy.
— What to pray for.
— Covenants and ordinances.
— Many other jewels that make up the gospel of Jesus Christ.

"It is beyond that barrier, near the end of the record, that you find a promise addressed to you and to everyone who will read the book with intent and sincerity. After you have read the Book of Mormon, you become qualified to inquire of the Lord, in the way He prescribes in the book, as to whether the book is true. Then you will be eligible, on the conditions He has established, to receive a personal revelation."

That is the introduction—that is the message—in substance, which every member and every missionary should present in his own words with every copy of the Book of Mormon.

To review, the person receiving the book should understand that

— Except for the Bible, the Book of Mormon is different from any book he will read.
— It is not a novel, it is not fiction, it is not biographical.
— It is not the history of a people but a saga of a message.
— It is written in scriptural language.
— There is a barrier of difficult-to-understand Old Testament prophecy, the writings of Isaiah.
— The reader is to persist through that barrier.
— There is the promise of a personal testimony to those who will persist.

To present such an introduction, the member and the missionary must know something of how and why the Book of Mormon is structured as it is. Learning that will increase the member's and the missionary's testimony of the book and allow them to present it with increased conviction and inspiration and testimony. Thus they may convey the book with a personal testimony of its truth as in no other way. Then we will have lifted the book from among all other books. We will have given it a dignity and a virtue that it fully deserves.

The history in the book has importance because it affirms that these were real events, happening to real people. We too are real people caught up in real events relating to this testament of Jesus Christ that are of equal magnitude. For we are custodians of that record.

Except we revere, above all else, preaching which is sacred and revelation which is great, and prophesying, we may be diverted from the ministry entrusted to us. Therefore we should soberly consider our responsibility, lest we fall into that circumstance which befell the Church so many times in the Book of Mormon days, when "because of their iniquity the church had begun to dwindle; and they began to disbelieve in the spirit of prophecy and in the spirit of revelation; and the judgments of God did stare them in the face" (Helaman 4:23).

This "voice from the dust" teaches, indeed warns us, the living prophets and Apostles, what we must do, and what we must not permit to be done with this sacred testament of the Lord.

When Nephi first began to keep his plates, the Lord instructed him that the record was to be "handed down from one generation to another, or from one prophet to another, until further commandments of the Lord" (1 Nephi 19:4).

Responsibility for the Book of Mormon, as well as for the Doctrine and Covenants, the Pearl of Great Price, and the other revelations, rests upon the prophets and Apostles today. They must be the things of *our* soul. We must convey them to the coming generation. In this we have no accountability but to Him who is our Master, whose church this is, and whose servants we are.

All of this we present as a testimony that the Book of Mormon is fully worthy of the unparallelled endorsement given to it in the Doctrine and Covenants (17:6) wherein the Lord said to the Three Witnesses:

He [Joseph Smith] has translated the book, even that part which I have commanded him, and as your Lord and your God liveth it is true.

30

The Pattern of Our Parentage

It's the Sabbath day, and outside is such a glorious day that all nature seems to bespeak the works of God. I can't refrain from saying with Helen Hunt Jackson:

> O suns and skies and clouds of June,
> And flowers of June together,
> Ye cannot rival for one hour
> October's bright blue weather.
>
> —"October's Bright Blue Weather"

I desire to share a few thoughts about a basic doctrine of the Church.

Sources of Understanding

What I say is based on these convictions:

First: Instruction vital to our salvation is not hidden in an obscure verse or phrase in the scriptures. To the contrary, essential truths are repeated over and over again.

Address given at general conference October 1984.

Second: Every verse, whether oft-quoted or obscure, must be measured against other verses. There are complementary and tempering teachings in the scriptures which bring a balanced knowledge of truth.

Third: There is a consistency in what the Lord says and what He does. That is evident in all creation. Nature can teach valuable lesson about spiritual and doctrinal matters. The Lord drew lessons from flowers and foxes, from seeds and salt, and from sparrows and sunsets.

Fourth: Not all that God has said is in the Bible. Other scriptures—the Book of Mormon, the Doctrine and Covenants, and the Pearl of Great Price—have equal validity, and the four sustain one another.

Fifth: While much must be taken on faith alone, there is individual revelation through which we may know the truth. "There is a spirit in man: and the inspiration of the Almighty giveth them understanding" (Job 32:8). What may be obscure in the scriptures can be made plain through the gift of the Holy Ghost. We can have as full an understanding of spiritual things as we are willing to earn.

And I add one more conviction: There is an adversary who has his own channels of spiritual communication. He confuses the careless and prompts those who serve him to devise deceptive, counterfeit doctrine, carefully contrived to appear genuine.

I mention this because now, as always, there are self-appointed spokesmen who scoff at what we believe and misrepresent what we teach.

As a young seminary teacher, I learned a valuable lesson from our principal, Abel S. Rich. He told me, "If you really want to know what a man is, and what he believes, do not go to his enemies. Go to the man himself or to his friends. He does not confide the thoughts of his heart to his enemies. His friends know him best; they know his strengths and his weaknesses. They will represent him fairly. His enemies will *mis*represent him."

The doctrine I wish to discuss concerns the nature of man and of God.

The Question

There is a question in both the Old and the New Testaments: "What is man, that thou art mindful of him? and the son of man, that thou visitest him?" (Psalm 8:4; see also Hebrews 2:5–7.)

The answer is taught most simply in the song we sang together at the intermission of the meeting:

> I am a child of God,
> And he has sent me here,
> Has given me an earthly home
> With parents kind and dear.
>
> I am a child of God,
> Rich blessings are in store;
> If I but learn to do his will
> I'll live with him once more.
>
> —*Hymns*, no. 301

Children of God

Those lyrics teach a basic doctrine of the Church. We *are* the children of God. That doctrine is not hidden away in an obscure verse. It is taught over and over again in scripture. These clear examples are from the Bible: "All of you are children of the most High" (Psalm 82:6), and "We are the offspring of God" (Acts 17:29).

Doctrinal truths are interrelated. There is an old saying that if you pick up one end of a stick, you pick up the other end as well.

If you concede that we are God's children you must allow that God is our Father. That, too, is repeated over and over again in the scriptures. There are so many references that I could not even begin to read them to you.

But I make this point: Christ did not speak only of *the* Father, or *my* Father; He spoke of *your* Father, and of *our* Father. He even put them together in one sentence, saying, "*your* Father, and *your* God, and *my* God" (D&C 88:75). God is addressed universally in the Christian world as Father. Were we not commanded to pray, "Our Father which art in heaven"? (Matthew 6:9.)

You may respond, "Every Christian knows that." Perhaps every Christian does, but some so-called Christians, with the help of clergymen, belittle in the most un-Christian ways our teaching that we are the literal sons and daughters of God.

Other ideals flow from that great truth. Once you know that, you know that all people are *brothers* and *sisters*. That realization changes you. Thereafter you cannot willingly injure another; you cannot transgress against anyone in any way.

After Their Own Kind

That simple, profound doctrine is worth knowing for another reason as well. It brings a feeling of self-worth, of dignity, of self-respect. Then self-pity and depression fade away. We then can yield to the discipline of a loving Father and accept even the very hard lessons of life.

Christ taught us to be "perfect, even as your Father which is in heaven is perfect" (Matthew 5:48); to take on His attributes; to follow the pattern of our parentage.

A little girl taught me a profound lesson on this subject. Surely you are not above learning from little children. Much of what I know that really matters I have learned from being a father.

Some years ago I returned home to find our little children waiting in the driveway. They had discovered some newly hatched chicks under the manger in the barn. When they reached for them, a protective hen rebuffed them. So they came for reinforcements.

I soon gathered a handful of little chicks for them to see and touch.

As our little girl held one of them, I said in a teasing way, "That will make a nice watchdog when it grows up, won't it?" She looked at me quizzically, as if I didn't know much.

So I changed my approach: "It won't be a watchdog, will it?" She shook her head, "No, Daddy." Then I added, "It will be a nice riding horse."

She wrinkled up her nose and gave me that "Oh, Dad!" look. For even a four-year-old knows that a chick will not grow to be a dog, nor a horse, nor even a turkey. It will be a chicken. It will follow the pattern of its parentage. She knew that without having had a course in genetics, without a lesson or a lecture.

No lesson is more manifest in nature than that all living things do as the Lord commanded in the Creation. They reproduce "after their own kind" (see Moses 2:12, 24). They follow the pattern of their parentage. Everyone knows that; every four-year-old knows that! A bird will not become an animal nor a fish; a mammal will not beget reptiles; nor "do men gather . . . figs of thistles" (Matthew 7:16).

In the countless billions of opportunities in the reproduction of living things, one kind does not beget another. If a species ever does cross, the offspring generally cannot reproduce. The pattern for all life is the pattern of the parentage.

This is demonstrated in so many obvious ways that even an ordinary mind should understand it. Surely no one with reverence for God could believe that His children evolved from slime or from reptiles. (Although one can easily imagine that those who accept the theory of evolution don't show much enthusiasm for genealogical research!) The theory of evolution (and it is a theory) will have an entirely different dimension when the workings of God in creation are fully revealed.

Since *every living thing* follows the pattern of its parentage, are we to suppose that God had some other strange pattern in mind for His offspring? Surely we, His children, are not, in the language of science, a different species than He is.

What is in error, then, when we use the term *godhood* to describe the ultimate destiny of mankind? We may now be young in our progression—juvenile, even infantile, compared with God. Nevertheless, in the eternities to come, if we are worthy, we may be like unto Him, enter His presence, "see as [we] are seen, and know as [we] are known," and receive "a fulness" (D&C 76:94).

This doctrine is in no way at variance with the scriptures. Nevertheless it is easy to understand why some Christians reject it, because it introduces the possibility that man may achieve godhood.

Plurality of Gods

Their concern centers on certain verses of scripture, for there are many references (at least twenty in the Bible alone) which speak of *one* God; for example, there is "one God and Father of all" (Ephesians 4:6). But if you hold strictly to a too rigid interpretation of those verses, you create serious theological problems for yourself.

There are many other verses of scripture, at least an equal number in the Bible, that speak in plural terms of "lords" and "gods." The first chapter of Genesis states: "And God said, let *us* make man in *our* image, after *our* likeness" (Genesis 1:26, italics added). Such references are found from Genesis to Revelation (e.g., Revelation 1:6).

The strongest one was given by Christ himself when he quoted that very clear verse from Psalm 82:1-6: "Is it not written in your law, *I said, Ye are gods?* If he called them *gods*, unto whom the word of God came, *and the scripture cannot be broken*; say ye of him, whom the Father hath sanctified, and sent into the world, Thou blasphemest; because I said, I am the *son* of God?" (John 10:34-36, italics added.)

The acceptance of this truth does not mean accepting the multiple gods of mythology nor the polytheism of the pagans, which was so roundly condemned by Isaiah and the other prophets.

There is *one* God, the Father of all. This we accept as fundamental doctrine.

There is only *one* Redeemer, Mediator, Savior. This we know.

There is *one* Holy Ghost, a personage of spirit, who completes the Godhead.

I have emphasized the word *one* in each sentence, but I have used it three times. Three is plural.

Paul used the plural *many* and the singular *one* in the same statement: "For though there be that are called gods, whether in heaven or in earth, (as there be gods many, and lords many,) but to us there is but one God, the Father." (1 Corinthians 8:5-6.)

Anyone who believes and teaches of God the Father, and accepts the divinity of Christ and of the Holy Ghost, teaches a plurality of Gods.

When the early Apostles were gone it was not long until those who assumed the leadership of the Church forsook revelation and relied on reason. The idea of three separate Gods offended them, for it appeared to contravene those scriptures which refer to one God.

To solve that problem they took verses from here and there and ignored all else that bears on the subject. They tried to stir the three *ones* together into some mysterious kind of a composite *one*. They came up with creeds which cannot be squared with the scriptures. And they were left with a philosophy that opposes all we know of creation, of the laws of nature; and that, interestingly enough, defies the very reason upon which they came to depend.

The Apostle Paul understood this doctrine and wrote to the Philippians: "Let this mind be in you, which was also in Christ Jesus: who, being in the form of God, thought it not robbery to be equal with God" (Philippians 2:5-6).

Lorenzo Snow, a modern Apostle, wrote a poem to his ancient counterpart Paul, from which I quote only one verse:

> A son of God, like God to be,
> Would not be robbing Deity;
> And he who has this hope within,
> Will purify himself from sin.

> —*Improvement Era*, June 1919, p. 661

What could inspire one to purity and worthiness more than to possess a spiritual confirmation that we are the children of God? What could inspire a more lofty regard for oneself, or engender more love for mankind?

This thought does not fill me with arrogance. It fills me with overwhelming humility. Nor does it sponsor any inclination to worship oneself or any man.

The doctrine we teach has no provision for lying or stealing, for pornography, for immoralities, for child abuse, for abortion, for murder. We are bound by the laws of the Lord's church, *as sons and daughters of God*, to avoid all of these and every other unholy or impure practice.

Knowledge Through Restoration

We did not invent this doctrine. Much of it was preserved in the Bible as it was revealed to prophets in ancient times. And as they foretold, further light and knowledge was revealed. With the restoration of the fulness of the gospel came the Book of Mormon, another testament of Jesus Christ. Other revelations were given and continue to be given as a result of which verses that seemed to oppose one another have harmony.

The Prophet Joseph Smith said, "It is the first principle of the gospel to know for a certainty the character of God" (*History of the Church* 6:305).

And that knowledge is given us.

The Father *is* the one true God. *This* thing is certain: no one will ever ascend above Him; no one will ever replace Him. Nor will anything ever change the relationship that we, His literal offspring, have with Him. He is Elohim, the Father. He is God; of Him there *is* only one. We revere our Father and our God; we *worship* Him.

There is only one Christ, one Redeemer. We accept the divinity of the Only Begotten Son of God in the flesh. We accept the promise that we may become joint-heirs with Him. Paul wrote to the Romans: "The spirit itself beareth witness with our spirit, that we are the children of God: and if children, then heirs; heirs of God, and joint-heirs with Christ" (Romans 8:16–17).

There are those who mock our beliefs in the most uncharitable ways. And we will bear what they do with long-suffering, for it does not change truth. And in their own way they move our work along a little faster. We will send our missionaries abroad to teach that we are the literal sons and daughters of God.

We will strive with every exertion to teach what Christ taught, to live as He lived, to endure as He endured.

We began with this question: "What is man that thou art mindful of him?" Christ, our Redeemer, our Elder Brother, asked, "What manner of men ought ye to be?" And then He answered, "Verily I say unto you, even as I am." (3 Nephi 27:27.)

I bear solemn witness that Jesus is the Christ, the Only Begotten of the Father in the flesh; that He is our Redeemer, our Savior; that God is our Father. This we know through the gift of the Holy Ghost. And I humbly but resolutely affirm that we will not, we cannot, stray from this doctrine. On this fundamental truth we will *never* yield! In the name of Jesus Christ, amen.

Index

— A —

Abinadom, 274
Abortion, 63–64, 228, 292
Abraham, 120
Academic training, 101–22
Accountability, 80, 109, 285
Adam and Eve, 78–79
Administrations to the sick, 17, 73,
    131, 185, 259–60, 264–65
Adversity, 227
Agency, 64, 78, 80, 81, 88, 133, 211,
    245
Agnostics, 62–63, 171
AIDS, 48
Alcohol, 176
Alma the Elder, 117
Alma the Younger, 14
    conversion of, 117
    on Atonement, 78
    on punishment, 79, 150–51
    on testimony, 154

Amaleki, 274
Amaron, 274
"America the Beautiful" (song), 70
Ammaron, 275
Amos, on spiritual famine, 124
Ancestors, 43
"Ancestral Home" (poem), 62
Angel, 14, 232
    destroying, 81
Angels, 88, 98, 127, 211
    ministering of, 216
    of Lucifer, 80
    presence of, 220
Apostasy, 130, 224
Apostates, 114–15, 120–21, 125
Apostles, 108, 126
    early, 34, 38, 291
    modern, 82–83, 272, 285
    receive revelation, 212
    See also Quorum of the Twelve
Apperception, 169
Armor of God, 52–53

Atheists, 62–63, 170–72, 218
Atomic bombs, 63, 165
Atonement, 75–81, 86, 228, 267
Authority, 10, 37–38, 40, 41, 126,
    129–36, 189, 212–13

— B —

Ballard, M. Russell, 82
Baptism, 128, 183, 210, 232
    covenant of, 81, 206, 233–34
    essential ordinance, 37–40, 228
    for the dead, 40–44, 214
Baptisms, 119, 177–78
Bates, Katherine Lee, "America the
    Beautiful," 70
Benjamin (Nephite prophet-king), 275
    on records, 270–71
Benson, Ezra Taft, on apostate
    writings, 114–15
Bergin, Allen E., 166
Berrett, William E., 108
Bible, 127, 150, 224, 256, 283, 284,
    287, 288, 290
    LDS edition, 6–11
Bill of Rights, 65
Birth, 223, 225, 227
Bishoprics, 16
Bishops, 16, 18, 20, 115, 212
    authority of, 131
    confession to, 204–5, 248
    counseling by, 102, 141, 236–37, 250
    home teachers assigned by, 183,
    185–86
    temple recommends given by, 257
Blessings, 72
    See also Administrations to the sick
Bodies, 50–51, 80, 98, 244, 253, 283
Bolivia, 131–32
Book of Mormon, 113, 127, 232–33,
    287
    another testament of Christ, 6, 8, 11,
    78, 227, 256, 269, 277–79, 282–85,
    292
    barrier in, 268, 279–85
    lost manuscript pages of, 277
    1981 edition of, 6–11, 214
    placement of copies, 281–85

    plates of, 269–77
    stick of Joseph, 6, 8–9, 256
    study of, 262
    teaching from, 150, 152–53
    testimony of, 154, 284
Bowen, Derek, 7–8
Boy Scouts, 167
Branch presidents, 177–78, 236–37
Brass plates of Laban, 269–71, 273
Brigham City, Utah, 229, 230
Brigham Young University, 27, 104,
    199, 202, 204
    Institute for the Studies in Values
    and Human Behavior, 166
Brother of Jared, 149, 155
Building fund, 72, 177
Busch, Noel F., on Theodore
    Roosevelt, 248–49

— C —

Cambridge Press, 6–7
Cars, 137–39, 141–42
Change, in the Church, 213–15
Chapels, 131–32, 134, 177
Character education, 158–74
Charity, 170, 205
Chemish, 274
Child abuse, 292
Children, 32–33, 35–36, 59–60,
    179–80, 203–4
    discipline of, 19
    learning from, 222–23, 289
    love of God for, 20
    obligation of, to parents, 137–42,
    183
    revelation received by, 210
    spiritual development of, 13–14, 68,
    159
    teaching, 67, 107, 174, 212
China, People's Republic of, 24, 165
Christian churches, 88, 123–28, 291
Christians, 10, 40, 288, 290
    ancient, 224
Church activity, 13–21
Church attendance, 67, 255
Church callings, 118, 212, 236
Church courts, 119

Church curriculum, 9
Church Educational System, 103
Church employees, 112
Church history, 103–22, 179
Church membership, 113, 207
Church of Jesus Christ, 40, 176
Church of Jesus Christ of Latter-day
    Saints, The, 38, 70, 83, 89, 100,
    116, 125, 126, 128, 183, 210
Church organization, 133
Church service, 71, 133, 178
Churches, 88, 123–28, 160, 167, 291
    See also Religions
Churchill, Winston, on war, 161–65,
    173
Citizenship, 67
City councils, 98–99
Clark, J. Reuben, on knowledge of
    God and Christ, 128
Clergymen, 70, 124–28, 224, 288
Cole, Abner, 6
Coleman, Roger, 7
Columbia University, 26
Comfort, 1, 2
Commandments, 181, 269
Commitment, 113–14
Communication, 141
Communism, 159, 165, 171
Compassion, 55, 120
Computers, 7, 168
Concord, Massachusetts, 54
"Condord Hymn" (poem), 55
Confirmation, 210, 232
Congress, 68
Conscience, 63, 67, 248
Constitution of the United States, 68
Conversion, 38, 113, 175, 280
Conviction, 70, 83, 89, 174, 283, 284
Cook, Gene R., 131
Corianton, 79, 150
Counseling, 102–3, 188
Counselors, 249–52
Courage, 50, 52, 61, 67, 128, 168, 169,
    174, 207, 223, 237, 250
Courtesy, 48
Courtship, 140
Covenants, 86, 109, 110, 111, 228,
    254–58, 269, 283

baptismal, 81, 206, 233–34
    marriage, 139, 176
    temple, 255–57
Cowdery, Oliver, 130
Creation, 80, 223, 227, 289–91
    of Adam and Eve, 78–79, 80
Crime, 64, 159, 160–61, 165
Cumorah Pageant, 262
Curtis, George William, on
    minutemen, 56

— D —

Dalebout, Peter, 94–96
Dating, 139–41
Death, 163, 223, 225, 227, 263
    life after, 41, 283
    overcome through Atonement, 79–80
    spiritual, 34, 79
    without baptism, 39–41, 43–44
Deaths, 188, 260, 266, 276
Decency, 62, 67, 68
Dedication, 70, 72
Democracy, 66, 68
Denmark, 172, 229–30, 234
Dependency, 249–50
Depression, 1, 247, 248, 289
Despotism, 66
Dickens, Charles, *A Tale of Two
    Cities*, 93
Dictatorship, 65
Discernment, 102, 105, 193, 212, 218,
    235
    See also Inspiration
Discipline, 2, 19, 51, 141, 289
Divorce, 14, 223
Doctors, 14, 155–57
Doctrine and Covenants, 7–8, 9, 78,
    150, 280, 285, 287
    1981 edition of, 6–11
Dogberry, Obediah (pseud.), 6
Donations, 72
Drake, Joseph Rodman, poem by, 65
Dreams, 216
    See also Inspiration
Drug abuse, 48, 64, 160, 176, 211
Durham, G. Homer, on writing
    history, 115

— E —

Ecumenical movements, 87, 124–26
Eden, Garden of, 78
Education, 22–30, 87, 158–74, 199–202
Education USA, 160
Elders, 129–30, 131
Elijah, 279
Emerson, Ralph Waldo, "Concord
    Hymn," 55
Emotional stress, 243
Endowment, 80, 257
    See also Temple work
England, 6–7, 159
Enoch, 78
Enos, 274
Ephraim, stick of, 5, 8–9, 11
Eternal life, 37
Ether, book of, 277
Ethics, 112
Evolution, theory of, 290
Exaltation, 15, 258
Excommunication, 110, 118–19
Ezekiel, 5, 9, 10, 256

— F —

Faith, 127–28, 206, 208, 287
    building, 104–5, 112, 120–22
    childlike, 218
    destruction of, 63, 102, 107–22,
        172, 251
    in future, 51–52
    in youth, 36
    keepers of, 145–57
    lack of, 98, 124
    of Nephi, 278
    resurgence of, 68
    trial of, 99
Fall of Adam and Eve, 79, 80
Family, 61, 83, 176, 224, 245
    benefitted through Relief Society,
        191–92
    responsibility to, 67, 95, 183, 238
Family prayer, 266
Family records, 42–43
Fast offerings, 72, 177

Fasting, 154
Fathers, 222–23, 236, 289
    See also Parents
Fear, 1, 51, 98, 244, 259
February, 247–48
Fellowship, 34, 121, 178, 181
Finland, 234
First Presidency, 115, 119, 132, 133,
    214, 261
First Vision, 85, 116, 126
Flag, 65
Forgiveness, 1, 51
Francisco, Peter, 56–58, 67
Franklin, Benjamin, on experience, 29
    Poor Richard's Alamanc, 29
Freedom, 61–62, 64–66, 80, 159, 211
    of speech, 65, 159
Frost, Robert, "Two Tramps in
    Mudtime," 69
Funerals, 192, 255, 259–67

— G —

Gareth (legendary knight), 49–50
Gazzeri, Ernesto, *The Mystery of Life*,
    223
Genealogy, 270, 271
General Authorities, 118, 132, 199,
    208–9, 237, 247
General conference, 152
Gentiles, 34, 269
Germany, 163, 165
Gethsemane, 75, 76
God, children of, 1, 50, 52, 183, 201,
    224, 227, 252, 288–93
    love of, 235
    nature of, 287
    relationship with, 243
    See also Heavenly Father; Jesus
    Christ
Godhead, 291
Godhood, 290
Gods, plurality of, 290–91
Gospel study, 2
Gossip, 106
Government, 67
Graduations, 22–23, 27

Grandchildren, 187
Grandin, Egbert B., 6-7
Grandparents, 48, 183
Grant, Ulysses S., 55
Gratitude, 81, 180-81, 182, 226
Great Britain, 162-63, 172-73
Grief, 1, 185, 250
Guilt, 51, 181, 245, 248

— H —

Habits, 181
Hale, Nathan, 60
Handcart pioneers, 179
Happiness, 28-29, 50, 79, 97, 140, 195
Harris, Martin, 6-7
Harris, Sydney, on independent action, 250
Harvard University, 25, 88, 113, 149-50
Haynes, Josiah, 56, 67
Hayward, James, 56, 67
Healings, 185
Health, 246
Heavenly Father, 2, 38, 85, 180-81, 228, 233, 288-93
  relationship with, 205
  separation from, 79
  See also God
Heavenly messengers, 116
Helaman, on the disbelieving, 213
Hendee, Hannah, 59-61, 67
Henley, William Ernest, "Invictus," 207
Henry, Patrick, 57, 60
Heritage, 84
Heroes, 30
High councilors, 16, 19, 98, 184
High priests, 131
Hinckley, Gordon B., 86
History, 61, 94, 103-22, 161
Holy Ghost, 127, 291
  Comforter, 2, 125, 253
  gift of, 206-7, 210, 232, 235, 287, 293
  promptings of, 125

speaking by power of, 123
testimony confirmed by, 15, 116, 154, 218
  See also Inspiration
Holy Spirit of Promise, 254, 256, 257
Home, 13, 186, 251
Home teachers, 13-16, 20-21, 131, 183-89
Homes, 61, 189
  broken, 181
Honesty, 23-24, 28, 168-69, 177
"How Gentle God's Commands" (hymn), 182, 189
Huacuyo, Bolivia, 131-32, 134
Human behavior, 166
Humanism, 170, 171
Humility, 52, 64, 83, 121, 124, 168, 177, 207, 223, 227, 235, 292
Hymns, 121

— I —

"I Am a Child of God" (hymn), 288
Idylls of the King, 49
"If You Could Hie to Kolob" (hymn), 148-49
Illiteracy, 25
Illness, 185, 244
Immorality, 28, 63, 76, 157, 176, 248, 251, 292
  See also Morality
Impressions, 73, 88, 210
  See also Inspiration
Incest, 223
Independence, 61
Indians, 58-59, 280-81
Innocence, 248-49
Inspiration, 17, 119, 122, 129, 173, 213, 276, 284, 287
  Church led by, 100, 104
  concerning call of leaders, 134-35
  failure to heed, 125
  in publication of scriptures, 8
  in work for the dead, 42
  living by, 230-39
  need for women who receive, 193
  Relief Society organized by, 195

seeking, 215
spirit of, 73
still small voice, 210, 232, 261
through gospel study, 2
See also Discernment; Dreams; Holy
    Ghost; Impressions; Promptings
Institute teachers, 104, 115
Institutes of religion, 145, 149
Integrity, 103, 112
International Council of Women, 194
"Invictus" (poem), 207
Isaiah, 273, 279-80, 282, 284, 291
Israelites, 256

— J —

Jackson, Helen Hunt, "October's
    Bright Blue Weather," 286
Jacob (son of Lehi), 274
  on Atonement, 79
  on great and abominable church, 77
  on small plates of Nephi, 272
James, on doers of the word, 15
Japan, 34-35, 63, 146
Jaredites, 269, 276
Jarom, 274
Jesus Christ, 10, 53, 225, 288
  appearance of, 85, 126
  atonement of, 75-81, 86, 228, 267
  Book of Mormon another testament
    of, 6, 8, 11, 78, 227, 256, 269,
    277-79, 282-85
  crucifixion of, 75-76, 81
  gospel of, 38, 89, 110, 228
  Light of, 67
  love of, 205
  Nephite ministry, 278-79, 283
  on feeding sheep, 36
  on gods, 291
  on Isaiah, 279
  on perfection, 289
  on strait gate and narrow way, 38
  prophecies concerning, 276, 283
  relationship with, 204-9
  Spirit of, 115-16, 235
  spirit world ministry, 41
  storm rebuked by, 100
  taking name of, 206

testimony of, 9, 20, 41-42, 81, 100,
    128, 154, 218
the way, truth, life, 37
witness of, 74, 181, 239, 267, 293
See also Church of Jesus Christ; God
Jethro, 236-37
Jews, 34, 269
"John Is Inactive . . . Why?" (article),
    13
Joseph, stick of, 5, 8-9, 11, 256
Joy, 140, 150
Judah, stick of, 5, 8-9, 11, 256
Judgment, 51, 66, 86, 179, 284
Justice, 39, 51, 76, 79, 150, 159, 283

— K —

Keys, 189, 214-15
  of presidency, 134
Kimball, Spencer W., 9, 118, 136, 264
Kingdom of God, 116
Kingdom of heaven, 179
Knowledge, 25-27, 49, 147-48, 151,
    153, 292
Korean War, 63

— L —

Law of Moses, 77, 279
Law of sacrifice, 81
Leaders, 20-21, 215, 235-37
Leadership, 193
Lee, Harold B., 182, 192, 259
Lee, Wilford B., on knowledge and
    Church activity, 13-14
Lehi, 10, 269, 277
  on brass plates, 270
  vision of, 134, 220, 278
Liberty, 67, 70
Logan Temple, 230
Loneliness, 181, 192, 264
Los Angeles, California, 161
Love, 67, 140, 168, 169, 170, 223, 259,
    292
  for children, 19, 20, 222
  of God, 20, 235
Lowell, James Russell, poem by, 54
Lying, 292

– M –

McConkie, Amelia, 260, 262, 263, 264, 266
McConkie, Bruce R., 82, 259–67
McKay, David O., 147, 203, 221
  on discipline, 141
  on freedom, 61
  on search for testimony, 220
Maeser, Karl G., 105
  on following the priesthood, 135
Mahonri Moriancumr. *See* Brother of Jared
Malachi, 279
Man, nature of, 243, 251, 252, 287
  origin of, 80
Mann, Horace, 202
Marriage, 23, 50, 97, 139, 176, 183, 187–88, 245
  broken, 181
  temple, 255–56, 257
Maxwell, Neal A., 172, 260
Mendelssohn, Felix, 105
Mercy, 39, 51, 76, 120, 283
Military service, 35
Ministers. *See* Clergymen
Minutemen, 55–56
Miracles, 13, 71, 127, 260–61
Mission presidents, 71, 94–95, 119, 131, 177, 237, 238
Mission reports, 17
Missionaries, 39, 68, 83–84, 125, 135, 146, 176, 177–78, 187–88, 224, 293
  all young men as, 33–34
  Book of Mormon presented by, 268, 277, 280, 281, 284
  dedicated service of, 70
  effect of weather on, 245
  illnesses of, 244
  interviews with, 115, 119, 199, 205
  member, 33, 131, 268, 277, 281, 284
  testimonies of, 153
Missionary work, 33–36, 38–39, 131, 148, 151–53, 175–81
Modesty, 48, 168
Monson, Thomas S., 261–62
Moral values, 158–74
Morality, 48, 62, 67, 112, 257
  See also Immorality

Mormon, 271, 275
  on charity, 205
  on plates of Nephi, 275–76
  on Spirit of Christ, 115–16, 235
  plates of, 269, 276–77
Moroni, 276–77
  on faith, 127–28, 148
Mortality, 29, 41, 52, 79, 116, 225–27
Mortimer, James, 6
Moses, 236–37
Mosiah, 270, 274
Moyle, Henry D., 71, 109–10, 146–47
Mulekites, 270, 274
Murder, 292
Murray, Madeline, 173
Mutual Improvement Association, 114
Mystery of Life, The (statue), 223

– N –

National Council of Women, 194
Nature, 287, 289–91
Nauvoo Temple, 214
Nelson, Russell M., 266
Nephi (son of Lehi), 285
  large plates of, 269, 271–72, 275, 277
  on Bible, 77
  on brass plates, 269–70
  on feeling, 14, 232
  small plates of, 269, 272–77
  vision of, 110–11, 278
Nephites, 61
  appearance of Christ to, 278–79, 283
Netherlands, The, 94
New England, 54
New England Mission, 34, 69–70, 145, 238, 244
New Testament, 8–9, 77–78, 87, 278, 280, 282, 283, 287
New York City, 175, 194
Norway, 229, 234

– O –

Oaks, Dallin H., 260
Obedience, 67, 76, 87, 170, 174, 213
"October's Bright Blue Weather" (poem), 286
Old age, 179

Old Testament, 8–9, 77–78, 279, 282,
283, 284, 287
Omni, 274
Ordinances, 37, 76, 86, 118, 128, 131,
228, 258, 283
vicarious, 40–44, 279
See also Baptism; Confirmation;
Endowment; Sacrament
Ordination, 102, 119, 126, 129–30,
152, 212
Our Town (play), 253

— P —

Packer, Emma Jensen, 73–74, 229–32
Packer, Ira Wight, 74, 230–32
Packer, Jonathan Taylor, 43
Packer, Mary Ann, 43
Pain, 51, 73, 76, 79, 223, 252
Pakistan, laborers from, 24–25
Palmyra Reflector (newspaper), 6
Parenthood, 228
Parents, 13–14, 48, 68, 137–42,
183–84, 248
See also Fathers
Parker, Ann, 179–80
Parker, Robert, 179–80
Passover, 81
Patience, 141
Patriarchs, 16, 32, 73
Patriotism, 55, 67, 68
Paul, 132, 264
on Atonement, 77, 81
on becoming joint-heirs with Christ,
293
on Christ's being equal with God,
292
on God, 291
on natural man, 102
on Saints' being fellowcitizens, 182
on things of God, 218–19
on turning from evil, 130, 133, 134
Peace, 1, 66, 79, 162, 164, 253
Pearl of Great Price, 7–8, 78, 150, 285,
287
Perfection, 256, 289
Persecution, 83
Perversion, 49, 64, 76, 107, 223, 250,
251

Pestilence, 64
Peter, 36, 75
on preaching to the dead, 41
vision of, 34
Peter, James, and John, 82, 264
Phelps, William W., 120–21
"If You Could Hie to Kolob,"
148–49
Philippines, 96
Philosophy, 10, 63, 291
Picnics, 31–33
Pilate, Pontius, 75–76
Pioneers, 84, 96, 179
Plan of redemption, 79, 266
Pledge of Allegiance, 65
Polytheism, 291
Poor Richard's Alamanc, 29
"Poor Student's Soliloquy, The"
(poem), 200
Pornography, 49, 159, 172, 292
Pragmatism, 170
Pratt, Parley P., 129
Prayer, 67, 88, 174, 218, 219, 283
for blessings, 96, 231
for guidance, 21, 119, 135, 151, 248
for testimony, 154, 178
of Alma the Elder, 117
of Joseph Smith, 85
public, 64
sacramental, 234
school, 171
with parents, 141
Prayerfulness, 233
Prayers, assigned to less active, 16
of Harold B. Lee, 182, 207
of Joseph Fielding Smith, 254
Premortal life, 80, 148–49, 154,
224–25, 228
President of the Church, 106–8, 117,
132, 236–37, 255, 263
See also Prophets
Pride, 14, 52, 64, 111
Priesthood, 133, 190, 193
duties of, 13, 131
guiding power, 103
restoration of, 126
revelation on, 9, 264
See also Administrations to the
sick; Home teachers; Ordination

Priesthood meetings, 194
Procreative power, 50
Promptings, 125, 210, 216, 233,
    238–39
Prophecies, 5–6, 68
    of coming of Christ, 276, 283
Prophecy, spirit of, 269
Prophets, 263, 272, 285
    ancient, 268, 292
    authority of, delegated, 189, 236–37
    revelation received by, 126, 212
    testimony of, 44, 89, 100, 108, 117,
        195, 221, 239
    undermining, 106–9
    See also President of the Church
Prosperity, 66
Provo Temple, 266
Psychiatrists, 249–52
Psychologists, 249–52
Psychosomatic illnesses, 244
Punishment, 79–80, 150–51

– Q –

Quorum leaders, 186
Quorum of the Twelve, 132, 133, 214,
    261, 266

– R –

Radio, 21
Rasmussen, Ellis T., 6
Records, 42–44
Redemption, 15, 41, 76, 228
    for the dead, 39–44, 224–25
Relief Society, 31, 185, 190–95
Religion, 174
    in public schools, 171
Religions, 39, 86
    See also Churches
Religious News Service, 161
Rembrandt, 105
Repentance, 1, 109, 183, 206, 257
    never too late, 51
    of William W. Phelps, 120–21
    redemption through, 76
    through punishment, 79–80, 151
    the sacrifice required since Atone-
        ment, 81

Responsibility, 64, 118
Restoration, 86, 122, 126, 292
Resurrection, 225, 283
Revelation, 269
    Church led by, 40, 100, 117, 212–16,
        291
    in work for dead, 42
    on priesthood, 9, 264
    personal, 210–16, 284, 287
    received by bishop, 102–3, 105, 212
    spirit of, 15, 269
    women blessed by, 191
Revelations, 10, 43, 251, 292
Reverence, 40, 54, 73, 168, 169, 177,
    223, 281, 290
Revolutionary war, 54–61, 67–68
Rich, Abel S., 107, 287
Richards, Elliot, 35
Richards, Stephen L, on
    "debunking," 109
Rigdon, Sidney, 120
Righteousness, 174, 239
Rights, individual, 64
    See also Freedom
Romney, Marion G., on speaking by
    the Holy Ghost, 260
Roosevelt, Franklin D., 164
Roosevelt, Theodore, 248–49

– S –

Sabbath, 177, 286
Sacrament, 81, 228, 233–34, 279
Sacrament meeting, 16, 183–84
Sacrifice, 120, 187, 223
Safford, Arizona, 43
Salvation, 37, 39, 40, 125, 157, 286
Samoa, 134–35
Sartre, Jean-Paul, 250
Satan, 76, 77, 80, 112, 116, 212, 235,
    287
Satan worship, 50
Sato, Chio, 35
Sato, Tatsui, 35
Scandinavia, 229, 234
School, 97
School Law News, 161
Schools, 64, 86–87
Scripture study, 1–2, 67

Scriptures, 15, 287
  new editions of, 5–11, 214, 261
  teaching from, 150–53
Sealing power, 279
Sealings, 255–56, 257
Secularism, 170
Security, 97, 176, 182, 195
Self-discipline, 2
Self-esteem, 52
Selfishness, 26, 72
Self-knowledge, 200–209
Self-respect, 1, 289
Seminary teachers, 102–4, 107, 115,
  141, 254, 287
Separation of church and state, 63
Service, 15, 20, 21, 27, 30, 70, 71,
  120, 178, 187
Setting apart, 131, 133, 212
Seventy, 133
Sex education, 107, 172
Shakespeare, William, on good name,
  108
  on self-knowledge, 203
Sin, 79–80
  remission of, 233, 234–35, 283
Skepticism, 171, 218
Slavery, 64
Smith, George Albert, 194–95
  on women, 191
Smith, Hyrum, 120, 263
Smith, Joseph, 40, 114, 117, 130, 154,
  214, 221, 239, 277
  birthplace of, 54, 70
  Book of Mormon published by, 6–7
  first vision of, 85, 116
  letter to William W. Phelps, 120–21
  on knowing God, 292
  on Relief Society, 190–91, 193
Smith, Joseph F., on workings of God,
  104
  vision of redemption of dead, 41,
  264–65
Smith, Joseph Fielding, 112, 203, 254,
  263
  on the Book of Mormon, 113
Smoking, 14, 18
Snow, Lorenzo, on becoming as God,
  98, 292

"Soul's Captain, The" (poem),
  207–8
South America, 24, 260
South Royalton, Vermont, 54, 58, 61
Spafford, Belle Smith, 194–95
Spirit world, 41, 267
Spirits, 50–51, 98, 225, 283
Spiritual death, 34, 79
Spiritual education, 27–28
Spiritual experiences, 8, 213
Spiritual growth, 97
Spiritual guidance, 105
  See also Inspiration
Spiritual strength, 33
Spiritual values, teaching of, 158–74
Spirituality, 30, 104, 140
Stake presidents, 16–18, 19, 118–19,
  131, 237
Stakes, 134
Standards, 19, 140, 170, 176, 178
Stealing, 292
Success, 28–29, 98
Suicide, 228
Sunday School teachers, 20
Supreme Court, 171, 173
Sustaining vote, 131, 133, 212–13
Sweden, 229, 234

— T —

Tale of Two Cities, A (novel), 93
Talmage, James E., 263
Teachers, 20, 101–22, 141, 170,
  201–2, 204
Teaching, 247–48
  by the Spirit, 21, 193
  of spiritual values, 67, 158–74, 212
Teenagers, 47–53, 137–42, 183–84,
  186, 282
  See also Youth
Television, 21, 49
Temperance, 65, 83, 176
Temple covenants, 103
Temple dedications, 254
Temple meetings, 182, 214, 265
Temple preparation, 257
Temple sealings, 255–56, 257, 279

Temple work, 40–42, 44, 266
  See also Endowment
Temptation, 1, 48, 51, 257
Tennyson, Alfred, *Idylls of the King*, 49
Testimony, 2, 72, 104, 150, 154
  after death, 263
  bearing of, 15–21, 88, 153–55,
    218–20
  loss of, 102
  moving power, 14–15
  of Book of Mormon, 154, 284
  of Christ, 9, 10, 89, 128, 154, 218,
    221
  of Joseph Smith, 116
  search for, 220
Testing, 52, 225–27
Three Witnesses, 285
Tingey, Dale, 251
Tithing, 67, 72, 177, 255, 257
Tolerance, 67
Transgression, 245, 248
Truth, 52, 88, 106, 293
Tuberculosis, 95
"Two Tramps in Mudtime" (poem),
  69
Tyranny, 64

— U —

United States Constitution, 68
United States Supreme Court, 171, 173
Unity, Christian, 124–28
Unwed mothers, 161

— V —

Values, 158–74
Vandalism, 160–61
Veil, 41, 43, 155, 188, 223
Vietnam War, 62–63
Violence, 160–61, 182
Vision, of redemption of dead, 41,
  264–65
Visions, 34, 85, 110–11, 116, 126,
  133, 155, 216, 278
Visiting teachers, 185
Voting, 67

— W —

Walters, Archer, 179
War. *See* Revolutionary war; Vietnam
  War; World War I; World War II
Washington, George, 56
Washington State University at
  Pullman, 84, 251
Weaknesses, 204
Weather, 245–46
Weber State College, 22–23, 27
Welfare program, 177–78, 184
Whitney, Orson F., "The Soul's
  Captain," 207–8
Wickedness, 76, 174
Widows, 183
Widtsoe, John A., 114
Wilder, Thornton, *Our Town*, 253
Wisdom, 50, 98
Women, 190–95
Woodruff, Wilford, 70, 267
  on Church history, 106
Word of Wisdom, 81, 211–12, 256
World War I, 61, 162–63
World War II, 7, 35, 61, 84, 96,
  163–65
Worry, 244, 247
Worship, 68

— Y —

Young, Brigham, 70, 105, 203
  on knowing oneself, 200, 209
  on perfection, 256
Young, S. Dilworth, on Bruce R.
  McConkie, 262–63
Young Women, 31
Youth, 124–25, 176, 183–84, 218, 282
  advice to, 31, 36, 47–53, 94–100,
    254–58
  car ownership for, 141–42
  obligation of, to parents, 137–42,
    183
  teaching, 103, 109–10, 147–57,
    185–86

— Z —

Zenos, 274